Vision and Sport

Also from the same publisher:
Andrews Essays on Physical Education and Sport

VISION AND SPORT

Edited by
Ian M Cockerill MEd PhD
Lecturer in Physical Education
University of Birmingham

and
William W MacGillivary MA PhD
Professor
and Dean of the Faculty of Physical Education and Recreation
University of New Brunswick

Stanley Thornes (Publishers) Ltd

First published in 1981 by
Stanley Thornes (Publishers) Ltd
Educa House
Old Station Drive
off Leckhampton Road
CHELTENHAM GL53 0DN
England

British Library Cataloguing in Publication Data

Vision and sport.
1. Visual perception
2. Sport
I. Cockerill, Ian M
II. MacGillivary, W W
152.1'4'024796   GV565

ISBN 0 85950 463 8

Text set in 11/12 Baskerville at Quadraset Ltd, Radstock
Printed in Great Britain by
Ebenezer Baylis & Son Ltd.
The Trinity Press, Worcester, and London

Contents

Preface

In 1980 the Wimbledon Lawn Tennis Championships included electronic devices to assist line judges, while for the first time at this tournament officials were required to undergo strict vision testing. It is also interesting to consider that judges for the men's vault in the gymnastics competition at the Moscow Olympics were assisted by pressure-operated lights located along the side of the horse in order to determine where the gymnast had placed his hands. Moreover, cricket umpires now carry a light-sensitive meter to facilitate their decision-making with regard to suspending play for bad light. Each of these examples highlights the importance of accurate visual perception in sport and especially in top-level competition where athletes have worked for many years to attain outstanding performances.

Vision and Sport seeks to provide information that will assist players, coaches and enthusiastic spectators to understand some of the psychological issues that influence the learning and performance of sports skills. The way in which the book came to be written was almost entirely fortuitous. One of us had recently been appointed to the University of Birmingham, while the other arrived there at a similar time from the University of New Brunswick to begin a year's study leave. Neither one knew the other until September 1978.

Following long conversations over several months about our various teaching and research interests, it became apparent that there were several overlapping areas, with visual space perception as the common thread. Since it is generally recognised that the eyes are an athlete's main receivers of information, we sought to identify a suitable text to provide the kind of material that physical education students, athletes, teachers and coaches might find useful.

There are three principal factors that contribute to success in sport. First, there must be skill, partly emanating from what is termed natural ability, but especially resulting from a long period of practice and coaching. Second, the athlete must be physically equipped to withstand the present demands of training and competition, with standards of performance showing little sign of levelling off. Third, there are those less tangible, but nevertheless important, variables to consider when preparing for competition. They include such aspects of personality as are manifest through anxiety, motivation and aggression. Despite the importance of this third group, athletes and coaches have surprisingly little material to help them understand the various problems that must be faced and overcome. It is hoped that as research progresses help will become increasingly available.

We have been most fortunate in obtaining world-wide contributions from knowledgeable and respected authors who could also be described as being actively involved in some practical aspect of sport. Having identified those areas of vision that we considered most relevant to sport and invited various professional colleagues to write about them, it became apparent that arranging chapters in a clearly defined sequence might prove difficult. Nevertheless, we have endeavoured to locate each chapter in its place for a purpose, and hope those who read the book will find the arrangement acceptable. Most of the contributions refer specifically to the author's own research, while some are more general reviews that identify what are believed to be potentially fruitful areas of study.

Chapter 1 outlines a taxonomy of sporting skills and raises problems that are dealt with later in greater depth. Chapter 2 identifies the probable association between an individual's personality and how he sees the world, while Chapters 7 and 14 review the research in visual acuity and colour perception as they are appropriate to motor learning and performance. Chapters 8 and 9 consider the effects of fatigue through exercise upon reaction time and upon the ways in which skilful players cope with a fast-moving ball. Both chapters are well supported by their author's work, and future research merits an investigation of the possible relationship between these two topics. Chapters 3–6 and 10–12 are applied to golf, ice-hockey, basketball, netball, hockey, rugby, association football and mountaineering, respectively, and reflect the research interests of the various authors as well as a sport each has enjoyed as a player. Chapter 13 is included to offer guidance, and possibly new ideas for lesson planning, to physical education teachers and, finally, Chapter 15 requests coaches to proceed with caution in their use of visual aids. It is stated that while the potential usefulness of videotape recorders is undeniable, they are not the solution to all problems and care must be exercised in their use.

We know that there are those who would have argued for the inclusion of additional chapters or different topics in the book. This is to be expected, but we are grateful to all contributors who responded to enthusiastically to the project throughout. In particular, we are indebted to Stanley Thornes for their continued encouragement.

January, 1981   Ian M. Cockerill
                                                                 William W. MacGillivary

The Contributors

Chantal Bard is an Associate Professor of Physical Education at the University of Laval, Quebec. After initial training in Paris she later obtained an MA in physical education at Michigan State University. Her doctoral studies were conducted at the University of Wisconsin, Madison. The majority of Dr Bard's many publications have been related to eye movement and sports performance.

Leslie Burwitz trained as a teacher at St Luke's College, Exeter, where he obtained a BEd degree. His graduate studies were carried out at the University of Illinois where he was awarded an MSc and subsequently a PhD. Dr Burwitz has wide-ranging research interests and he is currently course co-ordinator for the BA in Sports Studies at Crewe and Alsager College of Higher Education, Cheshire.

Brian P. Callington obtained a BEd (Hons) degree from Goldsmiths' College, London, after which he taught physical education for several years. He gained an MA in physical education at the University of Birmingham in 1979 and since that time has been Head of Physical Education at the Joseph Rowntree School, York.

Gerald H. Fisher is a Senior Lecturer in the Department of Psychology, University of Newcastle upon Tyne. Having initially trained as a teacher he later read psychology at the University of Hull which was followed by research leading to a PhD. Dr Fisher has made a significant contribution to many branches of psychology, but he is particularly well known for his work in visual perception. He is the author of more than a hundred scientific publications.

Michelle Fleury   is an Associate Professor of Physical Education at the University of Laval, Quebec, where she is also Chairperson of the Human Performance Research Group. Dr Fleury studied at Laval for her first degree and later at the University of Iowa where she obtained an MA. Her doctoral work was at the University of Liège, Belgium.

G. S. Don Morris   is a Professor in the Department of Physical Education at the California State Polytechnic University, Pomona. His main research interest is in visual perception, and in addition to publishing two books Dr Morris is the author of several papers on the developmental nature of vision and motor learning.

Helen E. Parker   is a Senior Tutor in the Department of Human Movement and Recreation Studies, University of Western Australia. She has a Diploma in Physical Education and an MEd degree from the University of Western Australia. Her main research interests are concerned with relationships between information processing and team-game performance.

Frank H. Sanderson   trained as a teacher at Carnegie College of Physical Education. His BEd degree was followed by an MA and subsequently a PhD at the University of Leeds. Dr Sanderson is presently a Senior Lecturer in the Department of Sport and Recreation Studies, Liverpool Polytechnic, and he has a special interest in squash, both as a player and as a national panel tutor and examiner.

Robert H. Sharp   is a Lecturer at Jordanhill College of Education, Glasgow. He has a first degree in mathematics from the University of London, an MA in physical education from the University of Alberta and his PhD research was carried out at the University of Leeds. In recent years Dr Sharp has become increasingly involved in the sport of mountaineering.

David A. Tyldesley   obtained a first degree in zoology and then trained as a teacher at Carnegie College of Physical Education. Dr Tyldesley's doctoral research was conducted at the University of Leeds and he is currently working with Professor H. T. A. Whiting at the Vrije Universiteit, Amsterdam.

Graeme A. Wood   is a Lecturer in the Department of Human Movement and Recreation Studies, University of Western Australia. He holds Diplomas in Physical Education and Education from the Universities of Otago and Massey in New Zealand. Dr Wood also studied in the Department of Exercise Science at the University of Massachusettes, Amherst, where he obtained MSc and PhD degrees.

1

Human Information Processing and a Taxonomy of Sporting Skills

Gerald H. Fisher

Recurring repeatedly throughout the history of scientific endeavour is the problem of explaining how man and his fellow creatures have gradually evolved biologically and developed behaviourally in order to be capable of processing information so reliably as they appear to do. Man himself may be essentially regarded as an organism possessed of fine capabilities for processing a wide variety of information. The highest levels of his potential ability for reacting to and interacting with the information content of the environment are exemplified by the quality of those sensory, motor, perceptual and cognitive skills which he finds himself uniquely capable of acquiring. Performing these skills efficiently depends upon the relatively precise ability to process information referring to the sizes of surrounding objects, their shapes and locations upon the one hand, and the meanings, implications and personal significance of those objects on the other. In highly skilled expression information processing operations become finely co-ordinated, whereupon they appear in appropriate space–time sequences. Should such operations prove unreliable, however, behaviour becomes disorganised and skills lose co-ordination. If the mechanisms whereby information is processed fall grossly into disfunction then skills deteriorate and may even be lost completely. It is to the analysis of particular skills and the synthesis of their components so as to consider how they might variously be acquired, improved upon and perfected that the present chapter, along with the main body of contributions in the remainder of this book, is addressed.

The view that many features of skilled human performance are recognised as processing the intrinsic content of particular information arrays is currently enjoying considerable popularity among behavioural scientists from a variety of callings. Having considerable intuitive appeal, and allying itself with the contemporary *cognitive* idiom, this view is now coming to be widely adopted by psychologists and others in cognate disciplines for a variety of theoretical, experimental and heuristic purposes. According to such advocates as Haber (1974, p. 313), the information-processing approach: "has caused a fundamental change in the way research is done and in the ways ideas are formulated". Nevertheless, others have the kind of reservations over the value of this approach as those which led Shaffer (1978, p. 580) to observe that: "The psychology of human information processing, like some modern atonal music, can produce fine sonorities from time to time but it does not convey a sense of overall form, or direction". The first reason for this apparent lack of direction is that even when engaged in what appear the most simple and commonplace activities we find ourselves implicitly involved in processing truly incredible amounts of information.

Sitting here at my desk, for example, a few minutes ago I inadvertently knocked a ruler on to the floor, whereupon glancing in its direction I reached out to retrieve it and, having grasped it, returned it to its former position. Performing an apparently simple series of operations as this demands relatively precise processing of the auditory information reaching my ears, the visual information reaching my eyes and both the proprioceptive and tactile-kinaesthetic information afforded when stretching out my arm to grasp the ruler. Moreover, despite the different types of information involved it must all be co-ordinated so as to yield an integrated and coherent account of the total situation.

This particular example may appear elementary, even trivial, but when the ruler is replaced by a ball struck by a squash opponent, my passive posture at a desk by active involvement in a basketball game, or the desultory reaching out of my arm by the rapid blocking of an attempted uppercut delivered by my boxing adversary, the relevance of an information-type approach to the analysis of sporting activity is brought more clearly into focus. In all such activities, mechanisms residing in the ears, eyes and body parts collaborate by performing their characteristic functions either successfully – so that the squash ball is struck cleanly by my racket head, the basketball intercepted from my team-mate's pass and the intended blow is warded off – or unsuccessfully, so that the point is lost, the basket missed and the blow reaches its target.

The information content of any situation exemplifying the exercise of some particular sporting skill may be readily analysed. Such analysis has long provided a major preoccupation of sports coaches upon the one hand and sports psychologists on the other. But as noted above, Shaffer (1978) insisted that it: "does not convey a sense of overall form, or direction". A further reason for the interest is that the focus of these analyses has tended to bear upon the nature of the information available for processing, rather than the mechanisms whereby it is processed. Accordingly, what is now required is an overall taxonomy of different types of information *processing,* exemplified with reference to specific sporting skills. The formulation of an appropriate taxonomy requires an exhaustive analysis of the behavioural operations involved when exercising particular skills. Such operations may be regarded as being performed in serial order and, if truly exhaustive, that order could be entered appropriately at different stages so as to accommodate sequences, or individual selections, relevant to the performance of any skilled activity.

During a recent weekend I found myself considering the implications of two sequences of sporting activity which, for me at least, exemplify opposite ends of a skill continuum that lends itself to analysis in information processing terms. The continuum forms part of the English game of cricket, but it is equally applicable to any fielding situation that might also arise, for example, in the North American game of baseball. First of all, Timothy, my four-year-old son, was selected to play cricket for his prep school. It was the first time he had appeared in such a role and he was naturally apprehensive. He was also somewhat overawed by the group of thirty or so spectators. Fielding in a position around silly mid-on, very close to the batsman taking strike, Timothy seemed to have a rudimentary understanding of what was going on. However, from time to time his attention wandered and he often appeared more concerned with activities taking place off, rather than on, the field. More by good luck than judgment Timothy occasionally succeeded, albeit inelegantly, in stopping the cricket ball with some part of his body. Yet he invariably failed to catch it, even upon those occasions when the ball seemed to be going directly to hand. Parental pride prevents me from judging his performance as being totally abysmal. However, even when apparently fully attentive to and engaged in the task of fielding, Timothy seemed to compose his activity in a curiously staccato, somewhat puppet-like, fashion. While distracted by the arrival of an ice cream van a typical sequence orchestrated itself in the following manner:

1.   his *attention* was caught by the sound of bat striking ball whereupon he
2.   *searched* visually for the ball in flight and eventually
3.   *engaged* it. He then
4.   *tracked* its trajectory while attempting to
5.   *position* himself so as to be capable of
6.   *intercepting* it and
7.   *bringing it under control* by
8.   *catching* it, and then
9.   *carrying* it prior to
10. *sighting* the wicket and
11. *aiming* in its direction before
12. *throwing* the ball towards the target, and again
13. *tracking* its trajectory towards that target.

Presumably, he was trying to:

14. *assess* the extent of error in the latter operation so as to be able to
15. *correct* for it in subsequent performances of a similar nature.

Regrettably, however, the boy's performance showed little significant improvement throughout the course of the afternoon; but what might one expect from a four-year-old? It would certainly not be the performance of, say, Derek Randall fielding for Nottinghamshire against Kent and which I had the pleasure of viewing on television the following day. The Kent opening batsmen soon took command of the bowling and, with the score at fifty for no wicket, from a full-blooded drive made off the meat of the bat the ball raced toward the cover boundary. "Another four runs", declared the commentator, but what he failed to appreciate was that acute reading of the situation and fiercely concentrated attention had enabled Randall to predict the flight of the ball even before the batsman had completed his stroke. Launching himself from a position around deep mid-off he covered a distance of approximately forty yards before gathering the ball cleanly and throwing it over the stumps directly into the waiting gloves of the wicketkeeper, for whom removing the bails was no more than a formality. At this time the astonished, non-striking batsman was still some four yards out of his crease. It was not 'four runs' but 'run-out' by one of the most brilliant fielding performances I have been privileged to witness.

The comparisons and contrasts between the performances of my small son and the professional cricketer are both clear and obvious:

four-year old boy	*professional cricketer*
first appearance	familiar with the situation
apprehensive	thoroughly relaxed
distracted	totally alert
rudimentary understanding	keen reading of the situation
wandering attention	keenly attentive

It is in these two sequences of skilled behaviour where the most obvious difference is to be found. Timothy's performance was staccato and produced in piecemeal fashion, much as a computer printout will proceed laboriously line-by-line from one stage to the next. By contrast, from the time it took to predict the line and length of the ball to delivering it speedily and accurately into the hands of the wicketkeeper Randall's performance was characterised by a seemingly simple and totally co-ordinated sequence of actions.

Although descriptive of my son's relatively inept fielding performance, the taxonomy outlined above appears irrelevant to analysing the unique ability of a highly skilled sportsman. Yet how did Randall acquire such exceptional skill? Although naturally endowed with such qualities as acute senses, an appropriate physique and adequate strength, his selection, acquisition and co-ordination of the component activities of his particular sport had to be developed by coaching by others and training on the part of himself. The skills of less able sportsmen than Randall fall at some point along a continuum between his and those of my small son. The primary tasks for all involved in proceeding along that continuum, either oneself or when assisting others to do so, are threefold; first, to improve each particular element of the individual activity, second, to co-ordinate those elements into coherent sequences and, finally, to blend those sequences into overall performances. However, improvements in performance will not necessarily be effected in this order. Certain blends may well come before sequences, which in turn may precede elements and here, as elsewhere, the whole performance may well prove something more than the sum of its parts.

Fielding, whether in cricket or baseball, provides an example of the taxonomy working itself out through a dynamic situation in the sense that the whole attention is, or should be, constantly engaged on the task in hand throughout. Other examples translating readily into similar terms include a variety of bat and racket games, along with the 'in play' components of virtually all team games. However, the 'starting play' elements of many games begin with some more or less static situation whereby the ball is addressed as in golf, served as in lawn- and table-tennis, or variously launched in some way by direct contact with a body part such as in football, or an extension thereof as in bat and racket games. Each of these starting play operations requires entry into the above sequence at stage (10) wherein the target, be it hole, service box, goal, cover-point boundary, net or tin, is sighted and the appropriate stroke decided upon and produced accordingly. 'One shot' games such as golf, archery, darts and various forms of rifle- and pistol-shooting proceed stroke by stroke, or shot by shot, from stages (10) to (13) and subsequently to (15). However, in 'continuous-play'-type games, whole 'in play' sequences cycle around continuously and periodically, punctuated at intervals by stoppages requiring the setting-up of new starting play sequences until the game draws to its conclusion. Again, each of these activities is characterised by its own continuum of skill, progression along which may be achieved by appropriate analysis into particular elements and synthesis of those elements into coherent sequences, whole strings of which blend into an overall performance of the particular sport concerned.

It is intended that particular features of the taxonomy outlined above will be elaborated elsewhere. Much research has been carried out upon the sensory, motor and sensory-motor elements referred to therein. However, how those elements become synthesised and blended together in a precise fashion remains to be understood. Certain of these issues are raised in subsequent chapters in this present book, while others will be addressed in a subsequent volume. None the less, attractive though this taxonomic approach may be found, it must be acknowledged as constituting something less than a complete analysis of those psychological processes, not to say skills, involved when engaging in virtually any form of sporting activity. The discerning coach may analyse particular skills into their elemental components and devise programmes whereby they may be variously synthesised. Being knowledgeable of the mechanisms and processes involved, the sports psychologist may assist in this task. In the present state of both these collaborative arts we can do much, even though a great deal awaits further research.

In returning to the comparison between Timothy, the four-year-old, and Derek Randall, a great fielder, the former was nervous and apprehensive before the game whereas, although apparently relaxed, Randall was fully aroused and tuned to the level required for producing a fine performance. Can this be coached? It is probably true to say that both individuals were highly motivated, but that motivation stemmed from different objectives, and whereas it almost certainly detracted from Timothy's performance it undoubtedly enhanced that of the highly skilled performer. Can this be coached? Both fielders probably found the situation stressful, albeit for different reasons, but they handled the stress quite differently. Can this be coached?

Being able to cope with factors such as arousal, motivation and stress constitutes in large measure that extra skill component of sporting performance referred to variously as confidence, style or charisma. These factors arise from the fact that, rather than being performed *in vacuo,* sporting activities take place within social contexts provided by others who find themselves playing out such ancillary social roles as characterise team-mates, opponents, referees, linesmen, umpires, captains and managers. The bigger the sporting occasion, the bigger the crowd; the bigger the reward, the bigger the elation; but greater may be the disappointment. Developing a taxonomic account of such factors as these and their effect upon performance leads into an entirely new area of human behaviour in which the skills involved are practised intuitively by a gifted few but, as yet properly understood, not to say explained, scientifically by none. Such is the present state of our particular art; not a philosophy of despair, but an exciting challenge for the future.

References

Haber, R. N. (1974) "Information Processing", in E. C. Carterette & M. P. Friedman (Eds.), *Handbook of Perception:* Vol. 1: *Historical and Philosophical Roots of Perception,* New York: Academic Press.

Shaffer, H. (1978) Review of *Attention and Memory* by G. Underwood, Oxford: Pergamon, 1978, *Quarterly Journal of Experimental Psychology,* 30: 580–1.

2

The Contribution of Perceptual Style to Human Performance

William W. MacGillivary

Over the past decade research in physical education and sport has employed the personality-perceptual dimension in attempting to explain a number of the factors assumed to contribute to the performance of perceptual-motor skills. Reference to such a dimension pertains to the evolving perceptual typologies, or styles, which have their roots in personality theory. Included in this category are levellers and sharpeners as defined by Klein (1951), augmenters and reducers as identified by Petrie (1960), and field–dependent/field–independent types as established by Witkin (1954).

The majority of research surrounding the topic of perceptual styles has concerned itself with the classifications of Petrie (1960) and Witkin (1954). The latter has received a great deal of attention from researchers, resulting in attempts to relate field dependence to a multitude of factors both within and outside the domain of human performance. In her research Petrie (1960) identified three perceptual types: the reducer, the moderate and the augmenter. She classified the reducer as one who tends to be tolerant of pain and reduces perceived sensations. The augmenter was described as one who tends to be tolerant of pain and subjectively increases the sensations which he or she perceives. The moderate resides somewhere between the other two extremes.

Research endeavouring to link Petrie's perceptual typologies to sport performers and sports performance has been somewhat limited. Ryan &

Kovacic (1966) based their work upon the assumption that the ability of an individual to tolerate pain is related to the nature of the activity in which he participates. They found a positive relationship between athletic participation and the way in which individuals were classified according to the augmentation–reduction dimension. According to their results, the individual who participated in contact sports, such as football, was more pain tolerant. He was classified as a reducer, while the non-athlete demonstrated an augmenting type of behaviour and the non-contact athlete tended to fit the moderate classification as identified by Petrie (1960). Ryan & Kovacic (1966) identified characteristics which differentiated athletic types based upon perceptual judgments. The contact athlete underestimated both time and kinaesthetic judgment, whereas the non-contact athlete demonstrated a moderate capability on these parameters. The non-athlete, however, was typified by overestimating time and kinaesthetic judgments. Thus, the study also demonstrated that athletes may be classified as reducers and augmenters based on their ability to tolerate pain, and additionally by the way in which they perceive such dimensions as time and size.

Petrie (1960) noted that reducers tended to describe themselves as alert, cautious, conscientious, dependable, efficient, precise, quick, relaxed, intelligent, self-confident and enthusiastic. Augmenters, on the other hand, described themselves as careless, imaginative, sensitive and serious. In contrasting these two perceptual styles it is important to note that there are obvious overlaps in the characteristics of both which have clear implications for human behaviour. For example, an athlete may demonstrate the general behaviour of a reducer, but still be imaginative and serious. It is, therefore, difficult to draw a clear line distinguishing the augmenter from the reducer. The results of the Ryan & Kovacic (1966) study have shown that within sport there are subtle differences between different types of athlete. In any use made of this perceptual dimension one must remember that it is essentially a continuum, and when speaking of augmentation or reduction it is a relative term. An important consideration in any future use of such a perceptual typology is the manner in which the augmenters, reducers and moderates are identified. The measure traditionally employed has been a proprioceptive one and merits further clarification with respect to its validity and reliability.

The major thrust in attempting to relate personality theory to perceptual behaviour came from Witkin (1954) and the many researchers who later developed his field-dependence/field-independence hypothesis. Witkin and his associates investigated the role of various individual differences in perceptual behaviour and the relative consistency of such differences in certain situations. The field-dependence perceptual dimension is frequently referred to in terms of the two extremes, field dependence or field independence; although strictly there are no extremes and this dimension is essentially a continuum. On occasions researchers have used arbitrarily determined extremes to identify differences of one kind or another. The use of such extremes has demanded an explanation, but from a perceptual standpoint the differentiation is quite basic. The field–independent individual is described as one who experiences the visual perceptual field as separate from the background. The field–dependent individual, on the other hand, is one who shows relative inability to perceive parts of the visual field from the whole and whose behaviour is characterised by an overall organisation of the perceptual field.

The voluminous research literature dealing with Witkin's (1954 & 1962) field-dependence hypothesis has been replete with inconsistency in terms of the manner in which this perceptual dimension has been measured. A review by Arbuthnot (1972) noted the large number of different measures employed by various researchers to identify what is generally referred to as field dependence or field independence. These measures have included such items as the embedded-figures test (EFT), the hidden-figures test (HFT), the rod-and-frame test (RFT), the portable rod-and-frame test (PRFT) and various combinations of each. It is evident from the literature that although there is some shared variance for these various measures, it is quite low and not significant. Arbuthnot (1972) indicated that the measures currently favoured bear little resemblance to Witkin's original measure and do not warrant their extensive use. More importantly, according to Arbuthnot (1972) future research involving this perceptual dimension should only be pursued using a combination of existing measures. He suggested that the standard rod-and-frame test in combination with the Witkin EFT, or a shortened version of the EFT, might be appropriate.

Physical education and sport research has attempted to draw relationships between human perceptual-motor performance and the degree of field dependence demonstrated by individual subjects. The research has taken several forms, ranging from an assessment of fine motor skills, learning and performance, to the identification of athletic sub-groups and their relationship with the field-dependence dimension. A study by Bard (1972) noted a relationship between athletes whom she classified as 'internally' or 'externally' oriented in terms of their activity participation and their performance on a standard rod-and-frame test. She found dancers and tumblers to be more field-independent, while volleyball players were more field-dependent, but cautioned others about drawing precise conclusions from her results. A criticism of this study would be that the sample size was small and the statistical treatment of the results inadequate. Green (1972) however, verified some of the results of Bard's study when using a perceptual style index comprised of the RFT and the Witkin EFT. In a study of the role of perceptual style among individual and team athletes Brown (1974) was unable to identify any significant differences between the two sub-groups whom she identified as 'team' and 'multi-sport' athletes. She did, however, report that secondary school female students who were individual sport athletes were significantly more field-independent than female team and multi-sport athletes. The measure of field dependence used in this study was the group-hidden-figures test.

Barrell & Trippe (1975), in a study which compared professional dancers, highly skilled tennis players, soccer players, cricketers and track and field athletes of varying ability levels, obtained some interesting data. Differences between the two athletic groups in tennis (high and medium ability) favoured the highly skilled as being more field-independent, with the highly skilled tennis group significantly more field-independent than the track and field athletes. The general tendency in this study was for the highly skilled category of athlete to be more field-independent, with the single exception of the track and field athletes. This finding is supportive of a claim by Kane (1972) that field dependency is usually associated with athletes who must interact with their environment. He used the portable rod-and-frame test with the mean absolute deviation representing the individual's field dependence score, but in retrospect one might question this measure on the basis of the manner in which the levels of ability for the various athletic groups was determined.

A favourite tool of many researchers has been the pencil-and-paper-type test such as the embedded-figures test, or the hidden-figures test. It is evident from Table 2.1 that much of the research dealing with sport and physical activity has used such devices. These tests have a number of advantages, but also some distinct disadvantages. In group form they are quick and easy to administer and require little time to score. Of greater importance is the regard the researcher must give to their valid use in a variety of situations, with a dynamic type of test of field dependence probably being more appropriate in situations where one is dealing with the concept of field dependence as it relates to skilled athletic performance.

Perhaps the most definitive study comparing various athletic sub-groups for perceptual style was that of Pargman (1974) who evaluated the perceptual style of 150 male athletes from five colleges. They used the group-hidden-figures test in comparing the perceptual style of 51 subjects classified as team sport athletes, and 64 subjects classified as

Table 2.1   Summary of Studies using Measures of Perceptual Style and
Physical Activity and Sport Skills

Author	Date	Perceptual Style Measure	Skill Classification
J. C. Kreiger	1962	EFT	Spatial location
J. Torres	1966	EFT	Catching
D. S. Siegel	1971	EFT	Hitting ball
F. Meek & V. Skubic	1971	RFT	Six motor skills
L. D. Schreiber	1972	RFT	Team choice
B. J. Shugart, M. A. Souder & L. K. Bunker	1972	RFT	Balance task
J. Jorgensen	1972	RFT	Alaskan yo-yo
C. Bard	1972	RFT	Various sports
J. Green	1972	EFT & RFT	Various sports
P. G. Brown	1974	GHFT	Individual-team sports
D. W. Bundy	1974	CEFT & PRFT	Body balance
J. G. Svinicki et al.	1974	RFT*	Active–inactive individuals
D. Pargman et al.	1975	GHFT	Basketball shoot
J. Williams	1975	GHFT	Fencing
G. V. Barrell & H. R. Trippe	1975	PRFT	Dance, soccer, cricket, tennis, track & field
P. Deshaies & D. Pargman	1976	GHFT	Football players
D. Pargman & K. Inomata	1976	GHFT	Tennis toss
W. W. MacGillivary	1977	PRFT	Catching task
A. Lee et al.	1978	CEFT	Ball handling skills
R. J. Rotela & L. K. Bunker	1978	PRFT	Reaction time
R. J. Robertson et al.	1978	EFT	Bicycle ergometry

*Used a single trial

individual sport athletes. The results of the investigation upheld the hypothesis that team sport athletes are more field-dependent than individual sport athletes. However, the presence of a football group in the team sport classification tended to confuse the issue, as most of the differences in perceptual style scores were between the two athletic sub-groups and thus was accounted for by the football group.

The likelihood that there is little, if any, relationship between perceptual style and perceptual-motor skills at the present time may be due in part to the procedures used to measure this dimension. In a study involving a group of fencers of varying ability Williams (1975) failed to find differences in their performance on a measure of field dependence. She did, however, suggest that as a group fencers tended to be more field-independent, although one might question her rationale for using the EFT in this study rather than the rod-and-frame test. Similarly, Deshaies & Pargman (1976) failed to differentiate between a group of varsity and junior varsity football players on the basis of their performance on several visual parameters including the EFT. Again, this study was dealing with subjects who were participating in a dynamic type of activity, once more questioning the use of this particular measure rather than, say, the rod-and-frame test. It can be argued that in a sport like football there is a certain requirement to be able to disembed an object as is expected in the EFT. Such a requirement, however, may be specific to the position played within an American Football team. For example, the flanker would be faced with this demand more often than the lineman, or the defensive back more than the tackle.

In addition to seeking to identify the relationship between field dependence, athletics and sport performance, there have been attempts to identify the importance of this particular perceptual dimension in the performance of more specific skills. Pargman, Bender & Deshaies (1975), for example, employed a correlational analysis of two basketball shooting skills and a measure of field dependence, but failed to find any significant relationship between them. The basketball skills were the free throw and field goal-shooting ability and they were compared with performance on the hidden-figures test of perceptual style. In the execution of a basketball shot it might be argued that an important factor is the ability to separate visually the basket from the backboard. This being the case, then it might also be considered appropriate to use a measure such as the hidden figures test to evaluate field dependence.

A more recent study by MacGillivary (1978) noted differences between various team athletes at the intercollegiate level, with a sex difference also evident among athletic sub-groups. Performance on the group-embedded-figures test (GEFT) showed significant differences between female field hockey players and male soccer players, and between male and female swimmers. Interestingly, the soccer players were more field-independent than the field hockey players, while results for the swimmers showed a reversal of this finding with females being more field-independent. In the case of the difference between soccer and field hockey it is difficult to readily identify a rationale for the outcome. In both sports there is a demand for a disembedding type of visual perception, and it can only be assumed that the difference favouring males as more field-independent was also evident in this study. The swimming data are more difficult to explain and it is suggested that the nature of the test of perceptual style may have contributed to the results. In the same study the female basketball players were found to be significantly more field-independent than the female volleyball players, further emphasising the need for more valid measures of this perceptual dimension. The measure chosen should be based upon the nature of both the task and the performer. In terms of athletic performance, one can readily identify some skills and some performers who might be better evaluated with the EFT rather than the rod-and-frame test. As an example, the athlete who is involved in performing skills which produce a conflict of cues, such as a skier, might be better tested for perceptual style with the rod-and-frame test. On the other hand the athlete who must visually disembed an object, such as a ball, from a rather homogeneous background, as in the case of a football flanker, might be better tested with the embedded-figures test.

A number of studies have tried to relate field dependence to the performance of perceptual-motor skills of a more specific nature. Kreiger (1962) indicated that there might be a link between performance demonstrated on the embedded-figures test and the ability to properly position a tennis racquet. The suggestion that the EFT, or figure–ground differentiation in general, is related to spatial localisation has, however, been refuted by Torres (1966). She found that there was no statistical relationship between performance on a ball-catching task and performance on the embedded-figures test.

The majority of studies reviewed in this chapter have considered the relationship between the various measures of field dependence and both type and level of performance of sports skills. There has been little research conducted to determine the contribution made to perceptual-motor performance as a result of a distinctive perceptual style. In one study which did consider the subject Jorgensen (1972) produced the interesting finding that there was an inverse relationship between field independence and the rate at which one learns a novel motor task. A more recent study by MacGillivary (1977) has lent support to these results when investigating the relationship of perceptual style to the acquisition of catching skill under varying environmental conditions. MacGillivary (1977) showed that there was a significant relationship between the amount of learning on the catching task, the time for which the ball was observed and the perceptual style of the subject. In other words, field-independent subjects learned the catching task better than those classified as field-dependent.

The research to date tends to be equivocal with respect to the role of a distinctive perceptual style in perceptual-motor and sports performance. There are indications that there may be a link between the way an individual *relates* to a performance situation and his ability to perform that task. That is, the literature indicates that there may be an association between the perceptual style of an individual and his ability to perform a particular skill. There is also evidence suggesting that type of sport involvement may be indicative of the perceptual style a person demonstrates; whether an individual or a team sport athlete. The failure to reach total agreement on the role of a perceptual style, or typology, for athletes and various types of athletic endeavour should not be considered a complete loss. The inability to achieve a consensus at this time may be largely due to the confounding variable of procedures for evaluating perceptual style. This chapter has, for example, noted that a number of studies have used a form of the rod-and-frame test, while others have employed some form of the embedded-, or hidden-figures tests. The somewhat indiscriminate use of these various instruments has been confirmed by Arbuthnot (1972) and the fact that results obtained in using these tests do not generally concur may account for much of the divergence apparent in the literature.

References

Arbuthnot, J. (1972) "Cautionary note on measurement of field independence", *Perceptual and Motor Skills*, 35: 479–88.

Bard C. (1972) "The relation between perceptual style and physical activities", *International Journal of Sport Psychology*, 7: 107–13.

Barrell, G. V. & Trippe, H. R. (1975) "Field-dependence and physical ability", *Perceptual and Motor Skills*, 41: 216–18.

Brown, P. G. (1974) Comparison of female team and individual sport secondary school athletes on traits of field independence–field dependence. Unpublished Master's Thesis, Florida State University, Tallahassee.

Bundy, D. W. (1974) Performance of kindergarten children on two measures of field dependence-field independence and a selected movement task. Unpublished Master's Thesis, Purdue University, Lafayette: Indiana.

Deshaies, P. & Pargman, D. (1976) "Selected visual abilities of college football players", *Perceptual and Motor Skills*, 32: 904.

Green, J. (1972) Perceptual style and athletic choice. Unpublished paper, University of Wisconsin, Madison.

Jorgensen, J. (1972) The relationship between perceptual style and the rate of learning a novel movement task. Unpublished Master's Thesis, University of Wisconsin, Madison.

Kane, J. E. (1972) "Personality, body concept and performance", in J. E. Kane (Ed.) *Psychological Aspects of Physical Education and Sport*. London: Routledge & Kegan Paul.

Klein, J. C. (1951) "The personal world through perception", in R. R. Blake & G. V. Ramsey (Eds.) *Perception: An Approach to Personality*. New York: Ronald Press.

Kreiger, J. C. (1962) The influence of figure-ground perception on spatial adjustment in tennis. Unpublished Master's Thesis, University of California, Los Angeles.

Lee, A., Fant, H., Life, M. L. & Lipe, L. (1978) "Field-independence and performance on ball handling tasks", *Perceptual and Motor Skills*, 46: 439–42.

MacGillivary, William W. (1977) Perceptual style and ball skill acquisition. Unpublished Doctoral Thesis, University of Wisconsin, Madison.

MacGillivary, William W. (1978) Perceptual style and intercollegiate athletics. Unpublished paper, University of New Brunswick, Fredericton.

Meek, F. & Skubic V. (1971) "Spatial perception of highly skilled and poorly skilled females", *Perceptual and Motor Skills*, 33: 1309–10.

Pargman, D. (1974) "Field-dependence of selected athletic sub-groups", *Medicine and Science in Sports*, 6: 283–6.

Pargman, D., Bender, P. & Deshaies, P. (1975) "Correlation between visual disembedding and basketball shooting by male and female varsity college athletes", *Perceptual and Motor Skills*, 41: 956.

Pargman, D. & Inomata, K. (1976) "Field-dependence, displaced vision and motor performance", *Journal of Motor Behavior*, 8: 11–17.

Petrie, A., (1960) "Some psychological aspects of pain and the relief of suffering", *Annals of the N.Y. Academy of Science* LXXXVI, 13–27.

Robertson, R. J., Gillespie, R. L., McCarthy, J. & Rose, J. (1978) "Perceived exertion and the field dependence-independence dimension", *Perceptual and Motor Skills*, 46: 495–500.

Rotela, R. J. & Bunker, L. K. (1978) "Field dependence and reaction time in senior tennis players", *Perceptual and Motor Skills*, 46: 585–6.

Ryan, E. D. & Kovacic, C. R. (1966) "Pain tolerance and athletic participation", *Perceptual and Motor Skills*, 22: 383-90.

Schreiber, L. D. (1972) Field-dependence–field-independence and athletic team choice in college males. Unpublished Master's Thesis, Boston University, Boston, Massachusetts.

Shugart, B. J., Souder, M. A. & Bunker, L. K. (1972) "Relationship between vertical space perception and a dynamic non-locomotor balance task", *Perceptual and Motor Skills*, 34: 43–6.

Siegel, D. S. (1971) Visual ambiguity and skilled performance. Unpublished Master's Thesis, University of Massachusetts, Amherst.

Svinicki, J. G., Bungard, C. J., Schwensohn, C. H. & Westgor, D. J. (1974) "Physical activity and visual field-dependency", *Perceptual and Motor Skills*, 39: 1237–8.

Torres, J. (1966) The relationship between figure-ground perceptual ability and ball catching ability in ten and thirteen year old boys and girls. Unpublished Master's Thesis, Purdue University, Lafayette, Indiana.

Williams, J. (1975) "Perceptual style and fencing skill", *Perceptual and Motor Skills*, 40: 282.

Witkin, H. A. (1954) "The nature and importance of individual differences in perception", in H. A. Witkin (Ed.), *Personality Through Perception*. New York: Harper.

Witkin, H. A., Faterson, R. G., Goodenough, D. R. & Karp, S. A. (1962). *Psychological Differentiation: Studies of Development*, New York: Wiley.

3

Use the Eyes to Control Your Putting*

Ian M. Cockerill

When a golf ball is superimposed upon a two-dimensional shape equal in surface area to a standard golf hole it may appear surprising that putting is considered a difficult skill (Figure 3.1). This 'game within a game' has become an increasingly crucial element of golf alongside the development of more sophisticated methods of course preparation. However, there are those who believe that it has become too important. Dobereiner (1972), for example, has emphatically stated that while putting was part of the game during the early days of golf's development it was a relatively minor ingredient. Skill has now replaced chance factors on the putting green, with the ball rolling smoothly on a surface prepared with the best aids that modern horticulture can provide.

Half the number of shots allocated to each round of golf are for putting, but what is the best method to adopt in order to ensure that the ball drops into the hole? When guidance is sought from the world's successful players they are often vague in advising the less able golfer, as Nicklaus's (1974) advice indicated:

> Your main concern on the course is 'feel'! That's what you want to develop on the practice green. My objective when I practise putting is to achieve a rhythmic feeling between my hands and the ball in a well-timed stroke. When I get the desired sensation in six or seven putts I stop.

*Part of this chapter was presented by the author at an International Congress in Physical Education, University of Quebec at Trois-Rivières, Canada, 26–30 June 1979. The paper is published in C. H. Nadeau, W. R. Halliwell, K. M. Newell & G. C. Roberts (Eds.), *Psychology of Motor Behavior and Sport—1979*, Champaign, Illinois: Human Kinetics Publishers, 1980, whose permission to include the material here is acknowledged.

hitting the ball correctly leading to greater inaccuracy? Second, would experienced golfers' putting be adversely affected by an "eyes on the hole" technique? Finally, would putting distance interact with the two vision conditions under consideration?

It is thought likely that without an opportunity for lengthy practice experienced golfers will not readily adapt to a new putting method, whereas non-golfing subjects, as a control, might usefully be tested on their ability to putt accurately when focusing the eyes on either ball or hole. The investigation described below was designed to determine how effort control in putting – a typical ballistic skill – might be facilitated among both low handicap golfers and subjects with no previous golfing experience.

The Investigation

Two groups of twenty right-hand-preferent males were designated 'golfers' (ages 22–42 years; handicaps 6 and below) and 'non-golfers' (ages 20–38 years).

A length of synthetic putting matt was placed upon a 10 cm high, flat platform and with a standard size golf hole, 11 cm diameter, cut towards one end. The platform was used to permit the ball to drop below the surface of the mat. Although using the platform necessitated subjects standing 10 cm below the putting surface to perform the experiment, a pilot study showed that operating in this situation neither assisted or impaired putting performance. At the other end two parallel beams of light, 10 cm apart, were set to shine across the mat. Holes, also 10 cm apart, were drilled through a wooden block placed directly opposite the light sources, and in both holes a light-sensitive device was connected to a timer. Any object obstructing the beam nearer to the end of the mat activated the timer until the furthest beam was obstructed. A centre-shaft putter and Dunlop "65" golf ball (1.62 in. diameter) were used throughout.

The effects of vision, target distance and golfing experience were evaluated using a ANOVA split-plot factorial design (SPF 2.22; Kirk, 1968). All subjects were required to putt towards the hole from 100 cm and 200 cm. Within both distances their vision was restricted by means of a triangular blinker made from stiff card and attached to the left or right side of the head according to whether the subject was required to watch the ball or the hole as he putted. The design also provided for comparisons to be made between the four sub-groups of subjects for the number of putts holed and for any tendency to hit to the left or right of the hole. Each subject received four blocks of twenty-five trials according to four operating conditions and the order of performing under each condition was randomised.

The mean time for the ball to travel between the two light sources, 10 cm apart, was calculated for each block of trials per subject. Times in milliseconds were later converted to distance putted in centimetres by referring to previously obtained data. This involved putting a golf ball towards a ball marker placed in each of forty positions on a length of putting mat 500 cm long. Distances from the 'start' beam of the apparatus were randomly presented in increments of 10 cm and ranging from 60 cm to 450 cm. Blocks of twenty-five trials were conducted at each distance; making one thousand trials in all. The mean distance associated with each time recorded was calculated and these data provided a set of norms for relating time for the ball to travel the initial 10 cm to overall distance putted.

Knowledge of results was available after each trial and holed putts were recorded by placing a mark on the data sheet, while missed putts were identified as rolling to the left or right of the hole. A standard form of instructions was read to each subject immediately before he took part in the experiment and after positioning the blinker to the appropriate side of his head.

An analysis of variance showed that distance was a highly significant source of variation among all subjects in respect of effort control ($F = 262 \cdot 73$; $df\ 1,18$; $p < 0 \cdot 001$); with an increase in target distance being commensurate with an increase in performance error. The manipulation of vision as an independent variable indicated that there was no significant difference between subjects' performance while looking at the ball ($F = 2 \cdot 35$; $df\ 1,13$; $p > 0 \cdot 05$). Golfing experience was also a non-significant source of variation ($F = 0 \cdot 23$; $df\ 1,18$; $p > 0 \cdot 05$); non-golfers were equally capable as golfers in their ability to putt the ball to the required distance of 100 cm and 200 cm. The interactions golfing experience with distance ($F = 1 \cdot 04$; $df\ 1,18$; $p > 0 \cdot 05$), golfing experience with vision ($F = 0 \cdot 94$; $df\ 1,13$; $p > 0 \cdot 05$) and distance with vision ($F = 0 \cdot 65$; $df\ 1,18$; $p > 0 \cdot 05$) were all non-significant.

Table 3.1   Group Mean Comparisons of Percentage Putts Holed in Both Vision Conditions

	Non-Golfers	Golfers	Putts holed per 1000
Eyes on ball	74·60	87·72	811
Eyes on hole	53·20	87·00	701

A preliminary comparison was made of the percentage putts holed between both vision conditions. Table 3.1 shows that whereas non-golfers scored better with eyes on the ball (74·60 per cent putts holed with eyes on ball) the golfers' performance was remarkably similar in both conditions (87·72 per cent putts holed with eyes on ball, 87·00 per cent putts holed with eyes on hole).

Table 3.2   Group Mean Comparisons of Putts Holed by Golfers and Non-Golfers

| | | 100 cm | | 200 cm | |
		Ball	Hole	Ball	Hole
Non-golfers	$\bar{X}$	21·40	16·70	15·90	9·90
	S.D.	2·67	2·91	3·54	4·12
Golfers	$\bar{X}$	24·00	24·00	19·80	19·50
	S.D.	1·25	0·94	3·49	3·10

Group mean comparisons of putts holed by both groups of subjects (Table 3.2) revealed surprising consistency by the golfers at both distances irrespective of viewing condition, while non-golfers performed less accurately over both distances when required to watch the hole as they putted.

Table 3.3   Effort Control as a Function of Distance Putted

| | | 100 cm | | 200 cm | |
		Ball	Hole	Ball	Hole
Non-golfers	$\bar{X}$	145·50	156·00	212·70	217·80
	S.D.	11·67	23·46	21·89	14·04
Golfers	$\bar{X}$	142·20	145·20	217·10	217·30
	S.D.	20·75	18·14	15·84	12·31

Table 3.3 indicates the mean distances putted by both groups of subjects within the vision and distance variables. There was marked similarity between golfers' and non-golfers' scores in all situations. In the case of holed putts, 'distance' was converted from time in

Table 3.4   Comparisons of Missed Putts Finishing to Left or Right of the Hole

	Chi-square	Level of Significance
Eyes on ball	3·31	$p > 0·05$
Eyes on hole	0·27	$p > 0·05$
Non-golfers	7·78	$p < 0·01$
Golfers	2·84	$p > 0·05$
100 cm	2·60	$p > 0·05$
200 cm	0·64	$p > 0·05$

milliseconds recorded for the first 10 cm of the putt as previously described.

Finally, comparisons were made for the effects of the three independent variables upon hitting to left or right of the hole (Table 3.4) and only lack of golfing experience was a significant determinant of putting off line ($X = 7 \cdot 78$; $p < 0 \cdot 01$).

The broad outcome of the results indicates no support for the findings of Whiting & Cockerill (1974) who demonstrated that watching a target facilitated scoring when a hand-held object was propelled along the ground. However, when an object was propelled by an instrumental extension of the hand as in golf putting, neither watching target or ball proved the better strategy. Although all subjects demonstrated relatively good effort control in their putting performance, errors revealed a tendency to overshoot from both the 100 cm and 200 cm distances (Table 3.3). It is acknowledged that both are short in terms of the range of putting distances that normally confront a golfer. While the longer of the two distances was limited by the overall length of the putting surface, it should be recognised that many putts are missed from within two metres of the hole in a game of golf.

The present data support the findings of Kelliher (1963) who identified a similar phenomenon of overshooting when putting from 6 and 13 ft. However, recent studies by Cockerill & Callington (see Chapter 11) and Cockerill & Raven (1980) have demonstrated that constant errors in perceptual underestimation occur among both adults and children for distances up to approximately 50 metres. These recent findings suggest that if distance to a target is underestimated, then associated errors in performance might reasonably be expected to result in undershooting. Only when Kelliher's (1963) subjects putted from 30 ft did this phenomenon occur. In Chapter 11 Cockerill & Callington discuss their findings and those of related studies in attempting to clarify the likely relationship between distance perception and sports performance.

Despite similarities between both groups for effort control the non-golfers holed fewer putts from 200 cm while watching the hole. It is proposed that beginners prefer to watch the ball to ensure that they make good contact with it and that this early behaviour becomes a habit which persists throughout their playing life. The need for inexperienced performers to watch the ball rather than locate its position kinaesthetically with the putter head is not surprising in the context of the well-known study of Fleishman & Rich (1963), which produced strong evidence for a dominant visual modality over kinaesthesis during the early stages of motor learning. The present data, in showing experienced golfers to be equally successful for both effort control and holing putts irrespective of viewing ball or hole, leads to speculation that if these low handicap players had used the 'eyes-on-the-hole' method from the beginning, they might be even more accurate on the putting green.

A recent study by Newell, Shapiro & Carlton (1979) investigating the problems associated with cross-modal compatibility may also have implications for the present experiment; although the tasks reported by Newell and his associates were of a slow, positioning nature, unlike those typically fast, ballistic movements of a ball game. Moreover, the distances they employed were relatively short, being within reach of the body, yet it was recognised that the problems of visual-kinaesthetic correspondence beyond the kinesphere are important ones, but at the present time await resolution.

Practical Applications

It is proposed that the accurate control of effort by both groups of subjects in the present investigation may have been an artifact associated with the necessity for a smooth putting stroke accompanied by a good follow-through when using the apparatus. A 'stabbing' action would have restarted the timer because of a 'rebound' effect by the putter, thus making it impossible to obtain information from the timing device.

A report by Ballantine (1980) emphasised the importance of this putting method, frequently referred to as 'blocking' or 'brushing', and he cited Tom Watson, the top money winner in American golf between 1977 and 1979, as an advocate of such a technique. The journalist's advice on putting was that:

> Length, not direction, is the prime requisite. If you don't believe it, try putting along your sitting-room carpet into a plain tumbler. Simply try to hole the ball, and don't worry if it speeds past. Hitting the target is easy, you'll find, if you don't have to worry about the ball 'dying' near it.

Ballantine (1980) suggested that the best way to hit the correct distance is to putt as if forearms and wrists are welded together and with a total lack of wristiness. There is abundant evidence that a smooth stroke, as enforced by the apparatus in this experiment, is the most effective putting method. Stuart (1974), a British Walker Cup player, was reported as attributing an improvement in his putting to this technique:

> At the Walker Cup at St Andrew's the only thing the team coach,

John Jacobs, spoke to me about was my putting. He got me to take a longer, smoother stroke instead of making a sharp jab at the ball. Ever since then I've putted soundly.

Finally, Faulkner (1973), a former winner of the British Open Golf Championship, commented upon the successful putting action of Lee Trevino during a match played between the two: "he is putting even better than last year – a nice, slow stroke and the blade so square".

In describing the present investigation it has been suggested that the reason for all group mean scores of distance putted falling within the criterion distances for holing putts at 100 cm and 200 cm was largely attributed to the adoption of the effective putting stroke identified above. Low (1974) drew attention to the importance of a good stroke in acquiring the much sought after quality of 'feel' in stating: "You can teach feel only up to a point . . . but good mechanics promote good feel." Allis (1973), on the other hand, saw importance in the relationship between the perceived distance from ball to hole and the amount of force required to make a successful putt. His reference to Jack Nicklaus playing the third round of the British Open Championship at Troon in 1973 is appropriate to this discussion: ". . . trying to picture the strength of his putt in his mind's eye", and an early statement by Hanley (1937) may have been the first to raise this issue within the context of golf. She wrote:

Hand in hand with the fundamentals the instructor should endeavour to instil in the mind of his pupil the idea of *thinking* the swing and recalling the correct movements by a sense of muscle feel.

A further outcome of the data analysis was that a greater number of putts rolled to the right of the hole when watching the ball as compared with watching the hole, although the result was non-significant (Table 3.4). It is proposed, therefore, that aiming is improved by focusing eyes on the hole and that a future investigation might seek to establish the reliability of this finding. Bowen (1968), for example, showed that irrespective of watching ball or hole, directional errors revealed a tendency to putt to the left, although he found, as in the present study, that focusing upon the hole when putting did not impair effort control. Accordingly, an experiment to examine the various parameters of aiming along the 'z' axis of visual space seems the most logical 'next step' for research into golf putting.

As pointed out in the introduction to this chapter, the main aim of the putting experiment was to determine the relative efficiency of using hand only or a hand-held instrument to propel an object along the ground in order to locate a distant target. The outcome suggests that watching the target in both these ballistic tasks may prove the better overall strategy, not only for effort control, but also for directional accuracy.

Golfers should take care to ensure that they strike approach putts to within two metres of the hole, from which distance effort control has been shown to be more or less accurate. Providing that beginners can be taught a mechanically sound, smooth putting stroke that is reliable over a range of distances and recognise the importance of a square club face at impact – because of a tendency for directional errors to be made to the right – then it is likely that watching the hole as they putt will prove more successful than watching the ball.

The implications of this study extend beyond the game of golf which has been used as a paradigm to illustrate just one kind of ballistic aiming task as maybe found in many sports. Acknowledging the specific nature of skill in sport it is, nevertheless, useful to attempt to identify and also classify those tasks which possess common elements. Such an exercise will surely promote a greater understanding of the nature of skilled motor behaviour generally and particularly within the context of sport, it is hoped for players, coaches and spectators alike.

References

Allis, P. (1973) BBC television broadcast, 13 June.

Ballantine, J. (1980) "Watson's way, putt for pay", *Sunday Times,* London, 2 March.

Bowen, R. T. (1968) "Putting errors of beginning golfers using different points of aim", *Research Quarterly,* 39: 31-5.

Cheatum, B. A. (1969) *Golf,* Philadelphia: Saunders.

Cockerill, I. M. (1975) Perceived distance and effort output control in ballistic aiming tasks. Unpublished Doctoral Thesis, University of Leeds.

Cockerill, I. M. & Raven, S. J. (1980) A developmental study of distance judgment in a standardised environment. Unpublished paper, Department of Physical Education, University of Birmingham.

Dobereiner, P. (1972) "In the interests of simplicity for the coarse golfer", *Golf Illustrated,* July, p. 637.

Faulkner, M. (1973) "Jacklin studies a defect and improves putting", *Daily Telegraph,* London, 10 July.

Fleishman, E. A. & Rich, S. (1963) "Role of kinaesthetic and spatial-visual abilities in perceptual-motor learning", *Journal of Experimental Psychology,* 66: 6-11.

Hanley, S. (1937) The sense of feel in golf, *Journal of Health, Physical Education and Recreation,* 8: 366-7 & 390.

Kelliher, M. S. (1963) "Analysis of two styles of golf putting", *Research Quarterly,* 34: 344-9.

Kirk, R. E. (1968) *Experimental Design: Research Procedures for the Behavioral Sciences.* Belmont, California: Brooks-Cole.

Low, G. (1974) "Choosing the right putter", *Golf World,* March, pp. 28-31.

Newell, K. M., Shapiro, D. C. & Carlton, M. J. (1979) "Coordinating the visual and kinaesthetic memory codes", *British Journal of Psychology*, 70: 87–96.

Nicklaus, J. (1974) "Putting: mental approach and strategy", *Golf World*, May, pp. 74–7.

Stuart, H. (1974) "Hugh Banks on his putting", *Sunday Express*, London, 2 June.

Valentine, J. (1974). "See the ball into the hole", *Golf World*, June, p. 70.

Whiting, H. T. A. (1969) *Acquiring Ball Skill: A Psychological Interpretation*, London: Bell.

Whiting, H. T. A. & Cockerill, I. M. (1974) "Eyes on hand – Eyes on target?" *Journal of Motor Behavior*, 6: 27–32.

4

Considering Eye Movement as a Predictor of Attainment

Chantal Bard and Michelle Fleury

Visual Search and Team Sports

A rapidly changing variety of information characterises the environment of the team sport player. He must quickly and constantly select relevant visual cues, while discarding or ignoring the irrelevant, in order to give an adequate motor response. Such selection is not randomly performed, with the human organism capable of determining visual strategies to minimise the cost of a response by sampling useful information by maintaining a high efficiency–cost ratio (Edwards & Slovic, 1965).

The coach usually pays attention to the learning of a motor response based on the player's experience. It might be as important for him to consider the visual dimension as a major learning and performance factor, grounded this time on the perceptual experience of the subject. Indeed, the literature shows that experience also plays a vital role in visual search patterns and in the corresponding outputs or responses (Gould & Schaffer, 1965; Kundell & LaFolette, 1972; Mourant & Rockwell, 1972; Bard & Fleury, 1976).

Visual exploration is one of the main factors for processing information, but because of the limited capacities of his sensory receptors man must *choose* the information to be analysed. Such an exploration, or search, has two essential functions: first to collect information and, second, to establish relationships between these obtained pieces of information, using them adequately to predict future events and prepare adapted responses.

Visual search seems to reflect which cues have been judged important enough to be retained among all potential cues. The selection made by visual search is both quantitative and qualitative: (a) the number of ocular fixations and the surface covered during exploration give an estimation of the number of pieces of information collected; (b) the scanpath, or sequence of exploration, generally reflects a search strategy and provides a way of determining to which elements of the stimulus the subject has chosen to relate; (c) the duration of the fixation over a definite spatial point corresponds to the time needed to register the information.

Oculo-motor activity is typically composed of successive ocular movements, or saccades, and pauses known as ocular fixations. Research indicates that afferent messages are more or less inhibited during saccades (Uttal & Smith, 1968; Ditchburn, 1973; Matin, 1974; Massaro, 1975) and information is registered during fixations or pauses. Saccades are, therefore, uninformational and in this area research has mainly focused upon information gathered during ocular fixations.

According to the literature, visual search strategy seems related to different factors: the nature of the task and the conditions in which the task is performed, the subject's characteristics, and the environmental conditions external to the tasks (Chambers, 1973). In team sports the nature of the task can be defined as problem solving and, as such, involves decision-making; namely rules of selecting an alternative response to given states of affairs. Temporal constraints are typical of the need for reference to such mnemonic rules, while task conditions or input characteristics can be classified into four categories: structural properties, qualitative properties, spatial properties and temporal properties, each one influencing performance (Gould, 1973; Christ, 1974; Teichner & Krebs, 1974).

Visual search processes and subsequent performance do not depend solely on task characteristics, they are also influenced by subject characteristics such as expertise and age. Schoonard, Gould & Miller (1973) registered the ocular movements of trained inspectors looking for defects in micro-integrated circuits. After a few months of training the mean duration of eye fixations was 200 msec and the longest fixations seemed to be centred on complex features of the display with less trained observers showing longest durations.

The number of ocular movements and the distribution of fixations vary with both age of subjects and nature of task. In familiarisation tasks three-year-old children show very little activity (Yarbus, 1967), with ocular fixations usually accumulating at the centre of the presentation. Around six years of age ocular movement trajectory follows the entire frame (contour), exploration is exhaustive, and while the number of movements increases, the duration of each fixation diminishes with age (Haber & Hershenson, 1973).

Visual scanpaths show trial-to-trial inconsistency, but explaining how so many different input sequences can be used to arrive at roughly the same perceptual experience remains a theoretical issue (Kolers, 1972). Nevertheless, instructions to the subject prior to the experiment largely influence his subsequent pattern. Yarbus (1967), for example, reported studies in which he varied the instruction to the perceiver. For each condition he alerted the viewer that he would be asked different kinds of questions after looking at a picture for three minutes. It became clear that fixation patterns are dramatically modified by instructions or immediate past conditions.

This brief review of literature illustrates that effective information processing is the key to adequate and prompt response to a given task. Therefore eye movement recording, a well-accepted measure of perceptual processing, can help the researcher and the coach to understand those perceptual processes underlying sport activities and, more specifically, team sports.

Eye Movement Recording

Several techniques are available for the recording of eye movements. The choice of a specific method generally depends on the type of eye movements studied, since each has its advantages and disadvantages. Extensive reviews of existing procedures and their characteristics can be found in Levy-Schoen (1969), Ditchburn (1973), Young & Sheena (1975) and Mounty & Senders (1976).

Ditchburn (1973) identified two different procedures: (a) methods which do not require an attachment to the eye, and (b) methods which do require such attachment. Most methods which do not require an attachment to the eye are less sensitive and less accurate in response to high frequency movements. Nevertheless, these methods have an important advantage in that they are convenient to apply to a large group of subjects and it is highly unlikely that eye movements are affected by the procedures used to measure them. Several techniques requiring no attachment to the eye are available; such as the corneal reflection technique, the after-image technique, the corneo-retinal potential technique, or electro-oculography, the scleral observation technique, and the double-Purkinje image technique (Ditchburn, 1973). The corneal reflection technique, widely used and easily applicable in sports situations, will be described.

The Corneal Reflection Technique

In this method a beam of radiation is reflected from the anterior surface of the cornea. The rotation of the eye about an instantaneous centre which does not coincide with the centre of curvature of the corneal surface causes a deflection of the beam (Ditchburn, 1973; Cumming, 1978). This deflection is an indicator of the subject's fixation and may be observed visually using a television camera or a ciné camera. In the studies presented in the next section the corneal reflection technique was used with the eye movement recorder fixed on the subject's

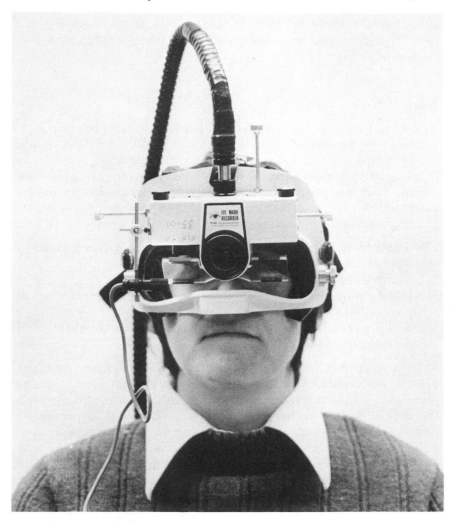

Figure 4.1   The NAC Eye Movement Recorder

head, thereby allowing free head movement (Figure 4.1). The technique permits the filming of the scene viewed by the subject with a bright 'V', representing the location of eye fixation, superimposed on the scene being filmed. The location of the 'V' corresponds to the region fixed by the subject with a precision of $\pm 2°$ of visual angle.

The Investigations

In a series of experiments conducted in both laboratory and field situations the strategies used by subjects in problem solving tasks specific to team sports were studied. Two sports, basketball and ice hockey, were investigated.

Basketball

Before making a decision a basketball player must process afferent information. To do that he must select and analyse visual information from the environment and then decide upon a response. Main sources of information are the locations of players on the court at a given time; that is, different positioning leads to different responses by the ball carrier when passing, dribbling and shooting.

The purpose of the following studies was to determine:

1. if experts in a given sport differ from less experienced players in their visual search patterns;
2. if experts are faster in finding solutions;
3. if, according to the type of responses required by the presentations, players respond differentially to visual cues;
4. if the complexity of situations affects the search strategy and performance of the players.

To answer these questions both expert and beginner basketball players were tested. Typical offensive basketball situations were presented to subjects on slides (Figure 4.2). At the onset of the stimulus the subject had to verbalise his answer as fast and as precisely as possible. The slide disappeared and timing was stopped as soon as the subject verbalised his answer. A single correct answer was linked to each slide shown. The possible answers were: shoot, dribble, pass to a specific and free partner, or stay (status quo). The measures were decision time and number of fixations, and choice of these parameters was made on the grounds that they best reflect the central analytical mechanisms (Just & Carpenter, 1975).

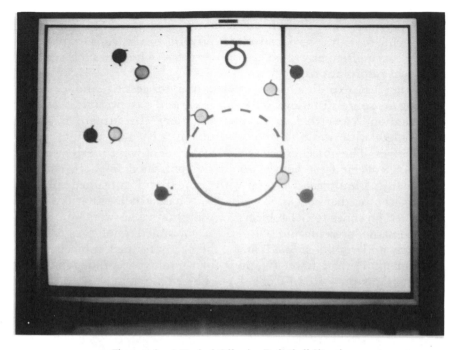

Figure 4.2   A Typical Offensive Basketball Situation

It was shown that expert basketball players have fewer fixations than novices (3.3 as compared with 4.9 fixations). However, there was no significant difference between experts and non-experts for decision time. It was also found that the type of problem-solving task presented to a subject (pass, dribble or shoot) significantly modifies the number of fixations and decision time. These initial results demonstrate an interesting point; the number of items on the slides were identical for all situations, yet they did not present the same informational load leading to different search strategies. Accordingly, it was decided to examine the locations of fixations according to type of problem-solving task and level of subjects' expertise.

The first finding was that search is never exhaustive. Subjects, whether experts or beginners, tend to select specific cues and, as soon as they possess sufficient information, respond. However, experts have a tendency to make repeated sequences of fixations on a pair of offensive–defensive players, giving importance to the opponent, while the beginner ignores the defensive player altogether, thus favouring his partner. The expert player more often fixates a significant empty space (a space between the ball carrier and the basket). This may, perhaps, be linked with the phenomenon that Kundell (1974) referred to as priority given by the subject to an element according to the use intended to be made of it. It is obviously more difficult for novices to exploit this empty space efficiently than it is for experts, who use such space as pertinent information.

In the first experiment on information processing and decision-making in sport situations only one solution was possible from the presentation. Nevertheless, in real situations the athlete is mostly confronted with multiple-choice problems; he has to face many alternatives. The object of the second experiment was to verify whether the data collected previously would be confirmed in more complex situations; with alternatives and with trained and untrained subjects. As on the earlier occasion, offensive basketball situations were presented on slides to the subjects, but alternative answers were added for the same presentation. Situations contained one, two or three solutions and results showed that experts, or trained subjects (as in Experiment 1), had fewer fixations than non-experts independent of the situations presented (Table 4.1). The results also showed that an increase in the number of choices (one, two or three choices in the presentation) facilitated decision-making (Table 4.1).

Table 4.1   Decision Time (DT) and Mean Number of Fixations according to Situation Complexity

		Complexity 1	*Complexity 2*	*Complexity 3*
Experts	DT (sec)	0.940	0.811	0.783
	NF	4.33	3.52	3.24
Non-experts	DT (sec)	1.361	1.080	1.000
	NF	5.09	4.59	4.18

With the influence of solution complexity on information processing and decision-making being established, it became interesting to compare the data from both experiments, where a subject was dealing with the same problem (only one solution), but was facing two different contexts. In the first experiment the subject was informed that all situations had a single solution ($\overline{W}A$: without alternative); in the second experiment with alternative choices (WA) the subject was told that the problem situations may have one, two or three solutions. For subsequent analysis only the situation with one solution was considered.

The results showed that all subjects were faster in making their decision and had fewer fixations when the context was without alternative ($\overline{W}A$) (Table 4.2).

Table 4.2   Decision Time (DT) and Mean Number of Fixations
according to Different Contexts

		Context without Alternative ($\overline{W}A$)	Context with Alternative (WA)
Experts	DT (sec)	0.937	0.940
	NF	3.30	4.33
Non-experts	DT (sec)	1.211	1.361
	NF	4.76	5.09

However, the context had more influence on task naïve subjects than experts. This result could be explained by a greater perceptual flexibility for experts; that is, an ability to adapt more rapidly to perceptual alternatives.

If we assume that the study was similar to the choice reaction-time studies, longer decision times could easily be predicted for a context involving alternatives because of the difference in the probability of appearance of the stimuli (Lambs & Kaufman, 1965; Teichner & Krebs, 1974). Nevertheless, it seems important in the present context not to entirely assimilate the experiments within multiple reaction-time studies but to examine how influential the context is for the number of fixations. As the analysis of the number of fixations revealed similar differences to those obtained for decision time (Table 4.2), one must concur with Pruit (1961) that in situations with alternatives a subject will need much more information than is necessary for the usual optimal level. In a WA context, fixations differ significantly from one problem-solving task to another – dribble and shoot or pass – and subjects are always faster and have fewer fixations when the solution only implies the ball carrier – dribble and shoot – than when it involves a relationship between two players – pass.

Moreover, subjects always favour, whenever they have the choice, those situations where only the ball carrier is concerned (75 per cent compared with 25 per cent). This priority afforded to the solution only involving the ball carrier confirms the assumption of independence between alternatives. In supporting Morrison & Slovic (1962) it is felt that a subject weights the cues and modifies his decision according to factors so far unidentified. However, it seems that three determinants might explain the predilection for the type of simple situations mentioned above: (i) economy – the reduced need for cues in solutions involving a single player; (ii) self-consideration – the need to first exploit one's own resources or ability; and (iii) simplicity of relation – the direct link existing between the subject and his aim will prevail over the creation of an indirect relation with another player (Bernard, 1962).

This contribution to the exhaustive, terminal nature of the cognitive process supports the terminal character of information search. It is clear from the present studies that even if a subject is faced with many alternatives he confines himself to the solution he found relatively easily and early in his search. The increase in performance for complexity levels two and three – where alternatives are present – is only due to the availability of a large number of relevant amounts of information (Table 4.1).

The basketball experiments clearly showed that search pattern is specific to the type of task presented. Subjects selected only the elements that were appropriate to solving the problem. It appears that a pre-attentive process (peripheral vision) allows a subject to bring exclusively into visual focus those elements considered important in the display. The context, or instructions, as mentioned by Yarbus (1967), modify fixation patterns and subject's strategy. Finally, search pattern is dependent upon subject characteristics, experts having fewer fixations and shorter decision time than non-experts.

Ice Hockey

Ice hockey, like basketball, is characterised by a rapidly changing environment and this is especially true for the goalkeeper. He must take instantaneous decisions based on a selection of relevant cues issued from a particularly dynamic environment and must also discard irrelevant information. Vision, the dominant channel for collecting data of primary importance, has not yet been systematically analysed. Visual search can be illustrated by comparing subjects of different levels of expertise, while Welford (1977) has stated that an individual makes use of specific strategies according to his own capacities, and these have been emphasised in the basketball investigation.

Two hockey investigations were conducted, one on ice with a few offensive combinations (two against one), and the other was set up on an artificial surface in the laboratory using an offensive player; without defence and where the duration of the attack was systematically manipulated. In the first experiment (Figure 4.3) a subject was presented with situations where the offensive player performed either a sweep shot or a slap shot, both executed with or without displacement (Figure 4.4).

Figure 4.3   Experimental Setting for the Ice Hockey Goalkeeper

Table 4.3   Mean Reaction Time (seconds)
according to Type of Shot and Level of Expertise

	Experts	Non-experts
Slap shot	0.165	0.325
Sweep shot	0.204	0.500

Results showed that expert goalkeepers initiate their 'block' (measured in terms of time elapsed between the moment where the puck leaves the offensive player's stick and initiation of the block by the goalie) much sooner than novice goalkeepers, whichever type of shot is being used (Table 4.3). However, the difference is even more important for the sweep shot. The analysis of the distribution of ocular fixations as the shot takes place reveals that all goalkeepers, experts and beginners alike, look at the stick and the puck. From all observations for all subjects one single fixation was registered on the lower part of the player performing the shot. Both groups of subjects, experts and beginners, did not have the same distribution of ocular fixations. Table 4.4 shows that experts, whichever shot was used, fixated the stick 65 per cent of the time and the puck 35 per cent. On the other hand, beginners facing a slap shot concentrated 70 per cent of their fixations on the puck and 30 per cent on the stick. For a sweep shot beginners looked 87 per cent of the time at the stick and 13 per cent at the puck.

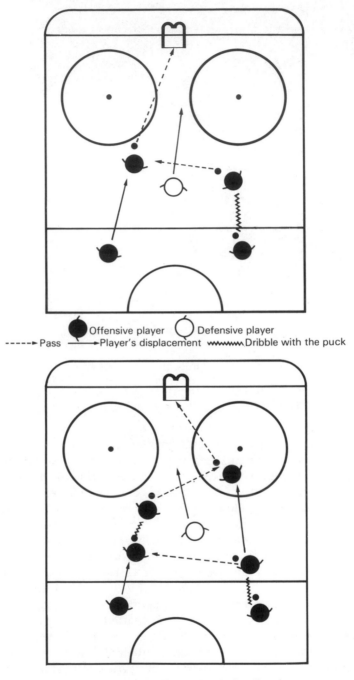

Figure 4.4   Typical Offensive Ice Hockey Situations

Table 4.4   Percentage Distribution of Fixation according to Type
of Shot and Level of Expertise

| | Experts | | Non-experts | |
	Stick	Puck	Stick	Puck
Slap Shot	71	29	30	70
Sweep Shot	60	40	87	13

In the second experiment an offensive situation was used with the offensive player executing a sweep shot. He initiated his shot having skated with the puck for one, two or four seconds. Results similar were obtained to the first ice hockey experiment. Experts were faster than beginners in initiating their blocking movement (Table 4.5). Temporal uncertainty created by the offence duration similarly affected experts and non-experts. Reaction time of experts decreased progressively according to the duration of the attack, while the tendency was less marked for beginners. The analysis of the distribution of ocular fixations during the shot revealed that all goalkeepers gave priority to the stick and puck. However, as noted in the earlier ice hockey investigation, beginners tend to have a greater number of fixations on the puck than experts.

Table 4.5   Mean Reaction Time (seconds) according to
Temporal Uncertainty and Level of Expertise

Offensive Duration	Experts	Non-experts
1 sec	0.190	0.229
2 sec	0.183	0.194
4 sec	0.169	0.200

The results of both investigations clearly show that experts react faster to the stimulus. They can anticipate or predict the shot's flight using cues from the stick's position and speed rather than the puck, while beginners make decisions on the shot's flight only when the puck is already on its way to the goal. Accordingly, it may be stated that subjects differ in the perceptual cues used to determine their subsequent action or motor response.

Practical Applications

The investigations in basketball and ice hockey described in this chapter provide a limited illustration of the vast amount of information that may be extracted by studying ocular movements in order to establish a better understanding of the way an athlete processes information. This type of investigation helps to determine how an individual selects and makes use of perceptual information for the planning and programming of an adapted and efficient motor behaviour. From such data it is also possible to consider the development of training programmes from which the coach might draw material for his players, particularly with regard to cues they could consider for solving perceptual-motor problems.

The study of ocular movements could also be extended to other types of activity where information processing is vital, such as diving or gymnastics judging. A recent study on gymnastics judgment for balance-beam routines (Bard, Fleury & Carrière, 1975) revealed that expert judges had fewer fixations than beginner judges and were not looking at similar elements. Expert judges had more fixations on the upper part of the gymnast (head, arm, trunk), while the non-experts concentrated their attention on the legs. Though other studies, as well as other approaches, are necessary to understand all the mechanisms underlying an adapted behaviour in sports activities, there is mounting evidence that the analysis of ocular movements can provide some answers to the problems raised by the controlled and systematic study of sport.

References

Bard, C. & Carrière, L. (1975) "Etude de la prospection visuelle dans des situations problèmes en sports", *Mouvement*, 10: 15–23.

Bard, C. & Fleury, M. (1976) "Perception et sports collectifs", *Mouvement*, 11: 23–38.

Bard, C., Fleury, M. & Carrière, L. (1975) "La stratégie perceptive et la performance motrice. Actes du 7eme Symposium canadien en apprentissage psychomoteur et psychologie du sport", *Mouvement*, 10: 163–83.

Bernard, M. (1962–3) "Une interpretation dialectique de la dynamique de l'équipe sportive", *Education Physique et Sport*, 62: 7–11; 63: 7–10.

Chambers, A. N. (1973) "Development of a taxonomy of human performance: A heuristic model for the development of classification systems", AIR-726 – 10/69-TR-AA, American Institute for Research, Washington Office Institute for Research in Psychobiology.

Christ, R. E. (1974) Predicting human performance: the accuracy of identifying simple visual target, NMSU-ONR-TR-741.

Cumming, G. D. (1978). "Eye movements and visual perception", E. C. Carterette & M. P. Friedman (Eds.), *Handbook of Perception*, volume IX, *Perceptual Processing*, Academic Press.

Ditchburn, R. W. (1973) *Eye Movements and Visual Perception*, Oxford: Clarendon Press.

Edwards, W. & Slovic, P. (1965) "Seeking information to reduce the risk of decisions", *American Journal of Psychology*, 78: 188–97.

Gould, J. D. (1973) "Eye movements during visual search and memory search", *Journal of Experimental Psychology*, 98: 184–95.

Gould, J. D. & Schaffer, A. (1965) "Eye movement pattern during visual information processing", *Psychonomic Science*, 3: 317–18.

Haber, R. N. & Hershenson, M. (1973) *The Psychology of Visual Perception*, New York: Holt, Rinehart & Winston.

Just, M. A. & Carpenter, P. A. (1975) "Eye fixations and cognitive processes", (CIP) Paper No. 296, Department of Psychology, Carnegie Mellon University.

Kolers, P. A. (1972) "Experiments in reading", *Scientific American*, 227: 84–91.

Kundell, H. L. (1974) "Visual sampling and estimates of location and information on chest films", *Investigative Radiology*, 9: 87–93.

Kundell, H. L. & LaFolette, P. S. (1972) "Visual search patterns and experience with radiological images", *Radiology*, 103: 523–8.

Lambs, J. C. & Kaufman, H. (1965) "Information transmission with unequally likely alternatives", *Perceptual and Motor Skills*, 21: 255–9.

Levy-Schoen, A. (1969) "L'étude des mouvements oculaires", *Revue des Techniques et des Connaissances*, Paris: Dunod.

Massaro, D. W. (1975) *Experimental Psychology and Information Processing*, Chicago: Rand McNally.

Matin, E. (1974) "Saccadic suppression", *Psychological Bulletin*, 81, 12: 899–917.

Morrison, H. W. & Slovic, P. (1962) "Preliminary results: effect of context on relative judgments of area", Eastern Psychological Association Meeting, Atlantic City, 1962.

Mounty, R. A. & Senders, J. W. (1976) *Eye Movements and Psychological Processes*, New Jersey: Lawrence Erlbaum Associates.

Mourant, R. R. & Rockwell, T. H. (1972) "Strategies of visual search by novice and experienced drivers", *Human Factors*, 14: 325–35.

Pruit, P. G. (1961) "Informational requirements in making decisions", *American Journal of Psychology*, 74: 433–9.

Schoonard, J. W., Gould, J. D. & Miller, L. A. (1973) "Studies of visual inspection", *Ergonomics*, 16: 365–79.

Teichner, W. H. & Krebs, J. (1974) "Laws of visual reaction time", *Psychological Review*, 81: 75–98.

Uttal, W. B. & Smith, P. (1968) "Recognition of alphabetic characters during voluntary eye movements", *Perception and Psychophysics*, 3: 257–64.

Welford, A. T. (1977) "La charge mentale de travail comme function des exigences de la capacité, de la stratégie et de l'habileté", *Le Travail Humain*, 40: 283–304.

Yarbus, A. L. (1967) *Eye Movements and Vision*, New York: Plenum Press.

Young, R. & Sheena, D. (1975) "Method and designs: Survey of eye movement recording methods", *Behaviour Research Methods and Instrumentation*, 7: 397–429.

5

Visual Detection and Perception in Netball[*]

Helen E. Parker

The assessment of superior athletes has interested researchers for many years and much is known about the physical and physiological characteristics of successful performers. However, to assess only the motor aspect of performance is to ignore the importance of central cognitive processes which detect and interpret changing stimulus patterns and make response decisions.

An overriding feature of performance environments like fast team games is the degree of stimulus uncertainty presented. This uncertainty arises from the great number of possible events which might occur, as well as from the changing pace and duration with which they take place. For information to be gained about the state of the stimulus environment the signal uncertainty must be resolved, or at least reduced (Welford, 1968). The process of uncertainty reduction is termed information processing and involves a chain of cognitive mechanisms; the perceptual (recognition of stimuli), decision-making (choosing the response) and effector (response organisations and control) mechanisms, each of which have limitations for the rate of throughput of information (Marteniuk, 1976).

Highly uncertain signals (high potential information) demand much processing space, time and conscious attention of the cognitive mechanisms in order to transmit the high information load. Overtly, responses are relatively slow and may be performed inaccurately

*This work was conducted on research grant form the Community Recreation Council of Western Australia. Thanks are extended to Dr J. G. Jones for his advice on the conduct of the study and in the preparation of the manuscript.

because processing the information takes time and response decisions are made in the face of uncertainty. Predictable signals, on the other hand, contain little potential information and require relatively little processing space in cognitive mechanisms. Responses to these types of signals appear automative or reflex-like. Spare attention not required for processing one information source can be taken up with information from other concurrent tasks.

The task of dealing with parallel information is an important one for the netball player. She must finely integrate all relevant information sources if she is to produce adaptable responses in the great variety of game situations which occur. The quality of her cognitive abilities, therefore, are particularly important for successful performance since the game environment is one in which stimuli regulate the spatial, temporal and force characteristics of the skill (Kay, 1957; Higgins & Spaeth, 1972; Jones, 1972).

Stimulation that provides information for the team player arises from both external and internal sources. The external source of information provides current and up-to-date input about the state of the game mainly through vision, although audition may also provide essential input. Internal information comes from the body proprioceptors (input from muscle, joint and balance receptors) which transduce force and position information, and from the brain which provides motivation and learned movements, tactics and strategies.

Of the many different inputs the netball player must take into account, visual signals provide most of the information that is immediately relevant for the performance. The game display presents a dynamic pattern of visual stimuli related to the movements of players and the ball. The ability to perceive motion and to respond appropriately to the perception of velocity and direction is widely acknowledged as being fundamental to successful ball skill performance (Whiting, 1969). The ability to judge motion by monitoring – or pursuit-tracking – of the ball's flight and player's movements requires perceptual analysis of the visual input in order to predict the future position of ball or player. Obviously, in ball games the future trajectory of the ball is not displayed ahead but anticipation is possible if the player recognises certain constants (statistical properties) in the flight path from past experience. Poulton (1957) has labelled this complex type of judgment "perceptual anticipation". Accordingly, successful catching or striking of a thrown ball depends upon accurate perceptual anticipation as well as accurate prediction of the degree of muscular contractions required (effector anticipation) and the duration of the movement (receptor anticipation).

However, a survey of skills performance literature reveals little research into the nature of cognitive processing abilities among skilful games players. In order to further knowledge in this area, investigations were conducted to examine both the visual perceptual ability and information-handling capacity of netball players of different skill levels and to establish whether these cognitive abilities relate to skill level in the game.

The Investigations

Players from six teams competing in the senior ranks of the major metropolitan netball competition were subjects for both experiments. The two top teams (fourteen players) from each of Al, Bl and Cl grade were chosen to represent a highly skilled, average and less skilled group respectively, resulting in a sample of 42 subjects. The highly skilled group included nine current and past state representatives. The ages of the total group ranged from 15 to 24 years.

Initially, visual-perceptual and velocity judgment abilities were assessed by measuring subjects' judgment of coincidence time of a moving* stimulus (travelling at 57, 85 and 166 cm/s) with a stationary target. In a totally dark room and from 4.6 m away subjects watched the stimulus move across the first 86 cm of the 176 cm slot and pressed a response button the instant they predicted the stimulus hit the target. The experimental set up is illustrated in Figure 5.1. Prediction error ($\pm$ ms) was recorded over ten trials for each stimulus velocity. No feedback was given to subjects until they had completed all trials. Players' velocity judgment ability was expressed in terms of judgment accuracy (constant, or algebraic, error) and judgment consistency (variable error).

The results are presented in Table 5.1 and Figures 5.2 and 5.3. Analysis of the error scores was conducted using a two-factor ANOVA repeated measures design with significant main effects for each factor (grade or prediction time) being tested by applying Tukey's post-hoc comparison test (Winer, 1962). Analysis of error scores was conducted in terms of prediction time, a consequence of the stimulus velocity and the occluded vision distance (86 cm). Previous research has confirmed that prediction time is a more potent variable affecting judgment performance than stimulus velocity (Sharp & Whiting, 1974; Buckholz, 1975).

---

*Stimulus motion was produced by the serial flashing of light emitting diodes from left to right across an 86 cm viewing slot. Viewing time and prediction time varied directly with the stimulus velocity; 1509 ms for 57 cm/s, 1012 ms for 86 cm/s and 518 ms for 166 cm/s.

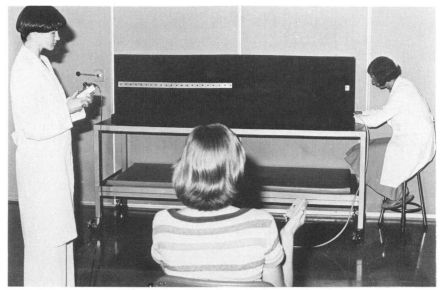

Figure 5.1   Set-up for Velocity Judgment Experiment

Table 5.1   Velocity Judgment Results

		Prediction Time		
		518 ms	1012 ms	1509 ms
		$\bar{X}$ $\bar{\delta}$	$\bar{X}$ $\bar{\delta}$	$\bar{X}$ $\bar{\delta}$
A1 Grade	CE	+ 38 ± 82	+ 29 ± 207	− 43 ± 214
	VE	91 ± 46	118 ± 35	155 ± 45
B1 Grade	CE	+161 ± 120	+116 ± 152	+ 44 ± 161
	VE	123 ± 73	150 ± 49	153 ± 61
C1 Grade	CE	+147 ± 222	+160 ± 297	+ 41 ± 157
	VE	143 ± 64	164 ± 78	188 ± 62

($\bar{X} \pm \bar{\delta}$ of Prediction Accuracy (CE) and Consistency (VE) in milliseconds (ms)

Analysis of VE scores showed significant main effects for grade ($F = 3.7$; $df 2,38$; $p < 0.05$) and for prediction time ($F = 7.9$; $df 2,78$; $p < 0.05$). Post-hoc comparisons revealed that A1 grade netballers showed significantly greater consistency in judging each prediction time compared with C1 players, while for prediction time the effect was due to significantly higher consistency of judgment for the shortest prediction time as compared to the longest.

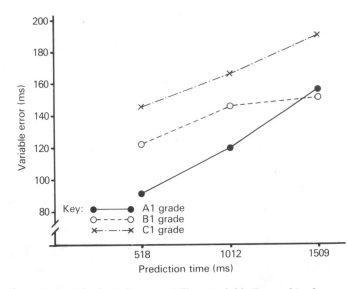

Figure 5.2   Velocity Judgment Ability: Variable Error of Performance

Results for velocity judgment accuracy (CE) did not show a consistent trend. A significant interaction was evident for grade and prediction time ($F = 26.1$; $df2,78$; $p < 0,05$), while only prediction time produced a significant main effect ($F = 730.4$; $df2,78$; $p < 0.05$) on CE scores. Examination of Figure 5.3 assists in the interpretation of these findings. This highly skilled group judged most accurately at the two shortest prediction times (518 ms and 1012 ms). For the longest prediction time there appears to be no difference in the judgment accuracy as the average accuracy of each group is within at least 44 ms of the coincidence time.

Overall, results support the notion that skilled players' visual perceptual ability is more efficient as reflected in high consistency and, to some extent, in judgment accuracy. Furthermore, it became clear that it was the shortest prediction time condition that clearly differentiated the judgment ability of the grades. Under this condition players had very little time to make accurate perceptual judgments about the speed of the stimulus before it disappeared behind the screen. The fact that skilled players were able to make reliable perceptual judgments in the very brief time period available concurs with earlier research which found that the critical period necessary for catching an object is shorter for experienced athletes (Bard, 1974) and that it can be reduced with training (Whiting, 1968). Through extensive experience in ball game situations the skilled group had developed their basic visual perceptual abilities to a more refined level in comparison with the other players.

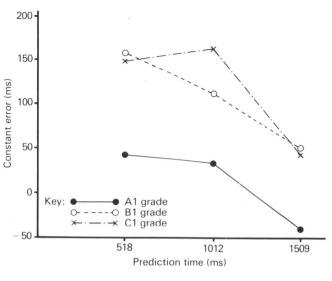

Fig 5.3

Figure 5.3   Velocity Judgment Ability: Constant Error of Performance

A noticeable feature of the data is high score variability within each group. This highlights the fact that poor velocity judgment *per se* does not necessarily preclude playing at a high level. Other characteristics, for example superior fitness, agility and physical size, can compensate to varying degrees for relatively weaker visual perceptual ability. The converse may be true for talented players – in terms of velocity judgment – in lower grades who play for friendship and social reasons and do not strive for selection in higher teams.

The second investigation was designed to measure the netball players' cognitive capacity to integrate several sources of sensory information at the same time. Two tasks were devised to simulate the cognitive processing demands of the real game. The primary task involved a player throwing from two metres to a series of targets fixed on a wall. In this task the player had to process incoming visual, auditory and kinaesthetic information arising from throwing accurately at whichever target was nominated, catching the rebound and performing footwork. The second, subsidiary, task involved visual scanning and required the player to call out the position of a signal – 'left' or 'right' – when it was detected. A player is shown performing the tasks in Figure 5.4. Subjects were instructed to concentrate on performing the primary task well at all times and to perform the subsidiary task whenever the primary task allowed it.

Figure 5.4   Set-up for Parallel Tasking Experiment

Within this dual-task research paradigm any reserve cognitive processing capacity not filled by one task (primary task) may be filled by information from the concurrently performed task (subsidiary task). Where the total information from both tasks exceeds the processing space available, errors result in the performance. In this particular example it was expectd that errors would be revealed in visual detection rate, since this task was simple and easy to trade-off in favour of attending to demands of the ball handling task.

Each player's ball handling and footwork skill was measured by timing a sequence of thirty accurate throws. An accurate throw was one which hit the correctly numbered target as randomly nominated on each throw by the experimenter. The average time for three trials of the primary task – when performed alone and also concurrently with the visual scanning task – was recorded for each player. In the dual-task condition visual detection errors, averaged for three trials, were also recorded.

Thus, the capacity to parallel process the combined sensory information was considered to be reflected in the player's accuracy in detecting peripheral visual signals under parallel task conditions. It was hypothesised that A1 grade players would have greater cognitive capacity to handle the resulting information overload than would less skilled players.

The findings are tabulated in Table 5.2. A two-factor ANOVA repeated measures design was conducted on both detection error and throwing time. Analysis of detection error indicated a significant main effect for grade ($F = 3.5$; $df\,2,39$; $p < 0.05$). A1 grade players detected significantly more signals while performing the basic game techniques than did the C1 grade players. When throwing time was analysed only the trial condition significantly affected throwing time ($F = 92.9$; $df\,1,39$; $p < 0.05$). There was a significant fall-off in all grades' skill under dual-task conditions. Even the most highly trained players were unable to maintain their previous performance levels when pressurised by concurrent task demands.

Table 5.2   Parallel Processing Results $\bar{X} \pm \bar{\delta}$

	Detection Error (%)	Throwing Times (sec)	
		Alone	Dual-tasking
A1 Grade	10.4 ± 7.9	38.5 ± 2.8	44.0 ± 5.1
B1 Grade	20.5 ± 14.0	42.3 ± 3.7	47.4 ± 4.0
C1 Grade	25.5 ± 18.8	42.7 ± 4.6	47.6 ± 7.2

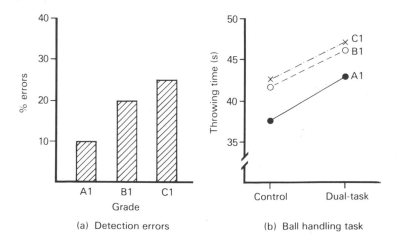

(a) Detection errors   (b) Ball handling task

Figure 5.5   Visual Detection and Ball-handling Ability Under Dual-Task Conditions

These results may be explained in terms of the most highly trained player's information processing capacity which enables her to attend to and integrate a greater range of input. For the less skilled player the visual and kinaesthetic feedback from ball handling and footwork movements constitute the major sources of information. This feedback contains much uncertainty owing to performance errors. Performance must be constantly monitored and wrong movements corrected. Hence, a major portion of the available processing space is taken up with the control of basic techniques. This player, then, has little spare attentional capacity to process other available input that is peripheral to the task at hand, but which is nevertheless essential to skilful application of movements and strategy and teamwork decisions.

For skilled players such basic movements are highly trained and result in both highly reliable kinaesthetic feedback and low input uncertainty. At automated performance levels skills are characterised by low error rates, high speeds and increased resistance to stress and interference from concurrently performed tasks (Fitts & Posner, 1967). Further, a task's level of automation may be considered with regard to the degree to which it can be performed while attention is on some other concurrently performed task (Posner, 1969). Little attentional space is needed to organise highly practised responses and to monitor their feedback. This reduced attentional load in performing basic game techniques also allows the skilled netball player to consider peripheral visual cues in her decision-making. With accurate perception and astute decision-making she can apply the basic techniques with finesse, perfect timing and adaptability to the game situation in hand.

Practical Applications

Overall, the unskilled player has a very limited capacity for information processing, thus accounting for inefficient perceptual judgments. These deficiencies can be improved by utilising appropriate teaching methods and setting up suitable practices for the task to be learned.

First, the coach working with beginners should recognise their limitations and provide extensive practice in the basic techniques of the game. Until some attention can be spared from the control of these movements more complicated drills will be useless and higher skill levels unobtainable. Even highly trained players benefit from basic technique practice in their warm-up drills in a training session; for example, footwork and agility drills without the ball or stationary ball handling.

Second, since motor techniques have to be applied in variable and complex game situations, the coach should build up drill complexity progressively until practice is as game-like as possible; for example, (i) practise footwork: dodging, slip-step, sprinting, stopping, leaping to pivot, hop to pivot; (ii) practise stationary ball handling: shoulder, bounce, lob passes, increasing the distance between pairs to improve effort judgment and control; (iii) introduce drills which include catching and throwing on the move, passing to a moving player; (iv) introduce passive opposition to attacking players, co-operative drills; (v) introduce active opposition; (vi) introduce variable speed of play, small unit teamwork, pressure drills.

Third, training sessions must include skill practices which tax the parallel-processing capacities of the player. A player who flawlessly performs the basic game techniques in practice but cannot maintain good performance under real game pressure is not truly skilful. For example, basic skill practices such as shuttle-ball, square-ball, side-shuttle do not require decision-making on behalf of the player. The various moves in the drill are well learned and so the player does not have to think beyond the task at hand. However, these same drills can be modified to tax her decision-making abilities, by including 'active' opposition players – one against one, one against two – so both thrower, attacker and defender must be alert to cues signalling when to throw or defend or what type of pass to make. Until players are put under pressure the coach is unable to judge their skill level. It was noted from the experimental results that even the highly trained A1 grade players were unable to perform under overload conditions without a fall off in performance. Weaknesses in technique that become apparent can be rectified by coach and player working together on specific remedial practices.

Fourth, the coach has an important role in acting as a selective attention device for beginners. Novices do not know what to look for among the signals and may consequently process some irrelevant information. There are many instances of these players performing basic techniques well under pressure yet making inappropriate decisions. That is to say they pass to a closely defended player, choose the wrong pass for the situation or crowd court space, rather than creating it for team-mates. In such instances the player is filling any spare-processing space with inappropriate information because she selects and attends to the wrong cues. These distractors do not contain relevant information which can contribute to successful performance. Thus, creating spare capacity in a player to attend to 'extra task' information does not necessarily mean that only crucial signals will automatically be selected and distractors ignored. The coach can assist in this selection by verbally or visually pointing out what to attend to through explanation or demonstration and by giving priority to various tactical decisions. Techniques such as 'freeze-replay' in which the practice game is stopped, the error indicated, the best alternative pointed out and the manoeuvre replayed again with the error eliminated, provide training in selective attention. Positive teaching is important in practice situations so that the player is given feedback about what she should do, rather than negative criticism such as "No, not that lead", "Don't throw there", but is not shown which lead or where to throw. The latter instruction does not reduce the uncertainty of the confusing game situation or inappropriate response for the beginner.

Fifth, the coach should recognise that individual differences in velocity judgment will limit to some extent the skill level attained by players. It may be that a player's ball handling and disposal is very weak because of associated inaccurate perceptual judgments. Since the critical period for making these perceptual judgments appears to be reduced with training (Whiting, 1974), coaching sessions should include work on such factors. Begin with stationary ball-handling, but move to drills which include players moving in different directions and at various speeds so the beginner practices both throwing and receiving on the move. Reaction drills, for example pepperball into shooting circle and reflex interceptions, allow players practice at making those instantaneous judgments so often demanded in fast team games.

In conclusion, the cognitive processing abilities of skilled netball players have been shown to be superior to those of less skilful players. These abilities included velocity and temporal judgments, anticipation of future events and information handling capacity to perform concurrent tasks. The various coaching strategies offered in this chapter are aimed at developing these particular cognitive abilities. The coach who recognises the importance to game success of cognitive skills alongside fitness and other physical capacities, and sets up practice drills to give players valuable experience of these skills is likely to produce adaptable, thinking and skilful team players.

References

Bard, C. (1974) "Rapidité et precision des judgements spatiaux 1: en fonction des variations de trajectories de balle", *Mouvement*, 9: 257–65.
Buckholz, E. (1975) "Human time estimation: Selected topics", in B. S. Rushall (Ed.), *The Status of Psychomotor Learning and Sport Psychology Research*, Nova Scotia: Sport Science Association.
Fitts, P. M. & Posner, M. I. (1967) *Human Performance*, Belmont, Calif.: Brooks-Cole.
Higgins, J. R. & Spaeth, R. K. (1972) "Relationships between consistency of movement and environmental condition", *Quest, Monograph Series*, 17: 61–9.
Jones, M. G. (1972) "Perceptual characteristics and athletic performance", in H. T. A. Whiting (Ed.), *Readings in Sports Psychology*, London: Kimpton.

Kay, H. (1957) "Information theory in the understanding of skills", *Occupational Psychology*, 31: 218–24.

Marteniuk, R. G. (1976) *Information Processing in Motor Skills*, New York: Holt, Rinehart & Winston.

Posner, M. I. (1969) "Reduced attention and the performance of automated movements", *Journal of Motor Behavior*, 1: 245–58.

Poulton, E. C. (1957) "On prediction in skilled movements", *Psychological Bulletin*, 54: 467–77.

Sharp, R. H. & Whiting, H. T. A. (1974) "Exposure and occluded duration effects in a ball-catching skill", *Journal of Motor Behavior*, 6: 139–47.

Welford, A. T. (1968) *Fundamentals of Skill*, London: Methuen.

Whiting, H. T. A. (1968) "Training in a continuous ball throwing and catching task", *Ergonomics*, 11: 375–82.

Whiting, H. T. A. (1969) *Acquiring Ball Skill: A Psychological Interpretation*, London: Bell.

Winer, B. J. (1962) *Statistical Principles in Experimental Design*, New York: McGraw-Hill.

6

Peripheral Vision and Hockey*

Ian M. Cockerill

It is frequently observed in team games that different playing positions demand varied physical, physiological and also psychological characteristics as well as functional training. Coaches are often faced with the problem of selecting players who possess the required "position-specific" characteristics in order to field a balanced team. Such a situation may arise when players are more or less equal in technical ability, fitness and motivation.

Morris (1977) has proposed that once a coach knows the dynamic visual acuity capabilities of his players and has assessed the requirements of the sport, assigning individuals to a playing position can be more realistic, training procedures can reflect a player's playing needs and practice can be designed more effectively and efficiently. If, for example, a hockey coach knows that a potential goalkeeper is velocity susceptible – that is, accurate perceptions are disturbed when objects are moving – perhaps the coach might encourage him to play in a different position where this variable is less critical.

It is interesting that one of the factors which many hockey coaches tend to neglect in selecting their teams is a player's perceptual skills. Although field hockey has become increasingly popular as a team sport in recent years for both men and women, the sporting literature contains little information about peripheral vision, either as an important component of the complex skills related to the sport or as a

* The author acknowledges the valuable assistance of Solomon Baah, graduate student in the Department of Physical Education, University of Birmingham, 1978–79, in the preparation of this chapter.

parameter relatively independent of other visual abilities (Low, 1946; McClure, 1946).

Whiting (1969) has stated that experimental work relating peripheral vision to motor skill performance continues to be limited and Wessel & Koenig (1971) have reported that little has been done to formulate hockey tests that measure and evaluate playing ability, while Cratty (1973) has suggested that a battery of perceptual tests should be used to assess different game requirements as well as the unique tasks of each team member. Accordingly, in order to contribute to a greater understanding of the sport of hockey this chapter reports an investigation that examined peripheral visual information processing among hockey players of the same team and also between hockey players and non-athletes.

Peripheral Vision as a Factor Affecting Performance

While Hopkins (1959) suggested that peripheral vision has generally been an unfruitful subject for research, producing comparatively few established facts and with experimental findings leading to conflicting results, a number of researchers have investigated the nature of varied visual behaviour among both athletes and non-athletes. For example, Brindley (1960), Koestler (1964), Leibowitz (1968) and Cox & Fisher (1975) proposed that proficiency in team games is influenced to a marked degree by such characteristics as being able to comprehend how a particular movement is carried out. Fitts & Posner (1967), in describing what is involved in acquiring complex skills in the early, or cognitive, stage of learning suggested that the learner attends to important cues, events and response characteristics that later go unnoticed. In team games the learner should make a conscious effort to attend to events such as locating the ball, synchronising trunk and limb movements to control the ball and being aware of the positions of other players. Later, when proficiency has developed, separate components combine to form a single skill that requires less attention demand and a player may then use peripheral vision to advantage.

Koestler (1964), Leibowitz (1968), Getman (1971) and Cratty (1973) have each suggested that peripheral vision is a critical factor relating to the efficiency of skill performance, while Ikeda & Takeuchi (1975) stated that we depend heavily upon peripheral vision for target recognition. Brindley (1960) related peripheral vision to sport in stating that the sprinter uses peripheral vision to locate his rivals, the basketball player controls the ball within his field of vision while scanning the display and the hockey player takes evasive action as a menacing stick enters his visual field during a dribble towards the circle. Brindley

(1960) also referred to the periphery of the retina 'shouting' its message to the brain as information is relayed from outside to within the field of vision.

Other research has reported the effects of eliminating peripheral vision during athletic performance. For example, the well-known studies of Krestovnikov reported by Graybiel, Jokl & Trapp (1955) showed that when peripheral vision is eliminated, greater difficulty in motor control is experienced than with occluded central vision. Javelin-throwing movements were shown to be significantly shorter and the javelin could not easily be thrown at right angles to the base line. Athletes complained that normal performance patterns were disorganised, expert skiers found it difficult to follow the course as their ski tracks became uneven and accurate distance judgment was almost impossible. Furthermore, discus-throwers, figure-skaters and gymnasts all revealed increased difficulty in performing their respective skills. These studies (Graybiel, Jokl & Trapp, 1955) emphasised the impairing effect of restricting normal peripheral vision, but at the same time did not report the relationship between individual differences in normal peripheral vision and skilled performance.

Peripheral visual ability has been found to vary between athletes and non-athletes. Stroup (1957) suggested that in general the ability to perceive objects or individuals at the extreme limits of the space field is an asset in most fast-moving team sports. Leibowitz & Appelle (1969) assigned importance to the ability to monitor peripheral visual stimuli as a factor influencing performance and Sanderson (1972) reported that situations arise in ball games when responses are made on the basis of peripheral cues. Johnson (1952) had earlier identified footballers and basketball players as significantly superior to non-athletes in peripheral vision, while Buckfellow (1954) and Gill (1955) subsequently found that athletes were superior to non-athletes in peripheral visual reaction time. McCain's (1950) study reported no differences between athletic criteria in static peripheral vision and Stroup (1957) found similarities in performance between basketball players and non-athletes on a motion perception test. More recently, Williams & Thirer (1975) demonstrated that both vertical and horizontal fields of vision are superior for both male and female athletes as compared with non-athletes. Thus, the general lack of consensus in these findings indicates the difficulty in determining whether the athlete has better peripheral vision than the non-athlete.

Despite the absence of agreement between researchers, peripheral vision may be important to the coach who is attempting to distinguish the superior from the inferior athlete and also in selecting players for specific playing positions. Different sports demand special perceptual abilities, for instance a lawn tennis player may use vertical peripheral vision to as great an extent as horizontal vision, while the hockey player is almost entirely preoccupied with the horizontal periphery. The majority of studies relating peripheral vision to sport have considered either the peripheral vision of the 'normal' subject as it affects his motor performance, or peripheral vision as a factor that distinguishes athlete from non-athlete. There has been little research describing the peripheral vision of superior athletes, despite Miller's (1960) claim that champions are more likely to possess superior visual perceptual abilities than those individuals whose performance of gross motor skills is at a relatively low level.

There are several situations in team sports when peripheral vision might be important. For example, when passing the ball, retaining it or shooting at the goal in a fast game such as hockey, the player in possession of the ball need not waste time turning his head to observe the movements of team-mates and opponents. Peripheral information might also be utilised when a player runs 'off the ball' to draw opponents and allows his colleague in possession to penetrate the opposing defence more easily, or when a player runs into space to place himself in a better position to receive a pass. In each of these situations a player should be able to use peripheral vision to advantage.

The Investigation

There is no known study relating peripheral vision to specific playing positions in hockey and the experiment described below was undertaken to supplement the data already available that relates visual factors with sports performance. Two hypotheses were tested; first, that there are no differences in horizontal peripheral vision between right flank players (outside right, right half and right back), central players (inside right, inside left, centre forward, centre half and goalkeeper) and left flank players (outside left, left half and left back); second, that there are no differences in left and right horizontal peripheral vision between hockey players and non-athletes.

Thirty subjects with a mean age of twenty-one years were identified as fifteen hockey players and fifteen non-athletes. The hockey players were of county and university first team standard while the non-athletes did not play any sport on a regular, or even recreational, basis. Personal data for all subjects are presented in Table 6.1.

The apparatus used in the experiment included: a stand perimeter and wand (Lafayette Instruments); an eye shade painted matt black on both sides; a Bausch & Lomb vision tester; a Kodak Ektagraphic Slide Projector (Model AF-2K) with remote control; and four colour slides,

Table 6.1   Personal Data for All Subjects

Subject	Hockey Players				Non-Athletes		
	Age	Height	Weight	Playing Position	Age	Height	Weight
1	24	5'11"	12 st 8 lb	Outside Left	19	5'9"	9 st 8 lb
2	19	5'10"	10 st 7 lb	Outside Right	24	6'0"	12 st 3 lb
3	19	5'10"	9 st 10 lb	Left Half	20	5'10"	10 st 1 lb
4	20	5'6"	9 st 7 lb	Centre Forward	20	5'9"	10 st
5	21	6'0"	12 st	Left Back	19	5'7"	9 st 7 lb
6	21	6'0"	11 st 10 lb	Left Half	19	5'6"	9 st 9 lb
7	21	5'10"	10 st 2 lb	Right Back	19	5'8"	9 st 7 lb
8	23	5'9"	11 st 6 lb	Goalkeeper	21	6'0"	12 st 4 lb
9	21	5'7"	9 st 7 lb	Right Half	20	5'10"	10 st 2 lb
10	20	5'9"	10 st 7 lb	Left Back	20	5'8"	9 st 9 lb
11	22	6'1"	13 st 2 lb	Centre Half	20	5'7"	9 st 8 lb
12	22	5'8"	11 st 2 lb	Centre Half	21	5'10"	10 st
13	21	5'10"	11 st 8 lb	Goalkeeper	24	5'9"	12 st 4 lb
14	22	5'10"	11 st	Outside Right	24	5'11"	11 st 7 lb
15	22	6'3"	13 st	Right Half	20	5'11"	11 st 1 lb
Mean	21.2	5'10"	11 st 1 lb		20.7	5'9"	10 st 8 lb

two depicting hockey situations and two of four geometric shapes (a circle, a triangle, a square and a five-point star). A projection screen was made from 5 × 2 m white, poly-cotton material and fixed to a 180° curtain rail with angles of 5°, 10° and 15° to left and right of zero marked at the top of the tachistoscope (slide projector). A small piece of black, diamond-shaped plywood 2 cm in length and 2 cm wide was suspended by a thin white thread from the top of the screen to the centre. A projection stand, lectern and a dentist's chair with adjustable head rest were also used.

Three tests were administered to all subjects:

1. visual angle was determined using the stand perimeter;
2. the vision tester was used to detect possible colour vision deficiencies;
3. peripheral visual acuity was measured by projecting the slides straight ahead of subject and at angles of 5°, 10° and 15° to his left and right. Exposure times for each stimulus presentation were 0.10, 0.50 and 1.00 seconds. Both angle and exposure were presented in a previously determined random order that was changed for each subject (Bennett, 1973).

Visual Angle

Each subject sat comfortably in front of the perimeter which was placed on a table in a well lit laboratory and adjusted to bring its arc parallel with the surface of the table. The subject was asked to cover one eye with the shade, rest the cheekbone of his other eye against the black plastic support and look into the mirror, reporting 'yes' immediately the target entered his visual field or 'no' immediately it disappeared from view. A yellow disc at one end of the wand was moved in and out of the subject's visual field along the curved arm of the perimeter and the exact limits of his binocular visual angle were determined.

Table 6.2   Visual Angle Scores for All Subjects

Subject	Hockey Players						Non-Athletes					
	Inwards			Outwards			Inwards			Outwards		
	Left	Right	Both	Left	Right	Both	Left	Right	Both	Left	Right	Both
1	90°	90°	180°	60°	60°	120°	90°	90°	180°	62°	60°	122°
2	90°	90°	180°	65°	65°	130°	85°	85°	170°	62°	55°	117°
3	90°	90°	180°	58°	60°	118°	90°	90°	180°	55°	56°	111°
4	90°	90°	180°	65°	65°	130°	90°	90°	180°	60°	65°	125°
5	90°	90°	180°	60°	65°	125°	82°	82°	164°	60°	60°	120°
6	90°	90°	180°	60°	55°	115°	90°	85°	175°	60°	55°	115°
7	90°	90°	180°	58°	60°	118°	90°	90°	180°	58°	58°	116°
8	90°	90°	180°	65°	65°	130°	90°	90°	180°	64°	60°	124°
9	90°	90°	180°	58°	58°	116°	90°	90°	180°	58°	58°	116°
10	90°	90°	180°	56°	62°	118°	88°	88°	176°	58°	58°	116°
11	90°	90°	180°	62°	65°	117°	90°	90°	180°	65°	60°	125°
12	90°	90°	180°	62°	62°	124°	90°	90°	180°	60°	60°	120°
13	90°	90°	180°	60°	58°	118°	90°	90°	180°	60°	60°	120°
14	90°	90°	180°	65°	65°	130°	90°	90°	180°	68°	68°	136°
15	90°	90°	180°	60°	58°	118°	90°	90°	180°	65°	65°	130°
Mean		180°			121.8°			177.7°			120.9°	

Colour Vision

Each subject was seated in front of the vision tester in turn and the Ishihara (1977) test for colour blindness was administered.

Peripheral Vision

Each subject was seated in a dentist's chair facing the tachistoscope that was placed 3·5 cm from the screen. The chair was adjusted so that the back of the subject's head rested comfortably against a rest and the diamond-shaped target on the screen was adjusted to eye level. He was asked to focus his eyes on the target and then to answer a question about each slide immediately after it had been projected on to the screen.

Mean scores for both left and right horizontal peripheral vision were obtained for the detection of stimuli at each angle and two, two-way analyses of variance (Ferguson, 1976) with repeated measures on one factor (peripheral vision) were conducted. The results of the first analysis of scores of the three sub-groups of hockey players – left flank, centre and right flank players – showed no significant variation in left and right horizontal peripheral vision between the three categories of hockey players. In addition, there were no differences between sub-groups in respect of angle of stimulus presentation. Moreover, the interaction of peripheral vision with angle of stimulus presentation was also non-significant. This finding indicated that left or right flank players, and also central players, did not have better or worse peripheral vision that might have determined their playing position.

The second analysis designed to show whether differences occurred between the horizontal peripheral vision of hockey players and non-athletes also revealed no differences or interaction between groups. However, as expected, highly significant differences ($F = 34 \cdot 74$; $df 2,56$; $p < 0 \cdot 001$) showed central vision to be significantly more reliable than left and right horizontal peripheral vision for all subjects.

Holson & Henderson (1941) and Low (1943) demonstrated that training has a positive effect upon peripheral vision, while Haith (1966) and Cratty (1970) indicated that peripheral vision is related to age. Thus, it is reasonable to expect support for the null hypothesis of no difference in peripheral vision between hockey sub-groups, since all players were aged between nineteen years and twenty-four years and had similar experience of playing the game. These data also lend support to Buckfellow (1954) who demonstrated that athletic groups differed significantly in central reaction time and peripheral visual reaction time from non-athletes, but not from each other.

The results from that part of the present study comparing horizontal peripheral vision upheld the null hypothesis that there were no differences between the groups. The reason for this finding might have been attributed to subjects falling within a fairly narrow age range (19–24 years) and also that no subject had any advantage over another through experience or specific training to improve peripheral vision. The results might lead to speculation that because of their active participation in hockey, players would have performed better in the horizontal peripheral vision test, since investigators such as Pieper (1963), Haith (1966), Cratty (1970) and Butts (1977) have suggested that the horizontal visual field could be significantly enhanced through training and experience. Moreover, Johnson (1952), Hopkins (1959) and Morris (1977) have argued that peripheral vision generally can be increased with practice. Regrettably, none of these studies stipulated the nature, length or frequency of practice that would merit such improvement.

Interestingly, the hockey players in the present study trained irregularly, but played matches once or twice a week over the winter period. If consideration is given to the ill effects which irregular practice and long periods between practices usually have upon performance, and the fact that the experiment was conducted during the close season, then the hockey players could not be said to have had any advantage over the non-athletes and there is good reason why the null hypothesis should have been upheld. As Low (1947) suggested, for effective improvement in peripheral vision there should be long, continued practice, forced fixation and unlimited viewing time.

Practical Applications

It is hoped that the results of the experiment described in this chapter, although rather inconclusive, might provide coaches with some guidance in the selection and training of hockey teams; especially in the light of a statement by Leibowitz (1968) that the difference between the skilled and the unskilled performer is the difference between efficient and inefficient processing of peripheral visual stimuli!

It may be concluded that despite an absence of clearly defined results to instantly benefit the player or coach, the evidence obtained is both useful and encouraging. When the hockey players were subdivided according to playing positions it was shown that, relative to peripheral vision, there is no reason why a player should not be selected to operate on either the left or right flank or in the centre. The fact that all players may be considered equal in terms of peripheral vision is noteworthy, inasmuch as team selection need only be based upon game skill considerations, rather than a perceptual parameter such as this. However, a word of caution is needed lest it might be implied that other features of the visual system may be thought to be relatively unimportant. Elsewhere in this book it is argued that such features as distance and colour perception, dynamic acuity and selective attention contribute in large measure to successful performance in sport generally, and to team games in particular.

At the present time research findings concerning the importance of peripheral vision in motor performance are equivocal. The experiment described in this chapter, using tachistoscopic procedures in the laboratory, is offered as a pilot study that may encourage the development of the method by other workers in vision and sport research. Although it has been shown that experimental subjects were unable to identify stimuli presented at exposure times less than $0 \cdot 10$ seconds and at angles greater than $15°$ from the mid-line, the use of the tachistoscope is recommended. Today, instruments may be controlled entirely by electronic means and it is likely that future psychomotor research will make extensive use of such apparatus. For a valuable text on instrumentation in psychology, attention is drawn to a publication bearing that title by Cleary (1977).

The pioneering report by Graybiel, Jokl & Trapp (1955) highlighted the importance of peripheral vision in sport. Later studies frequently produced conflicting data and the field remains open for investigations that will consider such issues as training, the effect of exercise and the developmental nature of peripheral vision in motor behaviour; especially the perceptual abilities of élite sportsmen and women.

References

Bennett, N. (1973) *Research Design: Educational Studies, A Third Level Course,* Methods of Educational Enquiry, Book 1, Open University Press.
Brindley, G. S. (1960) *Physiology of the Retina and Visual Pathway,* London: Arnold.
Buckfellow, W. F. (1954) Peripheral perception and reaction time of athletes and non-athletes. Unpublished Master's Thesis, University of Illinois: Urbana.
Butts, L. P. (1977) A parent training programme in observational methods and its effects on children's visual perception. Unpublished Doctoral Thesis, University of Arizona.
Cleary, A. (1977) *Instrumentation for Psychology,* New York: Wiley.
Cox, R. L. & Fisher, G. H. (1975) "The relevance of space perception to sports psychology", in H. T. A. Whiting (Ed.), *Readings in Sports Psychology,* London: Lepus.
Cratty, B. J. (1970) *Perceptual and Motor Development in Infants and Children,* New York: Macmillan.
Cratty, B. J. (1973) *Movement Behaviour and Motor Learning* (3rd edn.), Philadelphia: Lea & Febiger.
Ferguson, G. A. (1976) *Statistical Analysis in Psychology and Education* (4th edn.), London: McGraw-Hill.
Fitts, P. M. & Posner, M. I. (1967) *Human Performance,* California: Brooks/Cole.
Getman, C. N. (1971). "Concerns of the optometrist for motor development", *Foundations and Practices in Perceptual Motor Learning – A Quest for Understanding,* Washington, D.C.: AAPHER.
Gill, D. J. (1955) Effect of practice on peripheral vision reaction time. Unpublished Master's Thesis, University of Illinois: Urbana.
Graybiel, A. Jokl, E. & Trapp C. (1955) "Russian studies of vision in relations to physical activity and sports", *Research Quarterly,* 26: 480–5.
Haith, M. M. (1966) "The response of the human newborn to visual movement", *Journal of Experimental Child Psychology,* 3: 235–43.

Holson, R. & Henderson, M. T. (1941) "A preliminary study of visual fields in athletes", *Iowa Academy of Science*, 48: 331–7.

Hopkins, V. D. (1959) "A selective review of peripheral vision", Flying Personnel Research Committee. London: Air Ministry.

Ikeda, M. & Takeuchi, T. (1975) "Influence of foveal load on the functional visual field", *Perception & Psychophysics*, 18: 255–60.

Ishihara, S. (1977) *Test for Colour Blindness*, Tokyo: Kanehara Shuppan Company.

Johnson, W. G. (1952). Peripheral perception of athletes and non-athletes and the effect of practice. Unpublished Master's Thesis, University of Illinois: Urbana.

Koestler, A. (1964) *The Act of Creation*, London: Hutchinson.

Leibowitz, H. W. (1968) "The role of peripheral vision in sports performance", Paper presented at the meeting of the American College of Sports Medicine.

Leibowitz, H. W. & Appelle, S. (1969) "The effect of a central task on luminance thresholds for peripherally presented stimuli", *Human Factors*, 11: 387–92.

Low, F. N. (1943) "The peripheral visual acuity of 100 subjects", *American Journal of Physiology*, 140: 83.

Low, F. N. (1946) "Some characteristics of peripheral visual performance", *American Journal of Physiology*, 146: 573.

Low, F. N. (1947) "Peripheral visual acuity of fifty-five subjects under conditions of flash presentation", *A.M.A. Archives of Ophthalmology*, 151: 319.

McCain, S. R. (1950) A comparison of motion perception fields of athletes and non-athletes. Unpublished Master's Thesis, University of Alabama.

McClure, J. A. (1946) "The development and standardization of a new type of test for peripheral vision", *Journal of Applied Psychology*, 30: 340–53.

Miller, D. M. (1960) The relationship between some visual-perceptual factors and the degree of success realized by sports performers. Unpublished Doctoral Thesis, University of Southern California.

Morris, G. S. D. (1977) "Dynamic visual acuity: Implications for the physical educator and coach", *Motor Skills: Theory Into Practice*, 2: 15–20.

Pieper, A. (1963) *Cerebral Function in Infancy and Childhood*, International Behaviour Science Series, New York: Consultants' Bureau.

Sanderson, F. H. (1972). "Visual Acuity and Sporting Performance", in H. T. A. Whiting (Ed.), *Readings in Sports Psychology*, London: Kimpton.

Stroup, F. (1957) "Relationship between measurements of field of motion perception and basketball ability in college men", *Research Quarterly*, 28: 72–6.

Wessel, J. A. & Koenig, F. B. (1971) *Encyclopaedia of Sports Medicine*, The American College of Sports Medicine, New York: Macmillan.

Whiting, H. T. A. (1969) *Acquiring Ball Skill: A Psychological Interpretation*, London: Bell.

Williams, J. M. & Thirer, J. (1975) "Vertical and horizontal peripheral vision in male and female athletes and non-athletes", *Research Quarterly*, 46: 200–5

7

Visual Acuity and Sports Performance

Frank H. Sanderson

Increasing efforts to improve the excellence of performance in sport have involved the scientific investigation of those variables underlying human performance. Typically, subjects have been tested on various parameters supposed to be important in performance and findings have been related to athletic achievement. In the psychological domain many factors have been studied including simple reaction time, personality traits and particularly in the context of ball games, visual ability. It is the relationship between ball games and visual ability, specifically visual acuity, with which the present chapter is concerned.

In ball games a performer is normally highly dependent upon the visual system for providing cues about the fluctuating environment in which he operates. On the basis of such visual information he may have to make and act upon precise judgments with respect to moving objects as, for example, when catching or striking a ball. This being so, it seems logical that natural fluctuation in visual efficiency within an individual – and also variations in efficiency between individuals – would influence performance during those moments which require relatively high visual accuracy. An awareness of these considerations has generated a substantial amount of research on vision in sport and the essential elements of the visual acuity research so far conducted are outlined here.

Static Visual Acuity (SVA) and Sport

SVA is defined as the ability to resolve the detail of an object in the field of view (Riggs, 1965) and is specified in terms of the minimum dimensions of the critical aspect of a test object that a subject can correctly identify. An example of a static visual acuity test would be the Snellen wall chart used by an optician, in which the viewer's acuity score is based upon the smallest letter on the chart he can correctly identify.

The results of research have been equivocal. Banister & Blackburn (1931) noted that ability in ball games appears to be independent of visual acuity as many good players were below normal. They concluded that what is more important is "a very high innate visuo-muscular co-ordination". Tussing (1940) and Winograd (1942), both using ball games players, also discovered many subjects with visual defects and below normal visual acuity. More recently, Martin (1970) reported that of the hundreds of players he had tested for SVA, 22 per cent were defective, a fact which prompted the suggestion that the poor form of many athletes might be attributable to substandard vision.

However, refractive errors, which the SVA test detects, can be corrected by the use of optical aids such as spectacles and contact lenses and in all probability poor SVA would have a detrimental effect on performance in many athletic pursuits, particularly fast ball games, if refractive errors were not corrected. It might be assumed that when SVA needs correction an individual will use corrective measures, but apparently such an assumption is unjustified. It seems likely that many individuals, when not required to undergo compulsory screening, will avoid, by rationalisation or apathy, the acknowledgment of visual defects. Specifically, all those players who wear spectacles or lenses presumably need them, but many more without them have a similar need. It may be, then, that the demonstration of a positive relationship between SVA and ball games performance might be confined to a hypothetical situation in which a population has been totally without access to corrective optical devices.

Several other reasons might explain the shortcomings of visual acuity tests in differentiating among individuals other than in a gross fashion. For instance, there may be little relationship between visual capacity as measured and the use made of this capacity in the criterion task. Also, the task and/or the vision test(s) utilised may have low reliability. Another consideration is that ball games performance, though superficially dependent on visual efficiency, occurs in a rapidly fluctuating perceptual environment, whereas the measurements of visual capacity are obtained in highly artificial and strictly controlled laboratory conditions.

Such considerations do not preclude the possibility that an increment in acuity may have beneficial effects on an individual's efficiency in a ball game. In this respect, the investigations of the transient effect of athletic participation on SVA are relevant. Some evidence exists from Russian research conducted by Krestovnikov (in Graybiel, Jokl & Trapp, 1955) that SVA temporarily improves as a result of strenuous physical activity. Similar trends have been found by Whiting & Sanderson (1972) after a table-tennis task and by Vlahov (1979) after subjects had undertaken various workloads on a bicycle ergometer. Whiting & Sanderson (1972) found that auditory acuity can also be improved, a result which suggested interpretation of the phenomena in terms of sensory facilitation brought about by increased arousal associated with gross bodily exercise. Induced sensitivity may well be functional at the outset of a game, thereby emphasising the importance of warm-up. It is interesting that the general acceptance of the need to 'get the eye in' in ball games suggests a long-established subjective awareness on the part of sportsmen of the benefits of warm-up for efficient performance. The implications would be greatest for those fast ball games, for example cricket, in which warm-up is rarely fully undertaken prior to competition.

Dynamic Visual Acuity (DVA)

Whereas it is not inevitable that tests should imitate, either actually or symbolically, the requirements of the task to be evaluated, experimentation with more practically oriented visual tests appears to be a logical development. Here the task of investigators would be to refine and create tests in the light of the supposed visual requirements in ball games while maintaining acceptable standards of reliability. In ball games it is usual for the eyes to be used dynamically as, for instance, when the player is running, catching or viewing a moving object. A more relevant visual acuity test in the light of this is Ludvigh & Miller's (1953) dynamic visual acuity (DVA) test which was developed in order to provide a more relevant screening for would-be pilots. The parameter has been defined as "the ability of the observer to detect the detail of an object in the field of view when there is relative movement between him and the object". The speed of the object is described in terms of angular velocity since acuteness of vision diminishes as a result of angular, and not linear, velocity of the object viewed. Ludvigh & Miller (1953) described the test in more detail as follows:

> The test object suddenly appears travelling at a constant angular velocity. The CNS must estimate the direction and velocity of movement of the object. It must then send to the extraocular muscles innervation appropriate to place and hold the image of the object in the vicinity of the fovea for a sufficiently long period of time to permit

the resolution of the critical detail. It is the efficiency of this complex process which is measured by the test of dynamic visual acuity.

Notwithstanding Miller & Ludvigh's (1962) contention that DVA is a 'basic physiological function', it is not basic in the same sense as SVA. SVA measures the resolving power of the eyes, or 'optical resolution', which is the essence of basic acuity. But with the DVA test correct identification of the target image, although to some extent dependent on optical resolution, is primarily determined by the efficiency of eye movements in response to the moving object. A perspective of the DVA task is encouraged in which the emphasis is not on the ability to discriminate the detail of a moving object, but rather on the efficiency of these adaptive eye movements, and without such efficiency discrimination of the image would not occur. This perspective encourages the attempt to relate DVA to ball catching, since it is held that the latter also requires efficient visual adjustments. Miller & Ludvigh (1962) differentiated between 'velocity-susceptible', and 'velocity-resistant' subjects and it seems reasonable to hypothesise that good ball game players will be in the latter category, demonstrating a relatively slow deterioration in ability with increasing angular velocity (Figure 7.1).

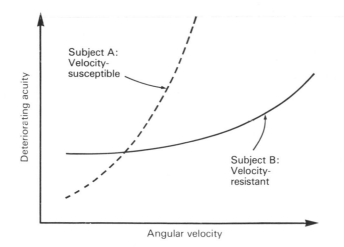

Figure 7.1   Individual Differences in DVA. (Note that performance at low angular velocities is not necessarily predictive of susceptibility or resistance. It is hypothesised that good fast ball game players are velocity-resistant.)

Miller & Ludvigh (1962) maintained that good DVA is an asset in flying, particularly during low-level reconnaissance work, but failed to test this assumption. Subsequently, Burg & Hulbert (1959 & 1961) have investigated the potential of the DVA test as a screening device for automobile drivers with reasonably promising results.

DVA and Sport

As playing ball games frequently demands the dynamic involvement of the eyes, for instance in tracking a ball in flight and perceiving the changing temporal and spatial patterns of the visual display, it is reasonable to assume that DVA's relationship with ability in ball games will probably be stronger than that of SVA. Because of low angular velocity the player tracking a distant ball or other object is not taxing his DVA capability. However, he may often be required to track a fast-moving ball at close quarters with a degree of difficulty compounded by his own superimposed movement, and it is in these circumstances that his DVA will be an important factor. For example, he may well encounter angular velocities in the region of 100 degrees per second.

Of course, a ball moves with deceleration and acceleration, thereby presenting more complex spatio-temporal problems than tracking a constant velocity target which remains at a constant distance from the eyes and in one plane. But the fact that there is a dynamic visual factor, even if somewhat ill-defined, common to both ball games and the DVA test, at least gives the latter face validity in its association with the former. In order to establish whether or not the DVA test can eventually be employed for purposes of prediction, investigation of its connection with both SVA and ball games ability is necessary. In this respect, Beals, Mayyasi, Templeton & Johnston (1971) found a high correlation between DVA and field shooting accuracy in basketball ($r = 0 \cdot 76$, $N = 9$, $p < 0 \cdot 01$). Their claim that SVA contributed "moderately" to the effectiveness of both field shots and free throws is suspect in view of the fact that only one player was responsible for this effect. More recently, Morris & Kreighbaum (1977) found no differences between DVA scores of high and low-ability female basketball players. However, under some of the angular velocity conditions the low-percentage field and free-throw shooters showed greater variability in their DVA scores. A relatively low correlation ($r = 0 \cdot 56$, $N = 10$, $P < 0.05$) between baseball batting average and DVA was reported in an unpublished study by Mayyasi (1972), which is again surprising since batting is more likely to involve a critical tracking function than basketball field shooting. Furthermore, he found that SVA was similarly correlated with batting average ($r = 0 \cdot 57$). Relevant in this context is a pilot study by Burg (1972) in which eight varsity baseball players were tested for DVA, with a 'high correlation' being found between DVA and batting average. Clearly, the preceding results do not provide impressive evidence of a relationship between visual acuity and ball games performance, but they do suggest that further research would be worthwhile.

The Investigation

The essential characteristics of a suitable test were assessed following an examination of the published research in the area. Methods of measuring DVA have included moving an individual relative to his environment, having the subject view a visual image of the target seen reflected in a rotating mirror, moving the test object in a circular path perpendicular to the line of sight and viewed through a rotating prism, moving a projected image by means of a mobile projector and physically moving the object itself. The last mentioned method was chosen for its technical simplicity.

The apparatus consisted of a horizontal beam with a vertical strut suspended from one end. Attached to the strut was a Landolt circle whose gap could be rotated about its axis from left to right (from the subject's aspect) by a variable speed motor (Figure 7.2). During rotation of the beam the image skirted the outer surface of a 189 cm opaque cylinder and the subject was seated in the centre of the cylinder with his head in alignment with the beam's axis of rotation. The subject viewed the image by looking in a forward direction through a horizontal slit in the cylinder. A sliding screen on the cylinder enabled the experimenter to vary the width of the slit so that both angular velocity and exposure time of the target could be varied independently. A second screen allowed the entire display to be quickly occluded or revealed to the subject. Parallel with the surface of the cylinder and 12·7 cm outside it the moving target was observed against a dark board. Three, 60-watt lamps attached to the board provided a homogeneous local illumination of 40 ft candles. During target exposure the subject attempted to identify the direction of the gap in the Landolt circle – top right, top left, bottom right, or bottom left.

Previous research attempting to relate ball games performance to visual ability has usually adopted game-based criterion measures, for example baseball batting average (Burg, 1972) and basketball field and free-shooting average (Beals, Mayyasi, Templeton & Johnston, 1971). But the intention in the present investigation was not to study the differential acuity of established ball game players, primarily because such a restricted range of subjects would be unlikely to yield meaningful results in terms of the acuity parameter. The aim was to obtain subjects

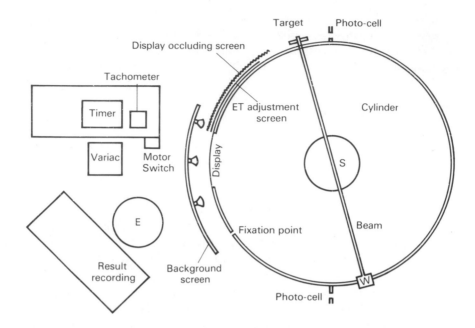

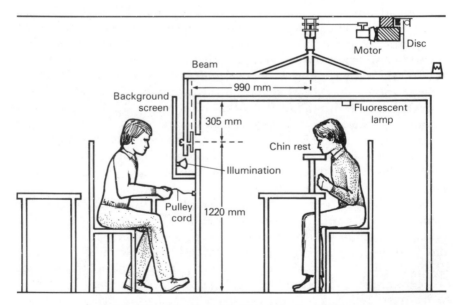

Figure 7.2:   The Dynamic Visual Acuity Apparatus

from a student population and have them participate in what would be generally regarded as a novel task, being relatively unfamiliar to all. Two general task categories in the performance of ball skills can be identified, both characterised by a marked visual-dynamic element:

1. Tracking the ball in flight followed by an "acquisition function", for example, catching it in the hands or an instrumental extension such as a lacrosse stick.
2. Tracking the ball in flight followed by its contiguous acquisition and despatch by the hand(s) or an extension of the hand(s), exemplified by volleyball in the first instance and by a cricket bat or a racket in the second.

For it to be a legitimate ball games task the measure needed to incorporate both the ball tracking and acquisition functions outlined above. It was decided that category 1, more specifically ball catching, provided the most practical framework for the task in that performance scores were quickly obtained even under laboratory conditions. The actual task was for the subject to catch tennis balls one-handed, with standardisation of conditions being achieved by the use of a tennis ball projection machine to propel the balls. In addition, each subject would operate under conditions in which ball viewing time was restricted for two main, interdependent reasons. First, the task needed to be of sufficient difficulty to discriminate adequately among subjects and demonstrate the underlying continuity of this ability. Second, the time available for viewing a fast-approaching ball is normally limited, largely because of its velocity, allied with the fact that the observer is usually in close proximity to the ball even before it begins its flight. In view of these factors a sufficiently demanding task was created by the artificial limitation of the viewing period.

The tennis ball projection machine was adjusted to fire a ball at approximately 12.2 metres per second over a fairly constant trajectory so that it reached the subject who was standing 6.1 m from the projection point. By using a photocell unit assembled immediately in front of the starting position of the ball and an interfacing two-channel interval timer, the time for which the dark room was illuminated could be varied and the onset located at any moment after ball projection. Illumination was provided by an 80 watt fluorescent tube, modified to operate on direct current to allow rapid rise and decay.

In the first experiment (Whiting & Sanderson, 1974) thirty male subjects from a university student population took part in the catching task in which there was a constant illumination period of 80 ms, but with the onset of this period varied systematically (Figure 7.3).

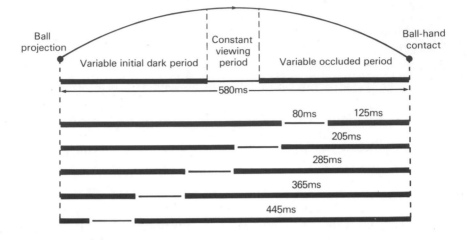

Figure 7.3   Viewing Conditions for the Catching Task in Experiment 1.

Additionally, the subjects' SVA and DVA were assessed, the latter at 100 degrees per second and under four exposure times of the target, that is 150, 200, 250 and 300 ms. Subsequent correlational analysis revealed that SVA was unrelated to either catching performance of DVA. The latter finding confirms that DVA is measuring factor(s) other than optical resolution alone. At all exposure times DVA was found to be significantly related to catching performance under the treatment level which best discriminated among individuals' catching abilities ($r = 0 \cdot 30$–$0 \cdot 45$; $p < 0 \cdot 05$).

This affords general support for the hypothesis that good ball-catchers tend to be velocity resistant. The reasons for this relationship are complex and will prove difficult to isolate. Possibly the correlation is a reflection of an ability to maintain information processing efficiency at a high level even when visual conditions are less than optimal. In a DVA task performance decrement is acknowledged to be due largely to the motion of the image on the retina (Methling, 1968), which has the effect of greatly reducing the information transmission rate (Mashhour, 1966). Similarly, in the catching task poor performance might be the result of low information transmission rate caused by the stressful nature of the task.

However, such postulations must be viewed in the context of the results which prompted them; at best there was only 23 per cent common variance between DVA and the catching task, a fact which encourages caution and certainly precludes the use of the DVA test *per se* as a predictive index of ball games ability.

In the second experiment (Sanderson & Whiting, 1978) the catching task was made easier since only 40 per cent of the balls were caught under the most discriminatory condition in the previous experiment. An illuminated period of 80 ms was included for comparison purposes, together with periods of 160 and 240 ms (Figure 7.4). Because DVA

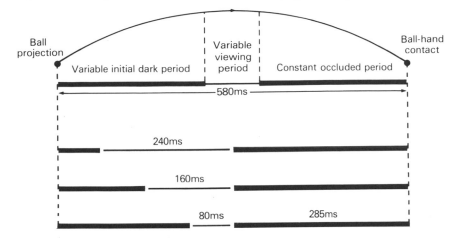

Figure 7.4   Viewing Conditions for the Catching Task in Experiment 2.

had been related to catching performance at all exposure times in the previous experiment a representative time of 200 ms was chosen and three angular velocities were used; 75, 100 and 125 degrees per second. SVA of the forty subjects was also measured. As expected, both viewing period in the catching task and angular velocity in the DVA task were significant performance variables. Correlation and principal components analyses confirmed the findings of the previous experiment in that SVA was unrelated to both DVA and catching performance. Further, DVA and catching were related under the majority of the combinations ($r = 0 \cdot 31-0 \cdot 43$; $p < 0 \cdot 05$) and most frequently at the highest angular velocity, suggesting that the dynamic element in both tasks is the common factor. The factor matrix illustrates a common factor embracing both the catching task and DVA, and also a second factor which is dominated by SVA (Table 7.1).

Practical Applications

A major impetus for the investigation of the relationship between DVA and ball games performance is that DVA is more likely than SVA to be a relevant parameter because of its 'dynamic' element and this argument may extend to the acuity increment context discussed previously

Table 7.1   Factor Matrix for the DVA, CT and SVA Tests

| Tests | Rotated factors | | Communalities |
	I	II	
DVA 75°/s	72*	28	60
DVA 100°/s	79*	30	71
DVA 125°/s	74*	32*	65
CT 80 ms	65*	−31	52
CT 160 ms	68*	−51*	72
CT 240 ms	74*	−25	61
SVA Landolt	06	86*	74
SVA checkerboard	05	85*	73
Variance	39·26%	26·91%	

$*p < 0·05$

(Whiting & Sanderson, 1972). More specifically, a productive line of enquiry might be to establish the effect of exercise on DVA, although this would not be without its problems, largely because of the existence of a practice effect in the DVA task. It is clear that an extended DVA testing period during the experiment would be incompatible with the requirement for a brief test after the exercise period in order that the duration of the effect could be established. The practice effect could be neutralised by giving subjects extensive practice prior to the experiment. For example, Miller & Ludvigh (1962) have demonstrated that when asymptotic levels of performance have been attained large individual differences still remain.

With reference to the nature of the DVA task, it is concluded that the major requirements are that the angular velocity should be relatively high (75 degrees per second or more) and that exposure time should be relatively low (400 ms or less), thus broadly simulating the visual demands with which the fast ball games player is frequently faced. It is apparent, however, that although it seems likely that DVA is an important contributory factor to ability in ball games situations, it is by no means the only factor and cannot conceivably be used as the sole predictor of ability or potential ability in ball games. This being the case, increased efficiency in predicting catching performance might be facilitated by isolating an array of perceptual-motor abilities likely to be associated with successful ball game performance. For example, Sanderson & Holton (1980) tested a group of cricket batsmen and found that speed of reciprocal tapping was significantly correlated with end-of-season batting average. The profile of the correlates of performance would provide a more precise picture of the attributes of a good ball player.

Although the catching task used by Sanderson & Whiting (1978) was a reliable index of a specific skill, it is not known how this ability related to the popular concept of 'ball game ability'. Game-based criteria that have been used include baseball batting average and basketball shooting ability, but to have validity these would need to be based on performance over a considerable number of games to counteract the inevitable biases that are present in individual games. Another problem is that teams of games players tend to be élite groups in terms of ability, which provides one reason why single-item tests have so often failed to be sensitive to differences among players. Herein lies the advantage of the ball-catching task in that it is a relatively novel test for all subjects, enabling non-games players, unhandicapped by experiential short-comings, to participate on a more or less equal basis with games players. It would be useful to establish to what extent the catching task, various game-based abilities and predictor test items are related. Such an investigation might indicate the validity of the catching task in terms of its ability to measure fundamental 'ball games ability' and delineating such esoteric variables as 'potential', 'adaptability' and 'ball sense'.

The DVA test as evidenced by its relationship to ball-catching has been found to measure visual efficiency in a dynamic environment, thereby rendering it a more appropriate test of the everyday functioning of the eyes than the SVA task. Several problems have hindered the commercial development of DVA testing apparatus, but no difficulty presents insurmountable obstacles. Apparatus can now be assembled easily and at low cost, as detailed by Anderson, Black, Hale, Mayyasi & Reeves (1971). The main residual difficulty inhibiting development is the necessity for a lengthy testing period because of the initial learning effect. This learning period could be reduced by the improvement of the testing conditions, for example comprehensive instructions, initial practice trials supplemented with coaching and feedback, and a generous anticipatory tracking time. The use of Crawford's (1960a) testing method which was adopted in the Whiting & Sanderson (1974) and Sanderson & Whiting (1978) experiments would also save time, as would restriction of DVA assessment to only one condition; namely a standardised exposure time and angular velocity.

It is maintained that the use of the DVA test in the fast ball games context is an integral part of an attempt to isolate the factors which underlie skilled performance and that to this end the basis of DVA performance needs to be understood. Early investigators tended to regard DVA as a 'basic physiologic function' thereby perpetuating, yet rarely elaborating or testing, the tentative theories of Ludvigh & Miller (1953). Their postulation was that accepting some negligible involvement of optical resolution, oculomotor co-ordination is the major factor underlying DVA. Whiting & Sanderson (1974) argued for a consideration of eye-movement latency, while Barmack (1970) added parafoveal acuity to the list of determinants on the basis of his research into human-simian differences in DVA. His results, together with the fact that Crawford (1960a) found differential tolerance among subjects to inexact foveal fixation of the target, indicates that parafoveal acuity may prove to be a more important variable than hitherto appreciated. Consequently, it is necessary for the role of, for example, parafoveal acuity, attention and eye-movement latency to be rigorously investigated both in relation to performance in fast ball games and the DVA test. This would involve a combination and elaboration of the kind of work undertaken by Hubbard & Seng (1954) who studied the eye movements of baseball batters, and by Crawford (1960b) who investigated the relationship of eye movements to DVA. The product of such efforts would be a greater appreciation of the factors underlying DVA and the reasons for the relationship between DVA and ball games performance if this was confirmed.

Anticipating the acceptance of DVA as a valid and reliable test of, say, 'oculomotor co-ordination', various potential lines of enquiry can be foreseen. One of these has already been mentioned, namely the involvement of the DVA test in the acuity-exercise investigation. A further possible research area not dependent upon, but stemming from, DVA considerations involves the effects of luminance on fast ball game performance. Indoor lighting conditions for ball games are varied and, when stipulated, somewhat arbitrary (Whiting, Alderson, Cocup, Hutt & Renfrew, 1972). Outdoor games usually relying on natural light, such as cricket and tennis, may be subject to interruption because of inadequate luminance. Visual requirements are, in some cases, similar for both DVA tasks and fast ball games, with low intensity contrast between the object being viewed and the background. Consequently, apart from the specific investigation of what constitutes adequate luminance in various ball games, there is the interesting possibility of demonstrating a relationship between DVA and the degree of tolerance to low luminance during fast ball game performance.

The other major possibility is for the study of DVA in a developmental context, together with consideration of the implications for the development of skill in fast ball games. As yet, and despite the adaptive role of oculomotor co-ordination, there has been little investigation of its development in childhood. Existing evidence illustrates that at birth, or very soon afterwards, primitive reflexive pursuit movements in response to a moving object are possible (Dayton, Jones, Steele & Rose, 1964). Abercrombie (1969) observed that for the normal child the precision of both saccadic and pursuit movements takes time to develop, showing a marked improvement between the ages of six and eleven years, but not maturing fully until late adolescence. Eye-movement latency, a probable factor influencing DVA, also develops with maturity as found by Miller (1969); adults revealed a mean latency of 270 ms, whereas that of eight-year-old subjects was 411 ms. This information, together with the knowledge of the sensitivity of many developmental processes to the effects of the child's early environment, and embracing such concepts as critical periods, environmental enrichment–deprivation and ages of readiness, would suggest that detailed investigation of the development of oculomotor co-ordination may have important implications of both a theoretical and practical nature.

From a theoretical standpoint a possible product of research would be a model of the development of dynamic visual behaviour from birth to adolescence which would be helpful in accounting for associated behaviours such as skill in catching a ball. Knowledge about children's ability to deal precisely with such important dynamic events and objects as a ball in sport, active peers in vigorous games and moving traffic has obvious social and practical implications. In the context of development, work on DVA has been limited to a series of hypotheses advanced by Sanderson (1972), some of which have been tested by Cratty, Apitzsch & Bergel (1973). Using children of both sexes between the ages of five and twelve years ($N = 475$), and target speeds of 60, 90 and 100 degrees per second, they found significant sex (in favour of boys) and age differences at each angular velocity. In addition, large individual differences were shown, suggesting that the velocity resistant–susceptible dichotomy is appropriate for children as well as adults.

The search for the factors underlying skill in ball games, typified by the experiments in which DVA has been found to be related to catching performance, or skill in any competitive sporting activity, will continue for two main reasons. First, there is the need to produce élite sportsmen, and this objective will be increasingly met by a scientific understanding of the bases of skilled performance. Second, and perhaps more important, is the need to provide opportunities for the non-élite majority to develop their potential in physical activities of their choice. By understanding those factors underlying skill, perhaps physical education and sports teaching may be so directed that the path leading to achievement of real enjoyment by children in athletic pursuits will be minimally traumatic and with success assured.

References

Abercrombie, M. L. J. (1969) "Eye movements and perceptual development", in P. Gardiner, R. McKeith and V. Smith (Eds.) *Aspects of Developmental and Paediatric Ophthalmology*, London: Heinemann.

Anderson, P. D., Black, T. L., Hale, P. M., Mayyasi, A. M. & Reeves, B. G. (1970) "An apparatus for measuring human visual acuity", *Test Engineering*, 24: 18–19.

Banister, H. & Blackburn, J. M. (1931) "An eye factor affecting proficiency at ball games", *British Journal of Psychology*, 21: 382–4.

Barmack, N. H. (1970) "Dynamic visual acuity as an index of eye movement control", *Vision Research*, 10: 1377–91.

Beals, R. P. Mayyasi, A. M., Templeton, A. E. & Johnston, W. L. (1971) "The relationship between basketball shooting performance and certain visual attributes", *American Journal of Optometry*, 48: 585–90.

Burg, A. (1972) Personal communication. 15 March.

Burg, A. & Hulbert, S. F. (1959). "Dynamic visual acuity and other measures of vision", *Perceptual and Motor Skills*, 9: 334.

Burg, A. & Hulbert, S. F. (1961) "Dynamic visual acuity as related to age, sex and static acuity", *Journal of Applied Psychology*, 45:111–16.

Cratty, B. J., Apitzsch, E. & Bergel, R. (1973) "Dynamic visual acuity: a developmental study", Paper presented at the 3rd International Congress for Psychology in Sport, Madrid, 25–29 June.

Crawford, W. A. (1960a) "The perception of moving objects. 1: Ability and visual capacity", Air Ministry Flying Personnel Research Committee Memorandum 150(a), Farnborough.

Crawford, W. A. (1960b) "The perception of moving objects. II: Eye-movements", Air Ministry Flying Personnel Research Committee Memorandum 150(b), Farnborough.

Dayton, G. O., Jones, M. H., Steele, B. & Rose, M. (1964) "Developmental study of coordinated eye movements in the human infant, II. An electro-oculographic study of the fixation reflex in the newborn", *Archives of Ophthalmology*, 71: 870–5.

Graybiel, A., Jokl, E. & Trapp, C. (1955) "Russian studies of vision in relation to physical activity and sports", *Research Quarterly*, 36: 480–5.

Hubbard, A. W. & Seng, C. N. (1954) "Visual movements of batters", *Research Quarterly*, 25: 42–57.

Ludvigh, E. J. & Miller, J. W. (1953) "A study of dynamic visual acuity", Joint Project NM 001 075.01.01, Pensacola: United States School of Aviation Medicine.

Martin, W. (1970) "What the coach should know about vision", Paper presented at the 3rd Annual Sports Medicine Seminar, Seattle, (March).

Mashhour, M. (1966) "Information transmission in speed perception and in locomotion", Reports from the Psychological Laboratories, No. 216, University of Stockholm.

Mayyasi, A. M. (1972) Personal communication. 16 November.

Methling, D. (1968) "Sehscharfe des Auges bei horizontalen Folgebewegungen", *Vision Research*, 8: 555–65.

Miller, L. K. (1969) "Eye-movement latency as a function of age, stimulus uncertainty and position in visual field", *Perceptual and Motor Skills*, 28: 631–6.

Miller, J. W. & Ludvigh, E. J. (1962) "The effects of relative motion on visual acuity", *Survey of Ophthalmology*, 7: 83–116.

Morris, G. S. D. & Kreighbaum, E. (1977) "Dynamic visual acuity of varsity women volleyball and basketball players", *Research Quarterly*, 48: 480–3.

Riggs, L. A. (1965) "Visual acuity", in C. G. Graham (Ed.), *Vision and Visual Perception*, New York: Wiley.

Sanderson, F. H. (1972) "Visual acuity and sporting performance", in H. T. A. Whiting (Ed.), *Readings in Sports Psychology*, London: Kimpton.

Sanderson, F. H. & Whiting, H. T. A. (1978) "Dynamic visual acuity: a possible factor in catching performance", *Journal of Motor Behavior*, 10: 7–14.

Sanderson, F. H. & Holton, J. N. (1980) "Relationships between perceptual-motor abilities and cricket batting performance", *Perceptual and Motor Skills*, 51: 138.

Tussing, L. (1940) "The effects of football and basketball on vision", *Research Quarterly*, 11: 16–18.

Vlahov, E. (1979) "Effects of different workloads varying in intensity and duration on resolution acuity", *Perceptual and Motor Skills*, 48: 1259–64.

Whiting, H. T. A. & Sanderson, F. H. (1972) "The effect of exercise on the visual and auditory acuity of table-tennis players", *Journal of Motor Behavior*, 4: 163–9.

Whiting, H. T. A. & Sanderson, F. H. (1974) "Dynamic visual acuity and performance in a catching task", *Journal of Motor Behavior*, 6: 87–94.

Whiting, H. T. A., Alderson, G. J. K., Cocup, D., Hutt, J. W. R. & Renfrew, T. P. (1972) "Level of illumination and performance in a simulated table-tennis task", *International Journal of Sports Psychology*, 3: 32–41.

Winograd, S. (1942) "The relationship of timing and vision to basketball performance", *Research Quarterly*, 13: 481–93.

8

The Effects of Exercise-induced Fatigue on Visual Reaction Time

Graeme A. Wood

The ability to respond quickly and effectively to visual cues is a key factor in many skilled motor performances. A cricket batsman has only a few hundredths of a second to make the appropriate stroke to a ball from a fast bowler, while a footballer may have little longer to effect a pass to an unmarked team member. Given the physical demands of these and many other sports activities it would seem reasonable to assume that with the onset of fatigue a deterioration in response timing to visual cues will occur. Indeed, Sir Frederick Bartlett (1953) has stated that:

> . . . the earliest and by far the most delicate criterion of change in activity due to the continuance of that activity is increasing irregularity in the internal timing lay-out of the successive items of the performance which must be repeated (p. 3).

There are many facets to the concept of timing referred to here, including the sequential ordering and temporal bounds of components of the the motor act, but one of the basic elements is undoubtedly the ability to react quickly to sensory cues. In its simplest form this ability can be assessed as a *reaction time*; a measure of the time delay between the presentation of a stimulus, for example a light flash, and the beginning of some predetermined motor effort such as pressing a telegraph key. This temporal delay, usually in the order of 200–399 ms, is a measure of the neuromuscular processing time required for simple voluntary motor acts and has been widely used in environmental, physiological and psychological research as an index of functional capacity (see extensive reviews by Woodworth, 1938 and Teichner, 1954).

It is widely accepted that exercise-induced fatigue adversely affects one's ability to respond quickly, but has been less frequently substantiated. This mistaken belief has partly arisen from psychological research in industry where fatigue, characterised by an impaired mental state, is often accompanied by reaction time changes (Kirihara, 1931; Banerji, 1935). In fact, even the mere hypnotic suggestion of 'tiredness' has been found to lengthen reaction times significantly (Graham, Olsen, Parrish & Leibowitz, 1968). A distinction can, however, be made between this form of 'mental' fatigue, arising from monotonous manual tasks, and that experienced by the sportsperson engaged in strenuous physical work.

Studies of the relationship between fatigue arising from strenuous physical work and reaction time change are surprisingly few and the results equivocal. A U-shaped response is typical of the relationship found between physical exertion and many human performance variables and is thought to reflect an arousal or activation effect which becomes suppressed with the onset of local muscular fatigue (Gutin, 1973; Dickinson, Medhurst & Whittingham, 1979). Clearly, such a phenomenon clouds the precise expression of a fatigue effect, particularly when no objective assessment of the contractile capabilities of the musculature involved in the performance of the skill is made. This deficiency has been evident in several reaction time studies and perhaps explains why reaction time in these instances has been found to improve (Elbel, 1940), worsen (Malomsoki & Szmodis, 1970), or to demonstrate no change at all (Meyers, Zimmerli, Farr & Baschnagel, 1969; Phillips, 1973). To confound the issue further, varying forms of physical exertion have been utilised in these studies, ranging from specific limb actions to a more general activity such as boxing. Response times have often been measured by a motor act totally divorced from that of the fatiguing activity, thereby resulting in meaningless data.

Several researchers have suggested that reaction time may vary as a function of the intensity of the physical activity. Malomsoki & Szmodis (1970), who examined finger reaction time performance during graded work on a bicycle ergometer, found reaction time to lengthen monotonically with increased work load. A similar trend was observed for oxygen consumption and the authors suggested that a decrease in cortical activity due to cerebral hypoxia was responsible for the reaction time change. More recently Sheerer & Berger (1972), in a study of shoulder flexion reaction and movement times following three levels of fatiguing activity resulting in 15, 30 and 45 per cent reductions in maximum arm flexion strength, found reaction times after 30 and 45 per cent strength decrement to be significantly longer than pre-exercise resting measures. Movement times were also observed to deteriorate under the most severe fatigue condition and the authors conjectured that ". . . the accumulation of lactic acid associated with increased work is reflected in the inability of skeletal muscle tissue to contract maximally" (p. 147).

Clearly, though, neither the locus nor precise mechanism of a fatigue effect can be deduced from such experiments of simple reaction time change, although to so do would contribute greatly to the elucidation of a problem that has absorbed work physiologists for decades.

In reviewing the wealth of physiological literature on fatigue, Simonson (1971) observed:

> . . . there are various types of fatigue as there are various types of work, involving different physiological functions to a different degree, different phenomena, different mechanisms and different locations. (p. xii).

Despite this problem researchers have continued to probe the effects of fatigue on neuromuscular processes and their implications for skilled motor performance. Several researchers have adopted the electromyographic (EMG) technique of Weiss (1965) in their reaction time studies, whereby a total reaction time (TRT) can be fractionated into a central, or 'pre-motor', component (= time delay from stimulus presentation to onset of EMG activity in responding musculature); and a peripheral 'motor' component, representing the electromechanical delay prerequisite for limb movement. The relationship between the premotor time (PMT), motor time (MT) and the traditional TRT can be expressed in simple equation form:

$$TRT = PMT + MT$$

In a series of studies Kroll (1973) has examined the effects of local muscular fatigue on fractionated reaction times. Kroll's (1973) studies of isometric and isotonic exercise effects on knee extension reaction time, and Hayes's (1975) study of plantar flexion reaction time following serial isometric contractions, both support the view that strenuous exercise has little effect on either the central or peripheral components of a reaction time. These investigators also measured tendon reflex times and both found the MT component of this involuntary action to be affected by fatigue. Kroll (1973) postulated that in the voluntary reaction time task the central nervous system (CNS) was able to compensate for peripheral deficiencies, whereas a reflexively evoked motor act, presumably brought about by invariant neural impulses, deteriorates in the face of local muscle fatigue. Support for such a compensatory mechanism can be found in the EMG literature, where decreases in frequency and increases in amplitude of voluntary electromyograms have been found to accompany fatigue (Person, 1960; Missiuro, Kirschner & Kozlowski, 1962) and are purportedly due to the recruitment of additional motor units and/or a more synchronous firing pattern to compensate for reduced muscular efficiency. Interestingly, however, Hayes (1975) found achilles tendon reflex motor times to shorten following exercise, but differing muscle morphology may account for this finding, the calf muscle being predominantly a slow-twitch muscle in contrast to most other muscles in the body.

More recent fractionated reaction time studies have shown that when greater decrements in maximum voluntary contractile capability (MVC) are induced, or when the mechanical demands of the criterion reaction time response are increased, fatigue effects are evident. These effects are principally a lengthening of the MT component and are evidence of peripheral fatigue in the form of a diminished rate of tension development.

Table 8.1 presents a summary of the findings of fractionated reaction time studies for comparison of changes observed in the light of these two deterrents. The tabulation suggests that a threshold level of MVC decrement must be reached for a fatigue effect to manifest itself, and the RT studies of Sheerer & Berger (1972) and Stull & Kearney (1978), in which varying levels of fatigue were studied, suggest that an MVC decrement in the order of 40 per cent is necessary before simple response timing is affected. However, when a more forceful motor response is required, as was the case in the resisted RT tasks of Morris (1977) and Wood (1979), the sensitivity level appears to be lowered.

Although fatigue effects seem to be primarily peripheral in nature, small but significant alterations in CNS processing have been observed (Hanson & Lofthus, 1978; Wood, 1979). It is also apparent that PMT co-varies with many other human performance variables, for example intentional set, motivation and age (Weiss, 1965), sex and preparatory interval (Botwinick & Thompson, 1966a; 1966b), and preliminary muscular tension (Santa Maria, 1970; Schmidt & Stull, 1970). To explore further the temporal dimensions of the central component of a reaction time an experimental model based on evoked potential (EP) recording techniques has been developed (Wood, 1977). By computer averaging of electroencephalographic (EEG) activity, time-locked to

Table 8.1   Fractionated Visual Reaction Time and Fatigue Studies – A Summary

Author(s)	RT Task	Fatiguing Exercise	MVC Decrement	RT Changes
Hayes (1975)	Ankle plantar flexion	Serial isometrics	15–34%	none
Hanson & Lofthus (1978)	Hand grip	Serial isometrics	∼48%	PMT and TRT lengthened
Kroll (1973; 1974)	Knee extension	Serial isometrics and isotonic (bench stepping)	24 & 27% respectively	none
Klimovitch (1977)	Hand grip	Serial isometrics	42 & 55%	MT and TRT lengthened
Morris (1977)	Knee extension (normal and resisted)	Serial isometrics and isotonic (squats)	57 & 35% respectively	MT and TRT lengthened for resisted task
Wood (1979)	Ankle dorsiflexion (normal and resisted)	Serial isometrics	33–42%	All components lengthened but MT under resisted condition showed greatest change

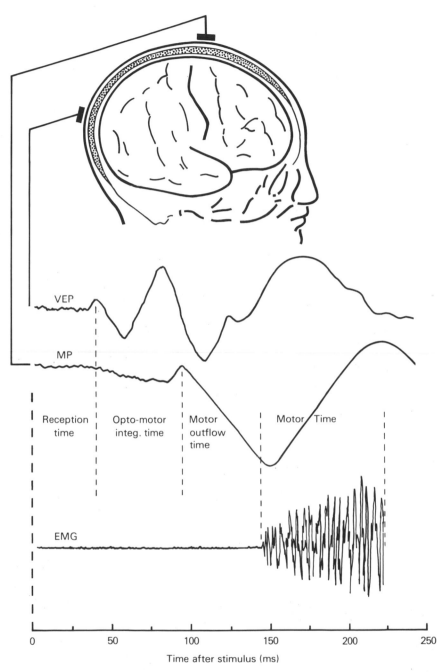

Figure 8.1   Schematisation of Visual Reaction Time Model (VEP = Visual evoked potential, MP = motor potential) from Wood, G. A., "An electrophysiological model of human visual reaction time", *Journal of Motor Behavior,* 1977, 9: 267–74. Reproduced by kind permission of the publishers.

the presentation of the visual stimulus and to the first appearance of the
response electromyogram, it has been possible to identify cortical
activity associated with sensory reception and motor execution. These
EP events then provided delimiters which enabled measurement of
visual reception time, opto-motor integration time and motor outflow
time as subcomponents of PMT (pre-motor time). A schematisation of
the reaction time model is presented in Figure 8.1, with formal
definitions of the components given below.

Reception Time (RCT): time delay between presentation of visual
    stimulus and the first appearance of visually evoked cortical
    activity as evidenced by the primary component of averaged visual
    evoked potential (Vaughan, 1966).

Motor Outflow Time (MOT): time delay between cortico-spinal
    outflow, evidenced by the onset of the dominant negative
    component of the averaged motor potential (Gilden, Vaughan &
    Costa, 1966), and the beginning of electromyographic activity in
    responding musculature.

Opto-Motor Integration Time (OMIT): time delay between cortical
    reception of visual stimuli and cortico-spinal discharge, that is,
    from the end of RCT to the beginning of MOT.

In a study of inter- and intra-subject variability of eighteen male
subjects performing a right foot dorsiflexion RT task, faster reactors
were found to display briefer OMITs and MTs, while an individual's
faster responses were characterised by shorter MOTs and MTs. These
differences are graphically presented in Figure 8.2 and suggest that
OMIT represents an inherent 'hard-wired' quality of an individual,
while moment-to-moment variability in performance is reflected more
in the labile MOT, which may be indicative of the state of the spinal
motor neurones' preparedness to convey the central command (Wood,
1977).

Fatigue effects on the dorsi-flexion reaction task were subsequently
investigated, with subjects required to perform the flexion response
against two levels of resistive force; one nominal, the other requiring
approximately 10 per cent MVC to register a movement. The fatiguing
activity was a series of thirty maximal voluntary isometric contractions
of the foot dorsiflexors which resulted in the order of a 38 per cent
reduction in MVC. Post-exercise measures of RT performance were
compared with baseline values previously obtained and the results of
this analysis are clearly apparent in Figure 8.3.

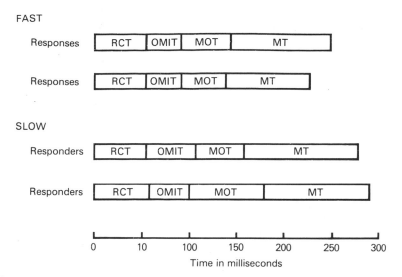
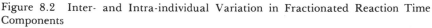

Figure 8.2   Inter- and Intra-individual Variation in Fractionated Reaction Time Components

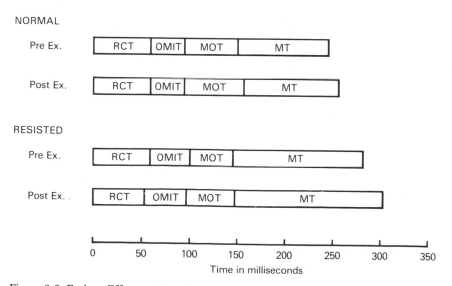
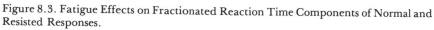

Figure 8.3. Fatigue Effects on Fractionated Reaction Time Components of Normal and Resisted Responses.

The quality of TRT was found to deteriorate, particularly when responses were resisted. A small (5 ms), but significant, lengthening of PMT was observed for both response conditions and this appeared to be largely due to a lengthening of MOT. As previously mentioned, this component can be primarily considered an index of spinal motoneurone excitability level, there being little variation in transmission delays even in the presence of fatigue (Simonson, 1971). Alterations in the state of spinal neural elements are known to occur as a result of exhaustive exercise (Kulenkampff, 1951), although the short delays evidenced in the present study may simply have been due to some alteration in the motor unit recruitment process, perhaps to achieve a more synchronous or extensive unit involvement as a means of compensating for peripheral deficiencies. Certainly MT changes only reached significant proportions in the instance of the resisted task, despite the dramatic reduction in maximum contractile capabilities. Limb motion was also recorded, however, and it was evident that even though the speed of response in peripheral musculature was preserved in the unresisted task, the extent and speed of the resulting flexion movement were diminished (Wood, 1979).

Clearly, then, local muscle fatigue induced by repeated isometric contractions has profound effects upon the quality of a simple visual reaction time. Changes in response timing are, however, largely manifest in terms of a lengthening of the peripheral motor time, indicative of a diminished rate of tension development, when the limb is loaded. These findings are in keeping with the suggestion by Merton (1956) that a breakdown in performance is only apparent "when working near the limits of reserve", while at other times a fatigue effect will not be apparent "owing to the excellence of the muscles' proprioceptive servo-control, which compensates automatically for fatigue" (p. 221). Such compensation has been shown to take the form of an increase in muscle spindle sensitivity to stretch (servo-loop gain) similar to that which occurs with increased load. It is not surprising, therefore, that researchers have found severe exertion impairs performance on such tasks as targetting (Cotten, Spieth, Thomas & Biasiotto,1974), tracking (Carron, 1969) and balancing (Ross, Hussman & Andrews, 1954; Schmidt, 1969) in so far as these motor skills require rapid adjustments to limb movements. Thus, in sports where the timing of a movement is an important factor and where a moderate degree of muscular force is required, muscular fatigue will seriously impair performance, while insufficiencies in the produced motion will require excessive correction and thereby inefficient movements.

References

Banerji, M. N. (1935) "Industrial psychology fatigue study", *Indian Journal of Psychology*, 10: 69–79.

Bartlett, F. C. (1953) "Psychological criteria of fatigue", in W. F. Floyd & A. T. Welford (Eds.), *Fatigue*, London: Lewis.

Botwinick, J. & Thompson, L. W. (1966a) "Components of reaction time in relation to age and sex", *Journal of Genetic Psychology*, 108: 175–83.

Botwinick, J. & Thompson, L. W. (1966b) "Premotor and motor components of reaction time", *Journal of Experimental Psychology*, 71: 9–15.

Carron, A. V. (1969) "Physical fatigue and motor learning", *Research Quarterly*, 40: 682–6.

Cotten, D. J., Spieth, W. R., Thomas, J. R. & Biasiotto, J. (1974) "Local and total body fatigue effects on learning and performance of a gross motor skill", *Medicine and Science in Sports*, 6: 151–3.

Dickinson, J., Medhurst, C. & Whittingham, N. (1979) "Warm-up and fatigue in skill acquisition and performance", *Journal of Motor Behavior*, 11: 81–6.

Elbel, E. R. (1940) "A study of response time before and after strenuous exercise", *Research Quarterly*, 11: 86–95.

Gilden, L., Vaughan, H. G., & Costa, L. D. (1966) "Summated human EEG potentials with voluntary movement", *Electroencephalography and Clinical Neurophysiology*, 20: 433–8.

Graham, C., Olsen, R. A., Parrish, M. & Leibowitz, H. W. (1968) "The effect of hypnotically induced fatigue on reaction time", *Psychonomic Science*, 10: 223–4.

Gutin, B. (1973) "Exercise-induced activation and human performance: a review", *Research Quarterly*, 44: 256–68.

Hanson, C. & Lofthus, G. K. (1978) "Effects of fatigue and laterality on fractionated reaction time", *Journal of Motor Behavior*, 10: 177–84.

Hayes, K. C. (1975) "Effects of fatiguing isometric exercise upon achilles tendon reflex and plantar flexion reaction time components in man", *European Journal of Applied Physiology*, 34: 69–79.

Kirihara, H. (1931) "The influence of factory work on psycho-physical functions", *Report for the Institute for Science of Labour*, Kurashiki, 2: 9–14.

Klimovitch, G. (1977) "Startle response and muscular fatigue effects upon fractionated hand grip reaction time", *Journal of Motor Behavior*, 9: 285–92.

Kroll, W. (1973) "Effects of local muscular fatigue due to isotonic and isometric exercise upon fractionated reaction time components", *Journal of Motor Behavior*, 5: 81–93.

Kulenkampff, H. (1971) "Des verhatten der vorderwurzelzellen der weissen maus uter dem reiz physiologischer tätigkeit", Z. Anat. Entwicklungsgesch, 1951, 116: 143. Cited in E. Simonson, *Physiology of Work Capacity and Fatigue*, Springfield, Illinois: Charles C. Thomas, 1971.

Malomsoki, J. & Szmodis, I. (1970) "Visual response time changes in athletes during physical effort", *Internationale Zeitschrift fur angewandte Physiologie, einschliesslick Arbeitsphysiologie*, 29: 65–72.

Merton, P. A. (1956) "Problems of muscular fatigue", *British Medical Bulletin*, 12: 219–21.

Meyers, C. R., Zimmerli, W., Farr, S. D. & Baschnagel, N. A. (1969) "Effects of strenuous physical activity upon reaction time", *Research Quarterly*, 40: 332–7.

Missiuro, W., Kirschner, H. & Kozlowski, S. (1962) "Electromyographic manifestations of fatigue during work at different intensity", *Acta Physiologia Polonica*, 13: 11–20.

Morris, A. F. (1977) "Effects of fatiguing isometric and isotonic exercise on resisted and unresisted reaction time components" *European Journal of Applied Physiology*, 37: 1–11.

Person, R. S. (1960) "Electrophysiological investigation of activities of the motor apparatus in man in a state of fatigue", *Journal of Physiology*, USSR 46: 945–54.

Phillips, W. H. (1963) "Influence of fatiguing warm-up exercises on speed of movement and reaction latency", *Research Quarterly*, 34: 370–8.

Ross, S., Hussman, T. A. & Andrews, T. G. (1954) "Efforts of fatigue and anxiety on certain psychomotor and visual functions", *Journal of Applied Psychology*, 38: 119–25.

Santa Maria, D. L. (1970) "Premotor and motor reaction-time differences associated with stretching of the hamstring muscles", *Journal of Motor Behavior*, 2: 163–73.

Schmidt, R. A. (1969) "Performance and learning a gross motor skill under conditions of artificially induced fatigue", *Research Quarterly*, 40: 185–91.

Schmidt, R. A. & Stull, G. A. (1970) "Premotor and motor reaction time as a function of preliminary muscular tension", *Journal of Motor Behavior*, 2: 96–110.

Sheerer, N. & Berger, R. A. (1972) "Effects of various levels of fatigue on reaction time and movement time", *American Correctional Therapy Journal*, 26: 146–7.

Simonson, E. (1971) *Physiology of Work Capacity and Fatigue*, Springfield, Illinois: Charles C. Thomas.

Stull, G. A. & Kearney, J. T. (1978) "Effects of variable fatigue level on reaction-time components", *Journal of Motor Behavior*, 10: 223–31.

Teichner, W. H. (1954) "Recent studies of simple reaction time", *Psychological Bulletin*, 51: 128–49.

Vaughan, H. G. (1966) "The perceptual and physiologic significance of visual evoked responses recorded from the scalp in man". In H. M. Burian & J. H. Jacobson (Eds.), *Clinical Electroretinography*, Proceedings of the Third International Symposium. London: Pergamon.

Weiss, A. D. (1965) "The locus of reaction time change with set, motivation and age", *Journal of Gerontology*, 20: 60–4.

Wood, G. A. (1977) "An electrophysiological model of human visual reaction time", *Journal of Motor Behavior*, 9: 267–74.

Wood, G. A. (1979) "Electrophysiological correlates of local muscular fatigue effects upon human visual reaction time", *European Journal of Applied Physiology*, 41: 247–57.

Woodworth, R. S. (1938) *Experimental Psychology*, New York: Holt.

9

Motion Prediction and Movement Control in Fast Ball Games

David A. Tyldesley

Action-oriented Studies of Vision in Sport

Modern western culture is largely dependent upon man's ability to use a sophisticated visual system. Lifestyles in industrial lands are determined and enriched by information acquired through the visual pathway. By the visual system is understood the head and neck, the eyes and eye muscles, the visual nerves and certain areas of the central nervous system (the lateral geniculate nucleus and the visual cortex).

Communication and the media, educational techniques and many forms of entertainment (including sport) are mediated by visual information. As a reflection of the importance of the system, the research effort directed towards it has been proportionally greater than, say, towards the auditory or proprioceptive (movement-sensing) systems. Indeed, this has always been so. As Polyak (1941) pointed out in his history of our knowledge of the human retina, the nature of sight and the structure of the organ of vision, have preoccupied philosophers "since the dawn of recorded history" (Le Grand, 1975).

Until the beginning of the nineteenth century, optics and vision were regarded as one field of study. However, with the identification of the frequencies infra-red, ultra-violet and X-rays, it became clear that light was only a small section of the range of electromagnetic frequencies. Research and study in *optics* then grew into an important part of pure and applied physics, while studies of *vision* became increasingly the prerogative of the physiologist and the psychologist. This chapter is directed towards certain contemporary problems in vision, and will attempt to review some aspects of vision research which have a direct connection with sport.

Psychological Approaches to the Visual System

Dodwell (1975) distinguished three main lines along which researchers are currently investigating vision. They correspond roughly to the traditional labels (1) the psychophysics of visual sensation, (2) pattern recognition and (3) object and event perception. The first of these so-called 'levels' regards the visual system as a *detector* of signals in a normally 'noisy' ambient stimulus environment. Underlying this approach is the concept that the retinal image may be broken down into a number of abstract features that are processed separately, and relatively automatically, by parallel channels. Since this is not a new idea it did not elicit much interest until a physiological basis for these sensory channels was revealed by modern techniques of neurophysiological testing. Using microelectrodes to record single cortical neuron activity, Hubel & Wiesel (1962) established that in the visual cortex of the cat exist classes of direction-specific neurons. The neurons fire at a high frequency when a properly oriented stimulus moves across the visual field in one direction, but at a much reduced rate when it moves in the other direction. Classes of such directional-specific neurons have been identified in several species of animal and it is now widely believed that *stimulus feature* (or possibly frequency) *analysers* are present in the human visual system. In general, these findings indicate that neurons exist which respond to specific stimulus features (e.g. colour, spatial frequency, orientation).

Two features of importance in almost all sporting activities are the perception of lateral motion in two dimensions and also *motion-in-depth,* which Regan, Beverley & Cynader (1979) have shown to be registered by physiological mechanisms. Using the psychophysical technique of selective adaptation (fatiguing the neural mechanism sensitive to a given stimulus), Regan and his colleagues were able to demonstrate that both the changing-size stimulation and stereoscopic motion disparity, generate signals which converge on *the same* motion-in-depth stage of a perceptual system. The model which results (Figure 9.1) suggests why certain illusions of motion-in-depth generated by changing stimulus size can be experimentally cancelled by adjusting the relative velocities of the retinal images and why sportsman may continue to perform reasonably satisfactorily, even after the loss of one eye. The loss of binocular vision cues can, in some circumstances, be compensated for by the changing size of object viewed.

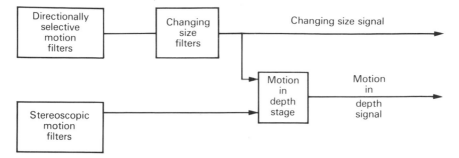

Figure 9.1   Early Feature Analysers in the Visual System (after Regan, Beverley & Cynader, 1979)

Such discoveries have greatly enhanced our knowledge of how the sensory *encoding* of important visual signals can occur, but they do not altogether satisfy the requirements of the cognitive psychologist concerned with the nature of visual perception *per se*. Regan, Beverley & Cynader (1979) commented that this work is based on the belief that carefully designed experiments (neurophysiological and psychophysical) could break down the operation of the visual system into elements that are more or less independent, and that a knowledge of these elements will advance the understanding of how vision operates in the complex everyday world. How we perceive things depends, in the first instance, upon the facilities of the sensory encoding process. As knowledge of coding grows and the constraints that it places on the central nervous system are recognised, then so too grows the realisation that it does not adequately explain how incoming information is actually dealt with in perceptual terms. The encoded information remains the substrate for further processing and it is wrong to directly equate electrophysiological findings with the phenomenon of perception. Though these stimulus feature analysers tell us much about the mechanism of pattern element recognition (level 1), they tell almost nothing about pattern organisation and synthesis (level 2) and about object and event perception (level 3).

Briefly, psychologists capitalised upon these findings at level 2 and suggested that some very complex visual patterns could be perceived as a whole by automatic stimulus analysers. Clearly, some of these applications were over-enthusiastic as was pointed out by Uttal (1971) in his paper "The psychobiological silly season, or what happens when neurophysiological data become psychological theories".

Instead, a reasonable view of the place of stimulus analysers in the perceptual system was provided by Haber & Hershenson (1973) who adopted an *information processing model* approach to the visual system (level 3). Here, the visual features output by the receptive field of the cortex form only the basic substrate for later processing. They are prerequisite in models of selective attention, which assume registration of all incoming signals in a storage system where selection on the basis of pertinence can occur (see Norman, 1968 & 1976). The third level of approach has proved helpful in considering visual functioning in real-life situations and has guided most studies concerning vision in sport. Only recently have certain limitations been exposed and these will be considered in more detail below.

An Information Processing Model

The model is constructed of a series of mental operations called processing stages which occur between the appearance of the stimulus and the production of the response. The given stimulus will have *potential information* (the amount of which will differ from one observer to the next), and its presentation initiates the sequence of processing stages in which each stage operates on the information made available by the previous stage. Stages may be arranged serially or in parallel, the output from one stage may feed into several subsequent stages and there may be temporal overlap between different parallel processes (for a further discussion of these problems see Macleod, 1977). The various stages have both *structural* and *functional* aspects where the structures may be loosely described as hypothetical computation mechanisms for dealing with the information, while the functional aspects are more general factors affecting the efficiency of the mental operations, such as available central capacity (Kahneman, 1973) and state of alertness (Posner & Boies, 1971). There is little doubt that between the appearance of a discrete signal and the production of a suitable response exist a series of time-consuming afferent and efferent processes, and it is one of the oldest hypotheses in psychology that reaction time (RT) comprises the sum of a number of finite processing times each of which corresponds to a stage in the translation from signal to response (Sanders, 1980). Welford (1968) indicated that identification of a signal and choice of a response constitute separate processing stages, while Smith (1968) distinguished the stages: pre-processing, identification, response choice and response execution. Perhaps the most clear identifications of RT stages stemmed from the work of Sternberg (1969) and Sanders (1967 & 1976). Sanders (1980) provided an information processing model (Figure 9.2) describing the reaction process (responding as quickly as possible to a given stimulus) which now serve as a basis for further discussion.

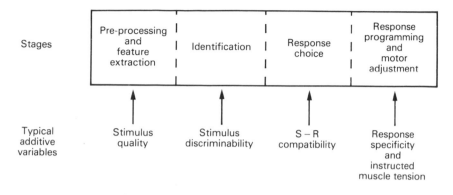

Figure 9.2   A Stage-Operations Model based on Sanders (1980). (No position is taken here regarding chronological order or directionality of the stages.)

Four processing stages are indicated here, though there may be many more. The model is in no way intended to be exhaustive, but only shows those operations essential for a simple reactive response. More complicated models could be drawn, involving all manner of *feedback loops* (see, for example, Norman & Rummelhart, 1970, or Pew, 1974), but the model shown above suffices for this treatment and is supported by a series of empirical studies. These studies mostly employ a methodology developed by Sternberg (1969) and suitable only for study of *reactive* information processing. The logic of this *additive factor method* proposes that if two independent variables (for example, stimulus–response compatibility and stimulus intensity) both have a main effect on RT, while their effects do not interact, then two different processing stages are likely to be involved. On the other hand, if the effects interact then the variables are likely to affect one common processing stage, since the size of the effect of the one variable depends on the state of the other. In the way inference can be made from experimental data as to which stages play a role in RT. Such a methodology is obviously open to criticism, summarised by Sanders (1980) under the headings: (1) concern about the basic logic, (2) the acceptance of RT as a single dimension, (3) the reliance of the method on statistical decision-making, (4) the notion of seriality and independence of stages, and (5) the precision of measurement and speed-accuracy trade-off. Moreover, Pachella (1974) has pointed out that much more must be known about individual subject *strategies* before the measures can be utilised in "subtle substantive controversies". Nonetheless, here is a fairly robust tool allowing empirical investigation of central nervous system functioning that would otherwise remain encapsulated in a general performance latency. Models developed with this technique allow understanding of a complex visual-motor system and are purely descriptive. They should not be localised to particular brain areas, though certain parallels can be drawn between identified stages and neurophysiological evidence for the preparation of movement (Gaillard, 1978; Brunia, 1980).

Upon leaving the problem of discrete stages it is noted that the static nature of such models is also criticised. The models have difficulty in coping with effects of past experience and practice, and circular models (Bernstein, 1967, Whiting, 1969; Adams, 1971) and schema constructions (Pew, 1974; Schmidt, 1975 & 1976) are used to overcome the problems of incorporating motor learning. Others have criticised the unidirectionality of such models and stressed that perception and decision-making are influenced by the set of possible actions that may be carried out. Perception is no longer seen as purely data-driven and the context in which the performer finds himself partly governs the factors in the display which gain his attention. Conceptually driven models of information-processing have appeared, wherein the importance of the information context is re-emphasised (Palmer, 1975). As Norman (1976) points out, signals do not go through a sequence of fixed neurological processes and come out "identified, labelled and tagged". Rather, ambiguous perceptions are interpreted in wholly unambiguous ways depending on their surroundings.

Stage Operations in a Perceptual Cycle

Neisser (1967) was a proponent of stage processing. A pre-attentive stage, where features were detected and analysed, was followed by an act of construction where the perceiver 'made' one perceptual object rather than another. But since that time certain authors (Fitch & Turvey, 1977; Whiting, 1980) and even Neisser himself, have come to doubt the value of such 'constructivism':

> It fails to explain the veridicality of perception. If percepts are constructed why are they usually so accurate? . . . The information must be specific enough in most cases to ensure that the constructed percept is true to the real object. (Neisser, 1976)

Laboratory experimentation is based so frequently on the *presentation* of discrete stimuli requiring immediate and simple response. Such experiments can deny the richness of the stimulus environment normally available, reduce the degrees of freedom of the subject's movements and do not allow him to self-pace his actions. Potential information should not have to be derived by the subject from a temporary stimulus, but should be chosen on the basis of an *information pick-up strategy* that he has learned. Such an 'ecological' approach to perception and skill learning is recognisably attributable to the work of the late J. J. Gibson of Cornell University. Gibson had for years challenged the simple analogy of the visual system as a passive receiver of information through a sort of retinal camera. To him, man acts as an active seeker of information, directly picking up information that the world offers him. Information 'pick-up' is "an act, not a response, an act of attention, not a triggered impression, an achievement not a reflex" (Gibson, 1979).

Gibson's theory of perception starts not with the retinal image, but with the ambient light reflected from objects that is available to be sampled by the eye at any point in space. This is the so-called *optic array*, a series of texture elements each of which reflects light differently from its neighbour. The light reflected from surfaces in the environment forms a densely structured optic array at the point of observation (for more detailed description see Lee, 1980). At each point of observation there is an unique optic array. If the head is moving, however slowly, relative to the environment, then this pattern of light at the eye is constantly changing. Gibson believed that this time-varying pattern or *optic flow field* is the normal stimulus for vision. In more complex mathematical analyses Lee (1974) has shown that the existence of a rectilinear optic flow field at the eye can directly specify that the eye is moving along a straight path through the environment, and empirical studies of human locomotion (Lee & Aronson, 1974; Lee & Lishman, 1975) have demonstrated the importance of 'exproprioception' made available visually for the control of movement relative to the environment. Clearly, if we accept that activity takes place within meaningful contexts and in a continuous fashion then a much more dynamic theory of perception is essential. Arbib (1972 & 1980) introduced the idea of 'action-oriented perception' and Neisser (1976), the perceptual cycle. In the latter model, the control of seeing is invested in anticipatory schemata (plans for perceptual action) which are continually updated and direct further pick-up of information. Each schema serves as an interactive mechanism integrating past information with what is picked up next, and the same external signals may be fed to different schema structures but used in entirely different ways. For example, a shoulder movement in football may, at one time, be seen simply as a displacement change for postural reasons, but in other circumstances as the beginning of a highly significant side-step, according to the currently active set of schema anticipations.

Neisser, however, could not completely deny the existence of internal cognitive processes. What he named in the schema was highly structured and involved the processing of information. It is a danger inherent in the ecological approach to perception that all notions of central processing are abandoned in favour of direct availability of environmental information. It is true that the optic array provides accurate information, but so is the idea that perception involves complex processing mechanisms. It is difficult to see how preparation for appropriate action can be explained without some postulate of further processing. Neisser takes what is a necessarily ambivalent position here. Grouping ecological and stage operations theorists with a third group, who describe perception as the testing and confirming of hypotheses (see Bruner, 1973), he suggests that each view simply focuses upon a single aspect of what is normally a continuous cyclic activity.

The researcher, currently concerned with understanding 'ordinary seeing' in an applied situation such as sport, is thus faced with a dilemma. His experimental situations must attempt to maintain the continuities of the 'normal' environment, and he must do this on the correct parameters and not simply provide face validity (Sanders, 1976). He must allow his subjects to engage anticipatory schemata and to plan ahead which information must be programmed. More cognitively complex movements should be employed than simple lever translations, and these skills should be measured at a more fine-grained level (kinematic analysis) than simply gross performance scores. In such constraints the control and elegance of an experimental methodology such as the additive factor method is difficult to maintain. The relative benefits of greater experimental validity must be weighed against increasing explanatory imprecision and a greater chance of confounding the independent variables.

The work on vision which finds application in the field of sport has been based almost exclusively upon information-flow principles. The research described in the rest of this chapter falls mostly into this category. However, by emphasising the use of vision in anticipation it is possible to see how these data may be integrated into an action–perception cycle.

Visual Information Processing in Sport

Though investigators have frequently used examples from sport to illustrate various phenomena in vision and hand–eye co-ordination, research which has as its main aim to understand the use of vision in sport *per se* is minimal. Stage processing models such as those described earlier have been used in theoretical studies and from these it is clear that the whole procedure, from starting to encode the incoming information to making the movement, costs a given amount of time (Sternberg, 1969; Sanders, 1977). This time will be affected by such factors as the discriminability of the stimulus, the compatibility of the signal and response and the relative frequency with which stimuli appear. In such work reaction time is more a *methodology* than the subject of the research. It is probably true to say that in the normal activities of daily life, reaction time is not so important. Poulton (1965) noted that there is no simple relationship between performance and reaction time. Measurements of the visual reaction times of top cricketers have indicated no above average RTs. Keele (1973) remarked that the heavyweight boxing champion, Muhammad Ali, could only produce a moderate SRT of 190 ms and suggested that the skill of the boxer lay not in his ability to react to an opponent's punch but his ability to anticipate it.

There are, in fact, few normal situations that require absolute reactivity. In laboratory situations this is achieved by the experimenter (or his computer!) switching on a light in the stimulus array, but in real life stimuli do not suddenly appear and require immediate reaction. Frequently, it is more important to make an accurate response, and in these instances time is taken, or 'traded-off' in order to achieve an optimum of speed and accuracy. Neisser (1976) has pointed out that entire events are perceived over time. "What is seen depends on how the observer allocates his attention, that is on the anticipations he develops and the perceptual explorations he carries out." Exploratory eye movements are made as a consequence of information already picked up and with the aim of obtaining more information. In fact, in sport we rarely react as quickly as possible to any single signal. Rather, we start gathering information ahead of time, which is important in later decision-making. Such predictions on only partial information are known as *perceptual anticipation*.

The anticipatory cycle is the essential link between output and input processes that simple stage operation models lack. The skilled performer anticipates the expected form of proprioceptive and exproprioceptive information which allow him to control his movements in a smooth fashion (feedforward). More central to this discussion is the notion that the expert can also anticipate the form of the visual afferent information that he must pick up in order to initiate a pre-planned movement sequence at the *correct instant*. The number of authors that have emphasised the close relationship between skill performance and anticipatory timing is legion (see, for example, Bartlett, 1947; Adams, 1961; Grose, 1967). Thus, before concentrating upon the role of vision in skill performance it is perhaps useful to review traditional theoretical approaches to anticipation:

Anticipatory Timing

Anticipation provides the means by which temporal and spatial judgments can be made in advance, thus avoiding unnecessary lags and allowing a smooth, co-ordinated response, coincident to a greater or less extent with external events. Yet anticipation has remained one of the least studied aspects of motor performance (Adams, 1966; Schmidt, 1971). Skill performance texts largely ignore the mechanisms of anticipatory responding, restricting their consideration of timing to the areas of simple and choice reactivity and studies of central refractoriness (Fitts & Posner, 1967; Welford, 1968; Singer, 1975). Marteniuk (1976) took the view that anticipation represented an ability of the performer, upon knowing or predicting a series of events, to coincide his response with the demands of the environment.

Such a general definition has satisfied some authors (Adams, 1964; Schmidt, 1968; Christina, 1970; Christina & Buffan, 1976), and although experimentally a separation between spatial and temporal anticipation is made, in normality they are confounding variables (Noble & Trumbo, 1967). Poulton (1952 & 1957) systematically investigated the role of anticipation in tracking tasks and distinguished two forms of anticipation dependent upon the source of information used in the predictions:

(a)   *Receptor anticipation:* arises when subjects can preview the approaching stimulus events and respond in a manner which eliminates the effects of RT delays. Here, preview provides information which is used to plan the time-course of future responses.

(b)   *Perceptual anticipation:* occurs when the subject cannot directly and continuously preview the approaching stimulus, but must base his predictions on learned regularities in the partial information made available to him. In the context of tracking tasks the separation provided by preview is easily understood, since subjects are either given or not given continuous sight of the target to be tracked. But the underlying mechanisms whereby predictions are made are probably not so distinct. Both involve learning, but in perceptual anticipation the task is made more difficult because the cue form which mediates the prediction is not continuously present. Subjects reduce spatial and temporal uncertainty through knowledge of some constant or probabilistic property of the input. It becomes necessary to sample the track at some point in advance in order to anchor the predictive judgments. However, as will be shown later, this cognitive aspect of timing is certainly not the only means to reduction of temporal uncertainty.

Perceptual and receptor anticipations are more important in the so-called "open skills". In these the environment is open to change, but only the skilled performer can predict with any degree of certainty what will happen in the next few minutes' play. Even then the unexpected can happen; the wind catches the football, the opponent makes a deception movement and so on. Examples of open skill are to be found in most competitive games, though the generality of such a statement is severely limited (for a further discussion of this problem see Whiting, 1975). In so-called "closed skills" the environment remains relatively stable and predictable. Examples are gymnastics, golf, rifle shooting and field events in athletics. Here the emphasis lies more on factors such as endurance, maximum effort and production of pre-described movement patterns; even so, a degree of anticipation is required. The performer must anticipate the form of the proprioceptive and exproprioceptive information associated with the correct movement pattern. Such intraresponse timing (Schmidt, 1969) plays an important role in controlling the expert's movements in a smooth, effortless fashion. Again, categorisation of sports along an open-closed continuum is dangerous. The movement patterns of the long jump, for example, have been shown to be continuously modified during the last few strides into the take-off board on the basis of visual information (Lee, Lishman & Thomson, 1977). The ultimate form of anticipation in movement control, that is rigid pre-programming, is obviously not taking place.

Vision and Movement Anticipation

Implicit within the work of Kay (1970) on ball catching in children was the importance of co-ordinated kinaesthetic and visual feedback in timing the closure of the hand around the ball. With great clarity he described how information about the flight of the ball might be integrated with control of the hand movements. In the same year Gibbs

(1970) modelled a movement control system and for the first time included a zone for modal integration; re-emphasising the psychological viewpoint of Konorski (1967) and Gibson (1968) that visual information can contribute a form of proprioception.

With regard to the control of movements themselves, the role of vision remains ambiguous. Functional combination of the two input streams has been shown to be both advantageous (Smith & Smith, 1962) and decremental to performance (Legge, 1965). In normal situations (that is, non-laboratory), and after sufficient practice, it is likely that the visual modality becomes *dominant*. Connolly & Jones (1970) and Salmoni & Sullivan (1976) provided evidence for an "equivalence dictionary" wherein location information can be translated from a visual to a kinaesthetic code. However, as these authors pointed out, it is uncertain whether the visual dominance noted is attributable to perceptual or output factors, or both. It was concluded that with sufficient practice an equivalence dictionary can be developed for any two modalities, but this would not usually be done since one modality is more appropriate.

This is certainly the case when one considers the nature of the visual information which may be picked up to aid the anticipatory movements of a limb (or limb extension) to meet a flying projectile. In an earlier paper, Bonnet & Kohlemainen (1969) suggested that any available cues in the visual display may be used to predict motion, but that the choice depends on the *relative accessibility* of each feature in the actual situation. It is to this problem of motion prediction, and the production of corresponding bodily movements, that the rest of this chapter will address itself. Two main questions will be considered. What is the *optimal time* for extraction of this information from the display? Which features of the display provide the most adequate predictive information of moving stimuli?

The Time of Extraction of Stimulus Information

A series of experiments initiated by Whiting (1967) considered not the form of the visual information, but the most efficient time to extract it for anticipatory movements. Although the findings of Whiting (1970) and Sharp (1975) were based upon ball flight anticipation, the timing principles apply equally well to other projectiles; moving body parts of the opponent and also for movements of one's own body toward a target.

Since ball flight velocities are much above the speed of smooth tracking with the eyes, and much of the latter part of the flight provides (theoretically) unusable information, Whiting questioned the idea of keeping the eye on the ball to bat–ball contact. In a continuous throwing and catching task Whiting (1969) illuminated only portions of the ball trajectory, and provided subjects had been allowed to practise in full light, performance was maintained even when only a restricted viewing period was available. Only the total darkness condition showed a performance decrement after training in full light. When subjects trained under restricted lighting, quadrants of the circular trajectory were noted, the illumination of which allowed performance equivalent to the full light conditions. A separate experiment (Whiting, 1970) allowed subjects more freedom to define their own viewing times and showed that with practice they shifted their vision *away from* the ball flight earlier and earlier before it reached their hands. In general, this series of experiments on a *self-initiated,* repetitive, throwing-catching task indicated that it was not necessary to view a ball in flight the *whole time* in order to catch it.

Catching the ball with one hand involves two predictions, one spatial, one temporal (though the two are not independent). Not only must the hand be in the correct position to receive the ball, but also the player must anticipate *when* the ball will reach the hand in order to start closing the fingers at the appropriate time. The required accuracy of this timing has been shown by Alderson, Sully & Sully (1974) who used high-speed film analysis to demonstrate that fine orientation of the fingers around the ball and closure of the hand is completed in approximately 65 ms. Taking into account the time it takes a ball to pass the outstretched finger tips and reach the palm and the rebound velocity of the ball from the palm, they calculated that the error margin for timing *grasp initiation* is between $+16$ ms and -30 ms of an optimal time. It is evident that the visual channel must allow for a predictive precision with a tolerance bandwidth of approximately 46 ms.

Similarly, the present author has demonstrated tolerances for timing bat–ball contact in a table-tennis situation. By allowing three subjects to repeatedly return consistently projected balls into a target on the opposite side of the table, displacement-time traces could be constructed for bat centre and ball movement over a number of attempts at the same shot. By separately regressing bat and ball movement over the final 100 ms to contact and representing these regression lines graphically, together with their 99 per cent confidence limits, it was possible to derive from the time axis a duration within which the trajectories overlapped with 99 per cent certainty. On this computation, and without consideration of the bat width, the temporal tolerances for successful contact were estimated for two conditions, performance under accuracy stress (A) and speed plus accuracy stress (SA). The tolerances shown in Table 9.1 for three subjects indicate that timing constraints vary with the task requirements and under

Table 9.1 Tolerances for Timing Bat–Ball Contact in Table-Tennis (ms)

		Condition	
		A	*SA*
Subjects	1	39	25
	2	46	23
	3	28	20

speed plus accuracy conditions, subjects had only a 20–25 ms interval wherein the bat centre could contact the ball. The slower movements of the accuracy condition gave an estimate of timing tolerance between 28 and 46 ms.

Sharp (1975) pointed out that Whiting had not controlled the time for which the ball could *not* be seen (the occluded period) and subsequently carried out experiments in which the viewing period (VP) and the occluded period (OP) were varied systematically. Results indicated that a minimum time (± 40 ms) is necessary to view the ball in order to extract ball-flight information. Furthermore, a certain amount of time is also needed to *process* the information and select the appropriate response, though this could occur in the dark. With an OP of zero, 40 per cent performance was achieved with a VP of 120 ms. With an OP of 80 ms, a VP of only 40 ms ensured 40 per cent success. Since an effective latency period of 150 ms (one RT) was included in his computations, it appeared that 40 ms viewing, beginning 270 ms (40 + 80 + 150) before contact allowed moderate performance. Increasing VP beyond 40 ms to 80 ms had no further beneficial effects. Possibly information obtained earlier could not contribute satisfactorily to the predictions, or subjects adopted a strategy of waiting until an optimal time to sample the ball-flight information.

However, increasing OP beyond 80 ms resulted in a performance decrement. Timing errors increased the longer the interval over which subjects must predict. This hypothesis has since been substantiated in simple movement time estimation studies by the present author. Coincidence of a linear hand movement with a moving target on an oscilloscope screen resulted in a rectilinear increase in absolute error of time estimation with duration (see Figure 9.3).

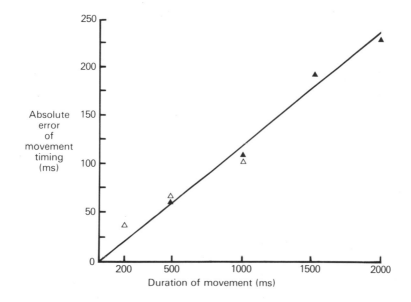

Figure 9.3   Increase of Absolute Error of Movement Time Estimation with Estimated Interval. (Data are extracted from two experiments with similar average velocities at all treatment levels.)

The VPs used by Sharp (1975) were minimal and resulted in only moderate performance. When, in a later experiment, subjects were provided with a greater range of OPs and VPs, catching performance maximised at 85 per cent when the ball was visible for 240 ms before an occluded period of 80 ms. Sharp (1975) speculated that the sudden increase in performance at long VPs was due to the greater possibility for clear foveation of the ball.

Given that this sampling takes place adequately, then the performer has two temporal predictions to make (Poulton, 1965). These are *when* to initiate the movement and *how long* it should last.* An efficient solution to this visuo-motor problem would be to standardise, with practice, the duration of the movement, thereby reducing the timing problem simply to that of initiating the movement at a specific moment before bat-ball contact (Tyldesley & Whiting, 1975; Lee, 1980).

*It is simple to give verbal description of these quantities. The author does not, however, mean to imply that such simplistic variables are actually employed in the CNS computations which result in movement timing.

Certainly, film analyses of table-tennis players under normal competitive conditions indicate that temporal consistencies are apparent in their movement patterns. A filmed sequence of a current English international player indicated that regardless of the current play conditions, the ballistic section of his forehand drive lasted 112 ms, with a standard deviation over 25 separate strokes of 7 ms. It seems that when free to choose how to control their movements, élite table-tennis players hold the duration of the stroke constant and vary other parameters. In more controlled laboratory studies it has been shown (Tyldesley & Whiting, 1975) that more highly trained players exhibit greater consistency of initiation of ballistic movements in relation to the time of bat–ball contact in both 'open' and 'closed' environments. Figure 9.4 shows the temporal and spatial variability of two groups of performers, trained and untrained, in initiating the ballistic section of a forehand drive over twenty trials in an open environment.

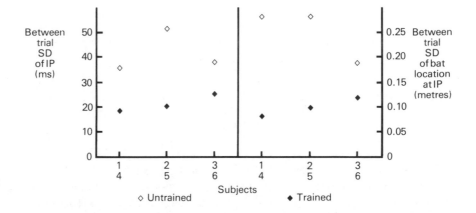

Figure 9.4   Consistency of Timing and Location of Ballistic Movements

These ballistic movements last between 110 and 150 ms and, despite current understanding of schema control of movement, can still be reasoned to be wholly under open-loop control (Keele & Summers, 1976). Laboratory studies using coincidence anticipation tasks with movement times of similar length have also shown that subjects tend to hold movement durations constant and that this tendency increases with practice (Schmidt, 1972; Schmidt & McCabe, 1976).

Using a similar linear movement timing paradigm it is possible to demonstrate a further advantage of a constant duration strategy. If the ballistic movement time in a striking action were to remain variable, then situations could be envisaged wherein too long or too short a time was made available for the required distance-to-contact to be covered. This would result in an increase or decrease in average velocity of the movement (distance covered/total MT), a variable which is related to the constant error of time estimations. Free (that is, not constrained by a cursor) linear hand movements, without preview and made in 200 and 500 ms over distances of 5, 10, 15 and 20 inches, provide timing response biases as shown in Figure 9.5.

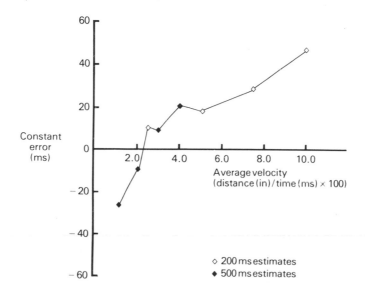

Figure 9.5   Effects of Increased Average Velocity of Movement on Constant Error of Movement Timing

Movements within a central range of velocities demonstrate a response bias of + 10 to + 20 ms regardless of the distance multiplied by time combination that comprised the movement. Subjects appear well able to keep the movement timing within the error tolerances discovered earlier for normal movements with preview. Movements slower than the central range tend to underestimate the MT (arrive early), while faster movements effectively overestimate the duration (arrive late).

It seems that a mechanism of *operational* timing is used to reduce the difficulties of movement control. A motor programme with a constant 'run time' is used by experts to reduce the timing degrees of freedom. The advantages of such a strategy lie in the reduction of attentional demands, the reduction of the length of the interval to be timed by input mediation and the easier prior planning of movement sequences.

The Nature of the Information Extracted

If such a strategy of coincidence timing operates under normal conditions, then more emphasis is laid upon the prediction of the initiation point (IP) of the movement rather than upon the time of contact itself. The exact form of the information extracted from the visual display to make this judgment is uncertain. Gerhard (1959) believed that estimates were based upon direct estimation of time intervals, but other authors favoured direct velocity perception and further computation of IP (Slater-Hammel, 1955; Bonnet, 1964). Such interpretations are in strict contrast to the Gibsonian approach described earlier. Lee (1980) has strongly argued that central differentiation of velocities from space–time relationships of approaching stimuli are largely unnecessary, and that all information regarding 'time-to-contact' is directly specified from the optic field in a dimensionless form.

In the table-tennis study already mentioned, it was possible to determine by film analysis over one hundred different kinematic features descriptive of the ball flight (input, variable over trials) and bat movement (output). Using a multiple regression technique, input para-meters were identified which influenced the timing of IP. The film analysis showed that all subjects had a variable 'dead' period at the top of the backswing, before initiating their ballistic stroke. By gradually refining the number of variables contributing to the predictive equation for IP, it was possible to identify five ball-flight parameters which substantially influenced the performer's decision when to release his ballistic movement. The occasions when these variables were signifi-cantly and independently related to IP time are indicated in Table 9.2.

An interesting interaction with training appeared. Subjects who had undergone a minimum of seven years' training for competitive table-tennis appeared to predict IP almost exclusively on the basis of some information that was available from the approaching ball when it reached a given *spatial location* (for example, size, angle subtended at the eye, or directly specified time-to-contact). Untrained subjects showed similar reliance on a displacement-linked ball-flight charac-teristic, but the timing of their actions showed traces of being influenced by velocity-linked features of the stimulus. Clearly, it is not possible to specify that velocity *per se* was influencing the decisions from such a regressional procedure. However, two hypotheses can be presented. The first is simply that the expert does cognise the velocity-related information, but at a time not sampled in this experiment. This seems untenable, since the kinematic analysis derived instantaneous velocity measures from within 25 ms of ball-projection. The second

Table 9.2   Beta Weights for the Various Significant Independent Variables within Each IP Prediction Equation (standard regression method)

	Ball Displacement Features		Ball Velocity Features		
	At IP	100 ms before contact	At projection	At IP	100 ms before contact
Untrained Group 1	−1·41**	0·30*	—	—	0·30*
2	−0·61**	—	—	−0·49**	—
3	−1·07**	0·46**	0·06*	—	−0·11**
Trained Group 4	−1·00**	0·13*	—	—	—
5	−1·05**	0·50**	—	—	−0·36**
6	−1·06**	—	—	—	—

$*p<0·05$ $**p<0·01$

hypothesis concurs with Lee's (1980) interpretation and suggests that the expert does not concern himself with velocity-related information, but extracts all the information needed about time-to-contact (or time-to-IP) from the ball at one given location. Whatever the correct answer, the general conclusion may be drawn, and emphasised for coaches, that the trained performer views more selectively and economically than the untrained. In purely operational terms, it appears that a 'progression' of cue forms (Fuchs, 1962) has been demonstrated from displacement plus velocity-related to displacement-related alone.

Perceptual Anticipation

The work described so far has concerned timing judgments based upon trajectory information from a projectile or moving limb. This may be strictly categorised as receptor anticipation, since continuous preview is available. Perhaps of more interest are those information sources, such as preparatory movements of the opponent's body, which provide partial information about his planned actions. Calculations are frequently made regarding the penalty situation in hockey and football. Drouin & Larivière (1974) estimate the puck flight time in ice-hockey to be under 100 ms for a penalty shot. Cues from the striker's body must be usable *prior* to the propulsion of the puck, if the keeper is going to anticipate and avoid RT delays. It is probable that full information regarding time-to-contact would not be extracted. Rather, certain parameters regarding the nature of the shot (direction, force) may be available to the expert keeper and could be used to prepare his movements. Increasingly, research in movement control has indicated that programming time for movements of different difficulty can be reduced by *pre-cueing* certain of the required movement parameters (Klapp, 1977; Kerr, 1978).

Few experiments have given attention to the cues which are available prior to the propulsion of a projectile. Salmela & Fiorito (1979) investigated the effect of both availability and quality of visual cues preceding the striking of the puck in the ice-hockey penalty situation. Film sequences of the striker were edited to end precisely 2, 4 or 8 images ($\frac{1}{12}$, $\frac{1}{6}$, $\frac{1}{3}$ second) before contact. Subjects were required to indicate verbally to the experimenter to which of the four corners the puck was believed to be directed. The results indicted a success rate well above chance, and the ratio success–non-success diminished significantly ($3 \cdot 2 : 1$ to $2 \cdot 1 : 1$) as the number of occluded frames increased from 2 to 8. Salmela & Fiorito (1979) concluded that information that can facilitate anticipation in a goal-tending task, is both available and usable in the period prior to the shot.

Stimulated by this work of Salmela & Fiorito (1979), studies are now being conducted to examine further the problem of the nature of the subtle cues available from the body movements of both (a) opponents in a game situation and (b) demonstrators in a teaching situation. In one study, unfortunately not yet complete, the author is further exploiting the idea of filmed displays. Instead of verbal responses, a choice reaction time paradigm is used, where discrete movements must be initiated as quickly as possible in the direction that the ball on the film is being kicked. Subjects view a head-on film of a penalty kick being taken from the required distances of association football. They are aware that only four different directions of ball flight are possible (high/low and left/right), and are provided with a central 'start' key on a board from which they must make a movement to the correct response key of four possibilities. Independent variables being manipulated in a series of experiments include (a) clarity of information presented by the film and the duration of its exposure, (b) probabilities of stimulus occurrence, (c) stimulus–response compatibility, (d) movement distances and (e) experience levels of observers. It is hoped that selection of variables will help to determine which stages are functioning in the production of a response. More importantly, however, an interaction between the experience level of the observer and the individual stage latencies is hypothesised. The direction of this interaction cannot be firmly predicted. Suppose the effects of skill level are interactive with both variable (a) (stimulus quality) and variable (c) (stimulus–response compatibility), then the indication would be that the stages *feature extraction* and *response choice* are major factors in acquisition of the skill. However, should skill level interact with, for example, stimulus quality, while remaining additive with S–R compatibility, then it is to be suggested that feature extraction alone changes with skill level. Motor learning is then identified on the perceptual side.

Since experimentation is not yet complete these hypotheses remain speculative and technical and theoretical problems have been encountered. With film displays how does the experimenter know the exact length of the RT interval? Already the broadening of the experimental validity has allowed anticipation to play a confounding role. Furthermore, the movements to be made are finger movements to a button, quite unlike the whole body movements of the goalkeeper. How can the action-orientation of the perceptual judgment be maintained when the experimental task requires only a very small movement? Finally, it is difficult to study the 'experience of years' possessed by professional goalkeepers without the confounding effects of practice on the task itself. Should all subjects be given equal task-practice, with the accompanying risk that novices learn the essential cues in this oversimplified situation? These and others are recognised, but not insurmountable, problems of attempting to make research more ecologically valid. It is hoped that results will justify the attempted marriage of experimental psychological methods with movement measurements under conditions of richer visual displays.

References

Adams, J. A. (1961) "Human tracking behaviour", *Psychological Bulletin*, 58: 55–79.

Adams, J. A. (1964) "Motor skills", *Annual Review of Psychology*, 15: 181–202.

Adams, J. A. (1966) "Some mechanisms of motor responding: an examination of attention", in E. A. Bilodeau (Ed.), *Acquisition of Skill*, London: Academic Press.

Adams, J. A.. (1971) "A closed-loop theory of motor learning", *Journal of Motor Behavior*, 3: 11–50.

Alderson, G. J. K., Sully, D. J. & Sully, H. G. (1964) "An operational analysis of a one-handed catching task using high speed photography", *Journal of Motor Behavior*, 6: 217–26.

Arbib, M. A. (1972) *The Metaphorical Brain: an Introduction to Cybernetics as Artificial Intelligence and Brain Theory*, New York: Interscience.

Arbib, M. A. (1980) "Perceptual structures and distributed motor control", in V. B. Brooks (Ed.), *Handbook of Physiology*, Bethesda: American Physiological Society.

Bartlett, F. C. (1947) "The measurement of human skill", *British Medical Journal*, 1: 835–8 & 877–80.

Bernstein, N. (1967) *The Coordination and Regulation of Movement*, London: Pergamon.

Bonnet, C. (1964) "La vitesse percue et la relation V = E/T", *Année Psychol.*, 64: 47–60.

Bonnet, C. & Kohlemainen, K. (1969) "Prediction of the future position of a moving object", *Scandinavian Journal of Psychology*, 10: 65–70.

Bruner, J. S. (1973) *"Beyond the Information Given: Studies in the Psychology of Knowing"*, London: Allen & Unwin.

Brunia, C. H. M. (1980) "Motor preparation, recorded on the cortical and spinal level", in G. E. Stelmach and J. Requin (Eds.), *Tutorials in Motor Behaviour*, Amsterdam: North-Holland.

Christina, R. W. (1970) "Proprioception as the basis for the temporal anticipation of motor responses", *Journal of Motor Behavior*, 2: 125–33.

Christina, R. W. & Buffan, J. K. (1976) "Preview and movement as determiners of timing a discrete motor response", *Journal of Motor Behavior*, 8: 101–12.

Connolly, K. J. & Jones, B. (1970) "A developmental study of efferent-afferent integration", *British Journal of Psychology*, 61: 259–66.

Dodwell, P. C. (1975) "Contemporary theoretical problems in seeing", in E. C. Carterette and M. P. Friedman (Eds.), *Seeing: Handbook of Perception V*, London: Academic Press.

Drouin, D. & Larivière, G. (1974) "Le temps de reaction et le temps de mouvement des gardiens de buts", *Mouvement*, 9: 21–5.

Fitch, H. L. & Turvey, M. T. (1977) "On the control of activity: some remarks from an ecological point of view", in D. M. Landers & R. W. Christina (Eds.), *Psychology of Motor Behavior and Sport*, Illinois: Human Kinetics Publishers.

Fitts, P. M. & Posner, M. I. (1967) *Human Performance*, Belmont, Calif.: Brooks/Cole.

Fuchs, A. H. (1962) "The progression–regression hypothesis in perceptual-motor skill learning", *Journal of Experimental Psychology*, 63: 177.

Gaillard, A. W. K. (1978) *Slow Brain Potentials preceding Task Performance*, Amsterdam: Academische Pers.

Gerhard, D. J. (1959) "The judgement of velocity and prediction of motion", *Ergonomics*, 2: 287–304.

Gibbs, C. B. (1970) "Servo-control systems in organisms and the transfer of skill", in D. Legge (Ed.), *Skills*, Harmondsworth: Penguin.

Gibson, J. J. (1968) *The Senses Considered as Perceptual Systems*, London: Allen & Unwin (1st American Edn. 1966).

Gibson, J. J. (1979) *The Ecological Approach to Visual Perception*, London: Houghton Mifflin.

Le Grand, Y. (1975) "History of research on seeing", in E. C. Carterette and M. P. Friedman (Eds.), *Seeing: Handbook of Perception V*, London: Academic Press.

Grose, J. E. (1967) "Timing control in finger, arm and whole body movements", *Research Quarterly*, 38: 10–21.

Haber, R. N. & Hershenson, M. (1973) *The Psychology of Visual Perception*, New York: Holt, Rinehart & Winston.

Hubel, D. H. & Wiesel, T. N. (1962) "Receptive fields, binocular interaction and functional architecture in the cat's visual cortex", *Journal of Physiology*, 160: 106–54.

Kahneman, D. (1973) *Attention and Effort*, Englewood Cliffs, N.J.: Prentice-Hall.

Kay, H. (1970) "Analyzing motor skill performance", in K. J. Connolly (Ed.), *Mechanisms of Motor Skill Development*, London: Academic Press.

Keele, S. D. (1973) *Attention and Performance*, Pacific Palisades, Calif.: Goodyear.

Keele, S. W. & Summers, T. T. (1976) "The structure of motor programs", in G. E. Stelmach (Ed.) *Motor Control: Issues and Trends*, London: Academic Press.

Kerr, B. (1978) "Task factors that influence selection and preparation for voluntary movements", in G. E. Stelmach (Ed.), *Information Processing in Motor Control and Learning*, New York: Academic Press.

Klapp, S. T. (1977) "Reaction time analysis of programmed control", *Exercise and Sport Sciences Reviews*, 5: 231–53.

Konorski, J. (1967) *Integrative Activity of the Brain: An Interdisciplinary Approach*, London: University of Chicago Press.

Lee, D. N. (1974) "Visual information during locomotion", in R. McLeod and H. Pick (Eds.), *Perception: Essays in Honor of J. J. Gibson*, Ithaca: Cornell University Press.

Lee, D. N. (1980) "Visuo-motor coordination in space–time", in G. E. Stelmach and J. Requin (Eds.), *Tutorials in Motor Behaviour*, Amsterdam: North-Holland.

Lee, D. N. & Aronson, E., (1974) "Visual proprioceptive control of standing in human infants", *Perception and Psychophysics*, 15: 529–32.

Lee, D. N. & Lishman, J. R. (1975) "Visual proprioceptive control of stance", *Journal of Human Movement Studies*, 1: 87–95.

Lee, D. N., Lishman, T. R. & Thomson, J. (1977) "Visual guidance in the long-jump", *Athletics Coach*, 11: 26–30 12: 17–23.

Legge, D. (1965) "Analysis of visual and proprioceptive components of motor skill by means of a drug", *British Journal of Psychology*, 56: 245–54.

MacLeod, P. (1977) "Parallel processing and the psychological refractory period", *Acta Psychologica*, 381–96.

Marteniuk, R. G. (1976) *Information Processing in Motor Skills*, London: Holt, Rinehart & Winston.

Neisser, U. (1967) *Cognitive Psychology*, New York: Appleton-Century-Crofts.

Neisser, U. (1976) *Cognition and Reality*, San Francisco: Freeman.

Noble, M., & Trumbo, D. (1967) "The organization of the skilled response", *Organizational Behaviour and Human Performance*, 2: 1–25.

Norman, D. A. (1968) "Toward a theory of memory and attention", *Psychological Review*, 75: 522–36.

Norman, D. A. (1976) *Memory and Attention: An Introduction to Human Information Processing*, London: Wiley.

Norman, D. A. & Rummelhart, D. E. (1970) "A system for perception and memory", in D. A. Norman (Ed.), *Models of Human Memory*, New York: Academic Press.

Pachella, R. G. (1974) "The interpretation of reaction time in information processing", in B. Kantowitz (Ed.), *Tutorials in Performance and Cognition*, Hillsdale, N.T.: Erlbaum.

Palmer, S. E. (1975) "Visual perception and world knowledge", in D. A. Norman, D. E. Rummelhart and the LNR Research Group, *Explorations in Cognition*, San Francisco: Freeman.

Pew, R. W. (1974) "Human perceptual-motor performance", in B. H. Kantowitz (Ed.), *Human Information Processing: Tutorials in Performance and Cognition*, Hillsdale, N.J.: Erlbaum.

Polyak, S. L. (1941) *The Retina*, Chicago: University of Chicago Press.

Posner, M. I. & Boies, S. J. (1971) "Components of attention", *Psychological Review*, 78, 391–408.

Poulton, E. C. (1952) "Perceptual anticipation in tracking with two-pointer and one-pointer displays", *British Journal of Psychology*, 43; 222–9.

Poulton, E. C. (1957) "On prediction in skilled movements", *Psychological Bulletin*, 54: 467–78.

Poulton, E. C. (1965) "Skill in fast ball games", *Biology and Human Affairs*, 31: 1–5.

Regan, D., Beverley, K. & Cynader, M. (1979) "The visual perception of motion in depth", *Scientific American*, 241: 122–33.

Salmela, J. H. & Fiorito, P. (1979) "Visual cues in ice hockey goaltending", *Canadian Journal of Applied Sports Sciences*, 4: 56–9.

Salmoni, A. W. & Sullivan, S. T. (1976) "Intersensory integration of vision and kinetics for distance and location cues", *Journal of Human Movement Studies*, 2: 225–32.

Sanders, A. F. (1967) "Some aspects of reaction processes", in A. F. Sanders (Ed.), *Attention and Performance 1, Acta Psychologica*, 27: 115–30.

Sanders, A. F. (1976) "Experimental methods in human engineering", in K. F. Kraiss and J. Moraal (Eds.), *Introduction to Human Engineering*, Koln: Verlag TÜV Reinland.

Sanders, A. F. (1980) "Stage analysis of reaction processes", in G. E. Stelmach and J. Requin (Eds.), *Tutorials in Motor Behaviour*, Amsterdam. North-Holland.

Schmidt, R. A. (1968) "Anticipation and timing in human motor performance", *Psychological Bulletin*, 70: 631–46.

Schmidt, R. A. (1969) "Movement time as a determiner of timing accuracy", *Journal of Experimental Psychology*, 79: 43–7.

Schmidt, R. A. (1971) "Proprioception and the timing of motor responses", Psychological Bulletin, 76: 383–93.

Schmidt, R. A. (1972) "The index of preprogramming (IP): A statistical method for evaluating the role of feedback in simple movements", *Psychonomic Science*, 27: 83–5.

Schmidt, R. A. (1975) "A schema theory of discrete motor skill learning", *Psychological Review*, 82: 225–60.

Schmidt, R. A. "Control processes in motor skills", *Exercise and Sport Sciences Reviews*, 4: 229–61.

Schmidt, R. A. & McCabe, J. F. (1976) "Motor program utilization over extended practice", *Journal of Human Movement Studies*, 2: 239–47.

Sharp, R. H. (1975) Skill in fast ball games: some input considerations, Unpublished Doctoral Thesis, University of Leeds.

Singer, R. N. (1975) *Motor Learning and Human Performance*, New York: Macmillan.

Slater-Hammel, A. T. (1955) "Estimation of movement as a function of the distance of movement perception and target distance", *Perceptual and Motor Skills*, 5: 201–4.

Smith, E. E. (1968) "Choice reaction time: an analysis of the major theoretical positions", *Psychological Bulletin*, 69: 77–110.

Smith, K. U. & Smith, W. M. (1962) *Perception and Motion*, Philadelphia: Saunders.

Sternberg, S. (1969) "The discovery of processing stages: Extensions of Donders' method", in W. G. Koster (Ed.), *Attention and Performance 2, Acta Psychologica*, 30: 276–315.

Tyldesley, D. A. & Whiting, H. T. A. (1975) "Operational timing", *Journal of Human Movement Studies*, 1: 172–7.

Uttal, W. B. (1971) "The psychobiological silly season, or what happens when neurophysiological data become psychological theories", *Journal of General Psychology*, 84: 151–66.

Welford, A. T. (1968), *Fundamentals of Skill*, London: Methuen.

Whiting, H. T. A. Visual motor coordination. Unpublished Doctoral Thesis, University of Leeds, 1967.

Whiting, H. T. A. (1969) *Acquiring Ball Skill: A Psychological Interpretation,* London: Bell.
Whiting, H. T. A. (1970) "An operational analysis of a continuous ball-throwing and catching task", *Ergonomics,* 13: 445–54.
Whiting, H. T. A. (1975) *Concepts in Skill Learning,* London: Lepus.
Whiting, H. T. A. (1980) "Information processing and skill modelling", Proceedings of the British Society of Sports Psychology Conference on *Information Processing in Motor Skills,* Bedford.

10

Distance Estimation and Sports Performance*

Ian M. Cockerill

Judging distance is an important feature of the striking skills associated with many team and also individual sports. In field games, for example, the distance to goal must be judged in a variety of conditions; either 'dead ball', such as a corner or free kick in soccer, or when shots are taken in dynamic situations. In racket sports, distances to baseline, service line and tramline must be estimated precisely, while golf also provides an interesting paradigm, since being able to hit the ball accurately over a given distance is the sole criterion of success; all aspects of the game lead to this end.

Team sport players are similarly involved in passing a ball to a colleague and before a long pass is made the player in possession may be seen to momentarily alter his attention from ball to target. This affords an impression of both distance involved and 'weight' of pass required. For example, a goalkicker in rugby football may make such estimations as he lifts his head and shifts his gaze from ball to posts. Likewise, the golfer invariably demonstrates similar behaviour before playing each shot. It is this second situation – with the ball stationary and sufficient time available in which to make the appropriate distance judgment – that provides the basis for the investigation described in this chapter. It examines the accuracy with which both games players and, for comparative purposes, non-games players are able to make estimations along the 'z' axis of visual space.

*The author acknowledges the generous contribution of Tony Sparrow and George Doganis, graduate students in the Department of Physical Education, University of Birmingham, 1978-79, who collected and analysed the data for this chapter.

Studies have long been conducted with the specific aim of determining those relationships that might exist between athletic performance and an individual's ability to make more or less precise judgments about the location of moving or stationary objects. For example, a review by Sage (1977) drew attention to attempts to associate measures of perception with athletic performance, while Ridini (1968) demonstrated that significant differences existed between athletes and non-athletes on a large number of psychological and sports skill tests. Conversely, Shick (1971) found no significant differences between subjects' basketball free-throw success and measures of depth perception. These studies are typical of many in the area inasmuch as they employ procedures for perceiving distance over a relatively narrow range and in a controlled, laboratory environment.

The apparatus described by Sage (1977) typically measures real – as distinct from apparent – depth, and involved a subject aligning two vertical rods from a distance of 20 ft. A different piece of commercially obtainable equipment designed to evaluate four features of vision includes distances up to 14 in as 'near', and not more than 20 ft as 'far' vision. Accordingly, such measures of depth perception appear inappropriate for the kind of estimations required in sport which frequently include distances up to 50 yd and more. A long pass in soccer or hockey, a kick for touch in rugby and a golf iron shot each exemplify motor skills conducted well beyond the range of the kind of laboratory equipment designed to test depth perception. Although distance estimation in applied situations may frequently be made using objects in the visual field as cues, a conscious awareness of the disparity between the stimulus and another object is unlikely to be a reliable cue to depth in a sports context.

In order to assess the accuracy of perceptual judgments in the location of a distant target the methodologies employed by Gibson, Bergman & Purdy (1955) and Cockerill (1969) might be considered more relevant. The former showed that with prior training – using a fractionation technique in which a subject was required to bisect the distance to an object by estimation – subjects were able to make accurate judgments about the location of a moveable target placed at distances varying between 52 yd and 395 yd. Cockerill (1969), in a developmental study of perceived distance, asked subjects to reproduce a specified distance by walking away from the experimenter. He challenged the Piagetian notion of a developmental progression toward veridicality – or 'true' perception – by showing that absolute judgments of distance do not vary reliably with age. Thus, on the basis of the findings of Gibson, Bergman & Purdy (1955) and Cockerill (1969) an investigation was designed to identify any differences, either innate or acquired, that might exist between games players' and non-games players' ability to make absolute distance judgments.

The terms depth perception, distance perception and distance judgment tend to be referred to interchangeably in many texts. Here distance judgment was used, since it is felt that it identified most accurately what was required from those subjects who took part. Distances were selected to represent the range reasonably expected in team games. There were 4 yd between the first four distances and 8 yd between the remainder; to identify more or less accurately any location at which significant errors of judgment might be made. Eight-yard increments provided a convenient number of distant points within an 80 yd range, while the 4 yd spacing was incorporated to test the null hypothesis that games players would not be more accurate in their distance judgments than non-games players beyond 7 to 10 yd. It is possible that those studies reviewed by Sage (1977) failed to reveal significant differences between athletes non-athletes because of the short, therefore inappropriate, distance judgments made in the tests of depth perception and sports tasks investigated.

Dickson (1953) and Shick (1971) used basketball shooting as a measure of athletic ability, Tomlin (1966) a badminton wall-volley test and a softball throwing task. A possible confounding variable in studies such as these concerns the selection of athletes for experimental subjects. Olsen (1956) and Ridini (1968), for example, did not sample subjects on the basis of sport played. It may be that sport makes differing demands on players' ability to judge distance and the wisdom of selecting an homogeneous group with respect to the type of sport played will be discussed.

Some studies of distance perception have emphasised other perceptual phenomena. Gogel & Tietz (1977), for example, examined the effect of eye fixation and attention upon the apparent location of a point of light, with 292 cm being the maximum distance to the light stimulus, while Collins (1976) investigated age changes in the accuracy of judgments up to 600 cm and identified a shift towards veridicality between seven and nine years. It should be noted that this finding differs from the results obtained by Cockerill (1969) and a further study to determine the reasons for disparity between these investigations would be worthwhile. Clearly, there are many basic developmental features of perception to be considered that are likely to have implications for the learning of motor skills. Moreover, despite variability in the nature of distance estimates obtained in the two studies, comparisons are possible because of similar age groupings used by both researchers. Also, in a study of ballistic aiming Whiting &

Cockerill (1972) showed that absolute error scores among four- to six-year-old boys were highly inaccurate for distances up to 160 cm, thereby supporting Collins's (1976) visual perception data from the standpoint of movement control and its ontogeny. The investigation described below, however, was designed to identify the efficiency with which adult athletes were able to make accurate spatial judgments in comparison with those by non-athletes.

The Investigation

Two groups of fifteen male subjects were randomly sampled from the undergraduate population of a British university. Games players were of university first team standard in either soccer or rugby union football. Non-games players were identified as having no active involvement or special interest in sport.

The stimulus object used was a solid, plastic traffic cone. It was easily visible and could be readily moved from one location to another. The cone was 75 cm high and 25 cm in diameter at the base, tapering to 14 cm at the apex. It was coloured fluorescent orange with a broad white band around the centre. Twelve white plastic discs, each 5 cm in diameter, were marked with one of each distance to be judged; that is, the first four ranged from 4 yd to 16 yd in 4 yd increments, and then to 80 yd in intervals of 8 yd.

The order of stimulus presentation was changed for each subject according to a previously determined random order. Each disc was held firmly in the ground by a 5 in nail that was invisible to subjects. A 150 ft steel tape was used to measure each judgment and subjects were provided with a clipboard, card and pencil to record their observations. The choice of site was considered especially important to avoid the proximity of trees, buildings or other objects likely to provide spatial reference cues for subjects. A suitable location was a large area of open ground adjacent to the university halls of residence. The terrain was judged to be sufficiently flat for the purpose of the study and, at the time, was uniformly covered with snow and ice.

Testing was conducted on four consecutive days and all subjects were task naïve and unaware that they had been allocated to a particular criterion group. Distance markers were placed prior to each subject arriving at the site and he was able to see only the cone, positioned at the final distance for the previous subject. Each subject was tested individually and upon arrival he was asked to stand facing away from the cone and follow a set of standard instructions.

Meanwhile, an assistant had moved the cone to the first distance; the initial judgment being considered a non-recorded trial to familiarise the subject with the procedure. As the subject turned away to note his score on each occasion the cone was moved to the next distance. This procedure was repeated until all twelve judgments had been made.

Mean algebraic error and mean ratio error scores were calculated for both groups and at all distances. These data were computed using a two-way analysis of variance with repeated measures on the distance variable. The analysis revealed significant variability in mean error scores between the two groups ($F = 5.02$; $df 1,308$; $p < 0.05$) indicating that the games players were more accurate in their judgments of distances than the non-games players.

Although the effect of distance was not significant, a one-way analysis of variance conducted independently for each group showed that whereas distance did not contribute to the variability of judgments by games players ($F = 0.906$; $df 11,154$; $p > 0.05$), it significantly influenced the judgments of non-games players ($F = 14.80$; $df 11,154$; $p < 0.001$). This finding explained the significant interaction between distances and groups in the initial analysis ($F = 6.36$; $df 11,308$; $p < 0.01$).

Furthermore, using both algebraic and ratio error scores, t-tests were conducted to evaluate the significance of differences between means for both groups at each distance. Algebraic error scores revealed a significant difference between groups at the nearest distance only ($t = 3.78$; $p < 0.001$). At 8 yd, 12 yd, 16 yd and 80 yd there were also differences, but they were nonsignificant. A graphical representation of these data is presented in Figure 10.1.

Ratio error scores produced quite different results. Mean ratio errors for games players were consistently smaller than for non-games players and these data are displayed in Figure 10.2, while Table 10.1 indicates those distances revealing significant differences between the two experimental groups.

Table 10.1   Differences in Mean Ratio Error
Scores Between Games Players and Non-Games
Players at Fixed Locations

Distance (yards)	t	p
32	1.70	<0.05
40	2.47	<0.05
48	2.55	<0.01
64	1.79	<0.05
72	1.94	<0.05
80	2.20	<0.05

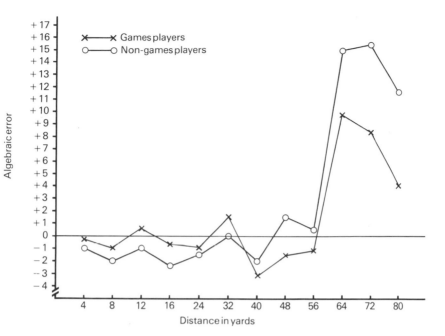

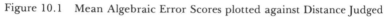

Figure 10.1   Mean Algebraic Error Scores plotted against Distance Judged

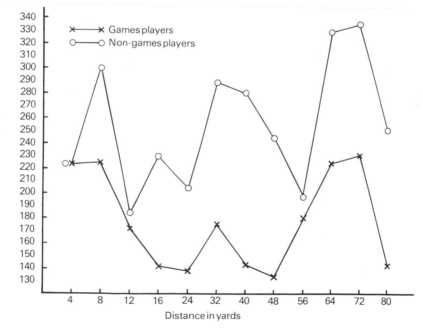

Figure 10.2   Mean Ratio Error Scores plotted against Distance Judged

The null hypothesis that there was no difference in the ability of games players and non-games players to make absolute judgments of distances up to 80 yd was rejected. Furthermore, differences were largely attributable to games players demonstrating greater accuracy in their estimation of the longer distances (Table 10.1). The notion that games players might reveal greater perceptual reliability beyond 7 to 10 yd was not substantiated and, using ratio error scores, significant differences between groups were only evident at 32 yd and beyond. This finding may have been due to the non-games player being unaccustomed to making relatively precise spatial judgments beyond, say, 30 yd in his normal daily activities.

Algebraic error scores were used to determine any systematic tendency for either group to over- or underestimate. As shown in Figure 10.1, non-games players consistently underestimated up to 45 yd, beyond which a reversal in error was shown. Apart from 12 yd and 32 yd, games players also tended to underestimate the shorter distances. Beyond 56 yd they over-estimated, which is consistent with the evidence produced by Cockerill (1969) that beyond 60 yd variability of judgment increases rapidly. The reduction in error at 80 yd by both groups in the present study may have reflected subjects' assumption that the maximum distance was 100 yd, therefore the 20-yd error represented a relatively smaller ratio error at that distance.

A possible explanation for these findings, being consistent with those of Cockerill (1969), may be found in Fisher's (1969) research. He calculated that when a standard stimulus is varied in distance, retinal projections are negligible at distances greater than 50 m from an observer. Following this principle, it is possible that retinal projection at distances even less than 50 m (approximately 55 yd), are equally so small as to make accurate distance judgment difficult also. Further consideration of the anatomical function of the eye suggests that the differences between groups occurring at 32 yd and beyond might be explained by accommodation and convergence; the former referring to the contraction of the ciliary muscles to change the convex property of the ocular lens. This facilitates focusing upon nearby objects. However, since there are only slight changes in the amount of accommodation beyond a few feet, such a mechanism is effective for short distances only. Convergence causes the extraocular muscles to converge the eyes and also assists in focusing an image of the stimulus object upon the retina. As pointed out by Sage (1977), this process is likewise only effective for judging the distance of objects up to 20 yd. From research undertaken to date it may be reasonably concluded that an unequivocal explanation has not so far been presented as to the exact nature of the mechanism for making precise judgments along the 'z' axis of visual space.

Practical Applications

Notwithstanding the above dilemma, a number of issues are raised from the results of the investigation described in this chapter and observations are made as to their implications for games players and coaches. Some doubt is thrown upon the extent to which a player is physiologically capable of making accurate judgments over the kind of distances appropriate to the ballistic hitting, kicking and throwing skills typical of most team sports. A golfer, for example, frequently requires augmented information to identify the precise distance to a target to supplement his perception of that distance. Since some sports demand that players perform without the availability of supplementary cues, a likely deduction is that the more skilful of them have either been endowed with, or have developed, the ability to judge target distances accurately. Gibson, Bergman & Purdy's (1955) conclusions that absolute distance judgment can be improved with practice provides empirical support for the suggestion that sportsmen might benefit from training with targets located at known distances. They might even learn to associate appropriate kinaesthetic information with the effort required to project an object a specific distance.

It is important to note, however, that there was a wide range of perceptual ability within the group of games players who took part in the present investigation. Mean ratio error scores for individual subjects over the twelve distances ranged from 0.92 to 4.57. Accordingly, these data cast some doubt upon the contention that being able to judge distance is a perceptual skill that contributes in large measures to playing success. Furthermore, Ridini (1968) has produced data that indicate no significant positive correlation between depth perception and specific sports skills. The highest correlation obtained related to a basketball dribble-and-shoot task and the lowest to a soccer volley.

In the light of these somewhat discouraging findings the frequently adopted practice of using apparatus that measures depth over distances unrelated to sport again comes into question. Perhaps the only advantage to be gained when, for example, the Howard–Dolman apparatus is used is that comparison between studies is possible. The procedures described here relied upon subjects' translation of perceived distance into yards and so raises doubts as to its reliability. It also highlights a conceptual problem common to many perceptual studies concerning the difficulty in obtaining an accurate measure of what is actually perceived by a subject. In order to overcome such a procedural difficulty the fractionation technique adopted by Gibson, Bergman & Purdy (1955) might prove more reliable. Similarly, the technique described by Cockerill (1969) overcame the problem associated with having to assume that individual variations in the translation of perceived distance into yards are randomly distributed within groups. The reliability of the method adopted in the present investigation could be established by a retest to learn whether such individual differences were random. The fact that the test successfully identified a range of distances over which games players judged significantly better than non-games players suggests that it may be considered a valid measure of the type of distance judgment required in team games; albeit in a static condition.

A further issue stemming from the present results relates to the problem of comparing the ages, sex and selected sport of the sample with those independent variables adopted by others. For example, Ridini (1966) used grade eight junior high-school groups while Shick (1971) tested a sample of female college students. The developmental study of Whiting & Cockerill (1972) reported that task performance based upon the perceptual judgment of target distance reflected an absence of fine control. Some perceptual discrimination *was* present, however, because an increase in effort to produce the required movement was commensurate with the further placing of the target. An extension of work in this field might usefully include subjects of similar ability from the same sport. This would provide a clearer understanding of the role of distance judgment in specific sports and also indicate whether this perceptual skill varies according to level of athletic attainment.

It is proposed that differences between groups in the experiment described here were not due to the intervention of confounding variables. The careful choice of site eliminated any of the classical cues of distance such as partial overlap, size and location of known objects, shading and texture. It is interesting to speculate that the results obtained may not have been due to differences in the ability of subjects to judge distance *per se,* but were a consequence of translating distance into yards owing to the games players familiarity with actual dimensions in team games.

The general conclusion that might be drawn from this investigation is that errors in perceptual judgments occur between groups of games players and non-games players, and also within them. It is proposed that further investigations are desirable and that problems associated with the need to make more or less precise judgments of distances are clearly evident. It is important that both players and coaches should be cognisant of the issues involved. The following chapter is an extension of the work described here and examines the probable relationship between distance perception and sports performance.

References

Cockerill, I. M. (1969) The development of perceptual and sensori-motor skills. Unpublished Master's Thesis, University of Newcastle upon Tyne.

Collins, J. K. (1976) "Distance perception as functions of age", *Australian Journal of Psychology*, 28: 109–13.

Dickson, J. F. (1953) The relationship of depth perception to goal shooting in basketball. Unpublished Doctoral Thesis, State University of Iowa: Dubuque.

Fisher, G. H. (1969) "Sizes of retinal images formed by distant objects", *Nature*, 221: 584–6.

Gibson, E. J., Bergman, R. & Purdy, J. (1955) "The effect of prior training with a scale of distance on absolute and relative judgments of distance over ground", *Journal of Experimental Psychology*, 50: 97–105.

Gogel, W. C. & Tietz, J. D. (1977) "Eye fixation and attention as modifiers of perceived distance", *Perceptual and Motor Skills*, 45: 343–62.

Olsen, E. A. (1956) "Relationship between psychological capacities and success in college athletics", *Research Quarterly*, 27: 79–89.

Ridini, L. M. (1968) "Relationship between psychological functions, tests and selected sports skills of boys in junior high school", *Research Quarterly*, 39: 674–83.

Sage, G. H. (1977) *Introduction to Motor Behavior: A Neuropsychological Approach*, 2nd edn., Massachusetts: Addison-Wesley.

Shick, J. (1971) "Relationship between depth perception and hand-eye dominance and free-throw shooting in college women", *Perceptual and Motor Skills*, 33: 539–42.

Tomlin, F. A. (1966) A study of the relationship between depth perception of moving objects and sports skill. Unpublished Master's Thesis, University of North Carolina: Bowling Green.

Whiting, H. T. A. & Cockerill, I. M. (1972) "The development of a simple ballistic skill with and without visual control", *Journal of Motor Behavior*, 4: 155–62.

11

Visual Information Processing in Golf and Association Football

Ian M. Cockerill and Brian P. Callington

The nature of the relationship between depth perception and sports performance has been of interest to sports psychologists for many years, but the precise implications of this variable for sports participants remain unclear. Banister & Blackburn (1931), Winograd (1942), Graybiel, Jokl & Trapp (1955), Olsen (1956), Miller (1960) and Ridini (1968) have provided substantial evidence in support of a relationship between the higher levels of achievement in sport and depth perception. Other researchers, notably Dickson (1953), Olsen (1956), Ridini (1968), Shick (1971) and Beals, Mayyasi, Templeton & Johnston (1971), failed to identify a positive correlation between such a feature of visual perception and sports performance. Accordingly, new measurement techniques and further research must be pursued before satisfactory and acceptable answers are found.

Anomalies exist when seeking to relate general findings with those of more specific studies and are clearly illustrated in an investigation by Ridini (1968). Using two groups of subjects, 91 athletes and 90 non-athletes drawn from the same junior high school male population, Ridini (1968) tested each on a motor skills test battery and also on the Howard–Dolman test of depth perception. Although the groups differed significantly on both measures, derived correlation coefficients were low.

The reasons for failure to obtain evidence of significant links between depth perception and sports performance at the specific level of analysis

126

could rest either with the particular sport skills selected, or with the tests employed to measure depth perception. Sports skills studied in isolation, either when examined in the context of a game or when extracted for inclusion in a test battery, may, in themselves, be unrepresentative of a performer's general ability, and in this respect fail to reflect fully the behavioural characteristics which comprise his total performance. With regard to tests of depth perception, it is questionable whether the standard tools for measurement are appropriate. Indeed, Miller (1960) was prompted to make the observation that "the most reliable indication of a person's depth perception in a certain situation is by tests in that situation or on a test in which the actual situation is most closely approximated".

The procedures used to measure depth perception in each of the studies already referred to were laboratory tests; either of the rod adjustment type – such as the Howard–Dolman test – or stereoscopic measures. In view of their nature, that is, being administered in a situation quite removed from sport, and being of a design which bears little relation to a sporting context, these tests do not appear to meet the criteria for reliability set by Miller (1960). It is, therefore, uncertain whether the elements of 'depth perception' vital to an accurate motor skill performance are the same as those being evaluated in such test situations. Clark & Warren (1955) used the Howard–Dolman apparatus when comparing a group of athletes with a group of unskilled subjects and were prompted to remark:

> Either depth perception as measured by the test is relatively unimportant in ball games of the nature of those included, or the test does not give an accurate measure of depth perception. In either event, the application of the results of this test to particular situations may be seriously questioned.

Dickson (1953) similarly queried the tests used for assessing depth perception, rather than the actual performance of this visual factor, in basketball shooting. Having used five different measures of depth perception, none of which produced results which correlated positively with performance levels in the particular skill chosen, Dickson (1953) drew the following conclusion:

> The findings in this study would appear to warrant the conclusion that the five tests of depth perception do not measure the factors of depth perception requisite to basketball shooting ability.

The standard laboratory tests of depth perception which have been used in sports research have focused primarily upon subjects being able to make discriminations of *relative* depth or distance. It can be readily seen that this visual measure must form an important part of the sports performer's perceptual behaviour, and also that ability along this particular dimension might be closely related to a general achievement level in sport. It is not so apparent, however, that the skill elements which comprise the total structure of a sport should rely to an equal extent upon this particular visual parameter, or that individual skills considered in isolation should have relative distance discrimination as the determining perceptual factor in their successful execution.

In many sports, the ability to project an object over an exact distance is of fundamental importance. Passing a ball in rugby, soccer, basketball or lacrosse, shooting for the ring in basketball, throwing a ball in cricket or baseball, aiming for the flag in golf, each require the precise projection of an object towards a known target. Relative proximity or distance of the target with respect to adjacent objects is of little consequence, with the *absolute* distance of the target from the player being the prime consideration. There appears to be some question as to the appropriateness of the dimension normally evaluated by standard tests of depth perception as it relates to some of the sports skills alluded to earlier. None of these investigations revealed a significant relationship between achievement levels in the skills studied and the various measures of depth perception employed. Pargman, Bender & Deshaies (1975) have offered an explanation for the inability of researchers to establish close links between sports skills and depth perception and have also provided an insight into an appropriate area for future work in this field:

> Research suggests that basketball shooting performance is meaningfully related to distance perception and dynamic visual activity, while relatively unrelated to measures of depth perception and visual imagery.

Whether or not *distance* is part of a composite psychological ability termed *depth* perception is incidental, but what is apparent from this quotation, and also the results of specific studies into basketball ability, is the fact that standard tests of perception do not appear to monitor skilful distance perception; if this is important in executing a skill efficiently. The possibility certainly exists that accurate *distance perception* may be that same visual factor which is crucial to successful performance in many sports.

Having categorised depth perception as that which is measured by standard depth perception tests evaluating the discrimination of relative distances, the distinction of depth from distance perception needs to be drawn. Gilinsky (1951) defined the former as: "phenomenal or apparent distance, comprising exclusively the direct product of stimulation (visual and muscular)".

He distinguished this process from one he referred to as 'estimated distance' which "includes an intellectual correlation of perceived distance derived from past experience and training, to arrive at a more informed inference or judgment of the true distance". In the following discussion, distance judgment, perceived distance, and estimated distance will be considered as one visual parameter relating to the quantitative appreciation of *absolute distance,* as opposed to the ability to qualitatively discriminate *between* distances.

The Investigation

An experiment by Cockerill (1969) identified a significant feature in the visual mechanism's ability to register absolute distance, wherein for shorter distances there is a tendency towards underestimation and for longer distances there is overestimation. The cross-over point in this phenomenon was shown to occur at a distance of about fifty yards. If the visual perceptual mechanism is prone to such error, and if this pattern is consistent for the majority of individuals, then the possibility exists that being able to determine absolute distance accurately may be influential in predicting success levels in sport in the same way that some researchers have attempted to link motor skill performance with measures of depth perception. Furthermore, the pattern of error evident in absolute distance judgment may afford insight into the reasons for particular performance errors such as over- and under-hitting a target and, as suggested earlier, it could be this visual dimension which is significant in the performance of many sports skills. It was upon the basis of this hypothesis that the present research was conducted to consider Cockerill's (1969) findings within a sport population and to discuss the implications of such an error pattern in absolute distance judgment for sports performance.

A preliminary study required seventeen university soccer players to estimate, in yards, eight distances over the surface of a soccer pitch. Two different locations were used in the experiment, with all subjects performing similar judgment tasks at both. The purpose of employing two locations was to determine the strength of any error pattern evident when judgments were made in situations familiar to a subject where potential cues were present. One site was a straight, unmarked path with no obvious cues to aid judgment and the other was a freshly marked soccer pitch familiar to all subjects. Judgments made by

subjects in the 'unfamiliar' location were followed seven days later by
the 'familiar' location test. Considering the group data (Figure 11.1),
there was a similar pattern of error in distance judgment as that noted
by Cockerill (1969). The one exception was that in the current study the
cross-over point for over- and under-estimation occurred at 30 yd rather
than 50 yd. This may well have been an artifact of the distance used in
this particular investigation, with the further distance being only 59 yd

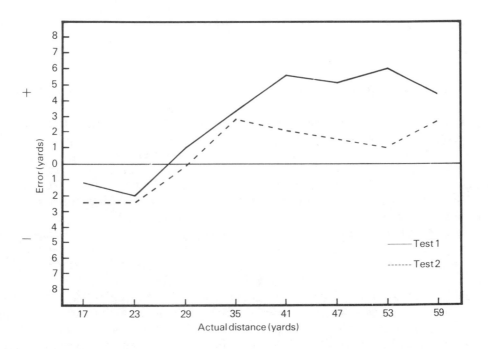

Figure 11.1   Error Distribution for Absolute Distance Judgment by Soccer Players

as opposed to the 130 yd used by Cockerill (1969). The error pattern was
also consistent for both locations and the subjects' familiarity with the
second test site and the presence of cues only benefited the judgment of
the longer distances.

   Once the error pattern in absolute distance judgments was established for the sports samples, it was then considered appropriate to
investigate the consequences of such perceptual errors in *performance*.
Based upon the reasons indicated earlier concerning the nature of visual
abilities considered important to skilful sport performance, a task

was selected which involved the accurate judgment of distance, namely the golf iron shot used in the approach to the flag. Cockerill (1969) demonstrated that the margin of error in such distance judgments is associated with the actual distance to be estimated. Since some golfers are capable of hitting a ball accurately to a target over relatively long distances, the particular task chosen provided an opportunity to relate sports performance to distance judgment. It also allowed an assessment of the impact of error for both variables, thereby providing evidence about the relationship between the two measures.

A total of 23 golfers, whose handicaps ranged from three to eleven, took part in the experiment. In an initial test subjects were required to judge the distance in yards to a flag placed randomly at thirteen different locations. The site for this test and for the performance test that followed was a large, flat, unmarked sports field with the same location being used for both. The data from the initial test of distance judgment again confirmed an error pattern in distance perception, with group mean scores conforming closely to Cockerill's (1969) results (Figure 11.2). The cross-over point for under- to over-estimation occurred at approximately 55 yd.

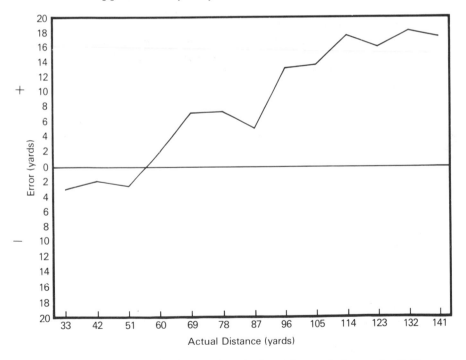

Figure 11.2   Error Distribution for Absolute Distance Judgment by Golfers

The performance test forming the second part of the investigation was designed to establish whether perceptual errors were associated with subsequently produced errors in performance. Seven distances were used, with the flag placed 33, 51, 69, 87, 105, 123 and 141 yd from the subject. Target distances were separately randomised for each subject. 12 subjects from the total sample of 23 were required to judge the distance to the flag in yards as they had done previously. After each judgment a subject was required to play seven shots, one at each distance, trying to hit the ball to drop at the base of the flag. The third to the seventh, inclusive, shots were measured according to the number of yards the ball fell short of or beyond the flag. Deviation of the ball to the left or the right was ignored, since the main concern of the investigation was the distance of the shot relative to the subject and the flag. Lateral error was accounted for by running a line to extend from the subject's hitting position to the point on the field where the ball landed. By pulling this line taut the outcome of any shot could be determined in similar terms, namely relating to actual flag distance. The first two shots in each block of seven were for practice purposes and were not measured. A folding, occluding screen was dropped in front of the subject after he struck each shot in order to eliminate visual feedback. He was not permitted to see the field until his shot was measured and the ball removed. Because subjects were deprived of visual feedback it was considered that each shot constituted an independent trial, and that it was possible to use the mean score of the five that were measured as a better representation of true performance at each of the seven test distances.

Group data from the performance test (Table 11.1) were computed to establish whether a pattern of error existed which was similar to that present in the pre-performance judgments. The distinctive error pattern revealed in the absolute distance judgment test data based upon the total sample was not revealed to the same degree by this sub-group. Although an apparent tendency for underestimation changing to overestimation occurred with increasing distance, the characteristics of this were somewhat different and an interesting finding was the high degree of judgment accuracy achieved by the group as a whole. Accuracy was

Table 11.1   Pre-performance Perceptual Error and Performance Error for
the Experimental Group

Distance (yards)	33	51	69	87	105	123	141
Judgment error	−4	−6.5	−6.9	−7	−0.8	+4.1	+10.7
Performance error	+2.54	+3.77	+1.47	+3.17	+2.83	+4.43	+10.01

compared with performance and individual subject data were examined more closely.

Distance judgment error and performance error scores for individual subjects were interesting in that they revealed that the golfers in the experimental group appeared to depend differently upon an estimation of flag distance during performance. The data for three subjects are presented in Table 11.2 to illustrate that absolute distance judgment may have been important for some of the golfers in terms of its effect upon their performance.

Table 11.2   Pre-performance Perceptual Error and Performance Error: three Experimental Group Subjects

Subject	Golf Handicap	Distance (yards)						
		33	51	69	87	105	123	141
T.S.	4							
Judgment error		− 5	− 9	− 24	− 32	− 40	− 43	− 36
Performance error		− 5	− 11.2	− 10.6	− 29.5	− 33	− 34.5	− 30.4
M.C.	7							
Judgment error		+ 7	− 1	+ 16	+ 23	+ 40	+ 42	+ 79
Performance error		+ 11.6	+ 22	+ 32.8	+ 42.8	+ 47	+ 31.5	+ 3.6
D.P.	10							
Judgment error		− 3	− 1	+ 11	+ 3	+ 20	+ 27	+ 29
Performance error		+ 10.8	+ 16.8	+ 24.2	+ 25.2	+ 27.6	+ 31.6	+ 45.2

The similarity between distance judgment error and subsequent performance error for the first subject (T.S.) is such that it is difficult to deny a causal relationship. With the other two subjects (M.C. and D.P.) there is a high degree of similarity in perception and performance patterns with some differences. Given the overall nature of the similarity between the error tendencies in each dimension, explanation for these differences was sought and it appears that the data for subjects M.C. and D.P. are evidence of a strong positive relationship, as do those of subject T.S. In the case of M.C.'s discrepancy at 141 yd, this subject judged all five measured trials to be 'short', which they were in terms of his estimation of the flag distance, although *in reality* they were not short. Subject D.P.'s discrepancies at the various distances are explained by referring to his absolute distance judgment test data where he recorded error scores of 2, 4 and 33 yd on the occasions when he overestimated. A change of mind following the initial estimation of the flag position – or during the performance trials – towards the direction of the earlier assessed distance values may have been responsible for the three large performance error scores.

Several subjects involved in the study explained their club selection during a game as estimating the distance to the flag in yards and knowing the approximate distance capability of each club. Other subjects did not conceptualise the requirements of a shot in this way and several stated that they 'viewed a shot' in terms of club number, judging the distance as an 'easy seven iron' or a 'full eight iron' shot. The relative merits of both strategies for playing golf shots became apparent from the data analysis. It proved to be of considerable significance to the overall purpose of the investigation and will be discussed later. It is appropriate to note, however, that before playing a shot some golfers estimate distance in yards, whereas others conceptualise the shot's requirements differently.

A further aspect of the investigation involved an enquiry into whether a knowledge of target distance beneficially influenced subsequent performance. Ten subjects from the initial sample were matched for performance accuracy and their ability to judge absolute distance with ten others from the group. This second, control group of golfers performed the same skill task as the experimental group, with the exception that they were informed of each flag distance before hitting their shots. All other aspects of the test for these subjects were identical to those previously described. A comparison of the overall accuracy for both groups of subjects revealed similar scores (Table 11.3).

Table 11.3   Performance Error for Experimental and Control Groups

	Distance (yards)							
	33	51	69	87	105	123	141	
Control group (N = 10)	4.70	6.27	9.46	10.43	10.94	12.73	8.90	Mean absolute error (yards)
	5.06	5.63	7.01	8.17	5.27	9.98	6.24	S.D.
Experimental group (N = 10)	5.46	5.88	9.24	11.27	10.58	16.37	18.48	Mean absolute error (yards)
	3.10	5.32	7.56	9.83	10.88	10.83	13.19	S.D.

Differences in accuracy and in consistency of performance for both groups of subjects only emerge at the two further distances. Thus, it may be concluded that a knowledge of the exact performance distance had no beneficial effect upon the execution of the task by subjects in the control group. However, having established that certain subjects in the experimental group showed no dependence upon prior assessment of yards to the flag while playing each shot, distance information provided for golfers in the control group would, presumably, have served no useful purpose. A significant difference between error scores for both groups could only have been expected if the control group had included the golfer who plays each shot according to his estimation of target distance in yards.

The main feature of the results linking absolute distance perception to skill in golf, and which argues for the importance of this particular visual factor in sport, was a highly significant positive correlation between the performance of the experimental group in the skill test and their ability to judge distance accurately. The 12 subjects in this group were ranked on their skill in judging absolute distance based upon a composite error score for their pre-performance judgment of each of the seven flag distances. They were also ranked on a composite error score for performance, the seven error values for the test being combined to determine an overall mean score. In both cases the algebraic signs representing positive and negative error were ignored in obtaining the composite values, since an indication of a *general* ability to estimate distance or hit to a flag was required; relating to an absolute rather than a constant error representation. The coefficient of correlation between these two sets of data was 0.82 ($p < 0.01$).

Practical Applications

It was suggested earlier in the chapter that a distinction needs to be drawn between depth perception and absolute distance perception. The nature of the positive relationship discovered between distance judgment and performance in the particular sports skill chosen for analysis appears to confirm this. While some studies into general levels of attainment in sport have shown a positive correlation between skill in sport and accurate depth perception, it may be concluded that the ability to discriminate relative distances has a more general significance; perhaps being present to some degree in most ball-type activities. However, performance in specific skills, such as golf, may depend greatly upon the facility for making accurate judgments of absolute distances. For those skills concerned with projecting a ball over an exact distance to a fixed target, standard tests of depth perception may be inappropriate. There is a need for greater specificity in the analysis of sports skills, particularly in ensuring that psychological capacities are carefully distinguished, as, for example, between depth perception and absolute distance perception, with valid and reliable tests to provide more objective measures. Moreover, the selection of skills is important in order that they, too, are appropriate to the particular variables under investigation.

The skill chosen for analysis evidently represented a unique element of play in golf, and this was borne out by a significant correlation between the performance of the experimental subjects in the skill test and their golf handicaps. A similar significant correlation was obtained between golf handicap and distance judgment for these subjects. The latter finding substantiated the earlier contention that the performance of a particular skill in isolation may not, in itself, provide a representative illustration of a performer's overall ability in a sport, or of the general visual-perceptual requirements of the sport. For researchers to look for links between depth perception and performance levels in highly *specific* skills as a means of substantiating relationships discovered at a *general* level of performance seems an exercise of doubtful value, particularly when the skills present within a single sport are so varied and the usefulness of particular psychological tests of visual perception questionable.

The identification of a positive relationship in the present investigation between performance level in one aspect of golf and absolute distance judgment is not only important for this sport, but for many others. The task used in the performance test closely approximated the requirements in playing approach shots to the putting green. Since it has been demonstrated that skill in judging distance may be closely associated with skill in playing golf iron shots, a distance judgment test such as the one used in the investigation could prove a useful aid to the golf coach for identifying the possible reason for a player's inaccuracy or inconsistency in approach play. In view of the probable relationship between absolute distance judgment and performance, and the obvious reliance upon distance estimation by some subjects in the experiment (Table 11.2), both golfer and coach are advised to consider the present findings. The degree of consistency between perceptual and performance errors presented in Table 11.2 suggests that regular training in distance estimation, and encouraging players to base approach shots upon a prior assessment of the actual target distance, could form a valuable part in golf coaching. Such a practice might result in reduced errors and be of general benefit to the development of this important aspect of a golfer's game.

The fact that performance test scores did not correlate with general golfing ability based upon handicap suggests that some of the better players in the sample needed to focus their attention upon medium iron play. In this respect both the performance test and the perceptual test used might prove beneficial in helping the better golfer to identify weaknesses in his game and also the reason for particular errors, such as consistently over- or under-hitting shots.

The category of skill focused upon here – the accurate projection of a ball to a target – is apparent in other ball-type sports and the implications of this golf study are relevant to them. Gibson & Smith (1952), Gibson & Bergman (1954) and Gibson, Bergman & Purdy (1955) demonstrated that absolute distance judgment can be trained. Accordingly, on the basis of the present discussion there is justification for investigations to be conducted into those sports where distance judgment is a major component, and within which accuracy is associated with successful performance.

References

Banister, H. & Blackburn, J. M. (1931) "An eye factor affecting proficiency at ball games", *British Journal of Psychology*, 21: 382–4.

Beals, R. P., Mayyasi, A. M., Templeton, A. E. & Johnston, W. L. (1971) "The relationship between basketball shooting performance and certain visual attributes", *American Journal of Optometry and Archives of American Academy of Optometry*, 48: 585–90.

Clark, B. & Warren, N. (1955) "Depth perception and interpupillary distance as factors in proficiency in ball games", *American Journal of Psychology*, 47: 485–7.

Cockerill, I. M. (1969) The development of perceptual and sensori-motor skills. Unpublished Master's Thesis, University of Newcastle upon Tyne.

Dickson, J. F. (1953). The relationship of depth perception to goal shooting in basketball. Unpublished Doctoral Thesis, State University of Iowa: Dubuque.

Gibson, E. J. & Bergman, R. (1954) "The effect of training on absolute estimation of distance over ground", *Journal of Experimental Psychology*, 48: 473–82.

Gibson, E. J., Bergman, R. & Purdy, J. (1955) "The effect of prior training with a scale of distance on absolute and relative judgements of distance over ground", *Journal of Experimental Psychology*, 50: 97–105.

Gibson, E. J. & Smith, J. (1952) "The effect of training on distance estimation on the judgement of size-at-a-distance", *Research Bulletin 52–59*, U.S.A.F. Human Resources Research Centre, Lackland Air Force Base, San Antonio: Texas.

Gilinsky, A. S. (1951) "Perceived size and distance in visual space", *Psychological Review*, 58: 460–82.

Graybiel, A., Jokl, E. & Trapp, C. (1955) "Russian studies of vision in relation to physical activity and sports", *Research Quarterly*, 26: 480–5.

Miller, D. M. (1960) The relationship between some visual-perceptual factors and the degree of success realized by sports performers. Doctoral Thesis, University of Southern California: Los Angeles.

Olsen, E. A. (1956) "Relationship between psychological capacities and success in college athletics", *Research Quarterly*, 27: 79–89.

Pargman, D., Bender, P. & Deshaies, P. (1975) "Correlation between visual disembedding and basketball shooting by male and female varsity college athletics", *Perceptual and Motor Skills*, 41: 956.

Ridini, L. M. (1968) "Relationships between psychological functions tests and selected skills of boys in junior high school", *Research Quarterly*, 39: 674–83.

Shick, J. (1971) "Relationship between depth perception and hand-eye dominance and free-throw shooting in college women", *Perceptual and Motor Skills, 33:* 539–42.

Winograd, S. (1942) "The relationship of timing and vision to baseball performance", *Research Quarterly,* 13: 481–93.

12

Visual Skills in Mountaineering

Robert H. Sharp

> I caught Dougal up at the bottom of the rock band and carried on up into the foot of the gully. I cleared the rope of ice as I jumped up, conscious of the struggle that Tut must have had, firstly traversing into the gully and then clambering over a giant snow-covered chock stone half way up. I noted the new perspective with interest, for the ropes led through a hugh gash – a veritable Devil's Kitchen of a chasm 300 feet deep into the rocks, whereas the rest of Everest had been wide slopes and broad open valleys. (Scott, 1976)

Mountaineering attracts people from many backgrounds and for a multitude of reasons and yet the visual world, with its infinite variety and detail, is a central source of stimulation and wonder for all. The interesting aspect is that while vision serves this very positive function, it is precisely this source of input which also provides the mountineer with some of his greatest challenges. Alongside other factors, such as the need to be physically fit and adequately clothed and the ability to recognise and deal with objective dangers and the determination to sustain confidence and motivation in the face of uncertainty, the mountaineer has to constantly make decisions, sometimes upon which his life may depend, about visual information. Visual skills are important not only for the Himalayan mountaineer, but also the low-level hillwalker and the rock climber. For many are common to all aspects of mountaineering; the only variable is the situation in which they are applied.

Perhaps the term 'skills' is not entirely appropriate, for by definition skilled behaviour is a learned activity (Whiting, 1975), yet many of the visual skills required by the mountaineer, although developed through experience, appear to be founded on either a basic physiological system (as in perceived depth and distance, see Chapters 10 and 11), or else upon an intangible 'sixth-sense' (as with some climbers who seem to have an 'eye' for spotting a new route). Accordingly, in this chapter the term 'skill' is used in its broadest sense. It should also be noted that the classification adopted below is in no way exhaustive – neither are the categories exclusive of one another – it has been chosen for clarity.

Route Judgment

Route-finding can be a problem in all kinds of mountaineering, ranging from the low-level ramble on a long-distance footpath, to rock climbing on a serious mountain buttress, to the Himalayan-type expedition extending over hundreds of miles. In all of these activities route-finding involves two phases, preparation before the walk or climb and judgments about the route while in progress.

The degree of preparation involved depends upon several factors, the two most important being the objectives of the walk or climb and prior experience on the same terrain, but consultation with relevant maps and guides is a central feature of all. More specifically, consider the example of an expedition to a locality in the British hills never before visited, and where the object is to camp at high level and climb several high peaks. The map must be carefully scanned to select a route which achieves these aims and which pays particular attention to the balance between the competing elements of challenge and safety. These factors demand empathy with the map which allows the reader to visualise the actual terrain to be negotiated from its two-dimensional representation.

Understanding contours and other methods of showing relief is important, but it is also vital for the reader to transform them internally into distinct, but related, topographical features; that is, to construct a valid, internal *visual image* of the terrain. The ability to synthesise detail from the map and extrapolate to the real world provides the evidence required to know, for example, how steep and narrow a ridge is and whether it will pose any scrambling or navigation difficulties, where the best 'escape' or alternative routes are should the weather turn bad and where suitable campsites are, taking into account water supply, shelter and prevailing winds. It is an ability which requires *absolute,* rather than relative, visual judgments in that it is insufficient to know that contours spaced nearer together indicate steeper slopes. It must be evident exactly how steep the terrain is as represented by the contours. This kind of knowledge emanates from an active visual comparison between topographical features as they appear in the terrain and their map representation, and by taking account of any errors in judgment. One difficulty in making absolute judgments is that the *transformation rules,* dictating the relationship between map and terrain developed through experience, need to be adjusted whenever a different scale map is used. Thus, the rules dictating the relationship between contour width and terrain gradient on a 1:50,000 scale map will be different from those on a 1:25,000 scale map.

Problems such as this are presently apparent with the Ordnance Survey changing from imperial to metric measures. The kinds of errors produced when transferring to larger scale maps are often pronounced; boulder fields are viewed as steep crags, minor streams are seen as rivers and gentle slopes can be interpreted as steep ridges. The situation is further compounded by the presence of other detail which can confuse the display. However, the overall advantages gained with the extra information far outweigh the limitations. For expeditions to remote regions of the world advance preparation is paramount, with route planning based upon personal experience as well as that of others, together with the analysis of aerial photographs and maps. Uncertainty in route prediction is increased by poorly detailed, and sometimes inaccurate, maps and also the distorted view presented by two-dimensional photographs. This was noted by Gillette (1979) in his account of an expedition to climb Mount McKinlay:

> Chance was not to be denied its part. Despite careful plotting with the aid of aerial photographs, the route down from Traleika Divide proved far steeper than we anticipated. At one point we were forced to rappel and had to abandon our only two ice screws, essential protective devices for ice climbing.

The situation is increasingly complicated by sudden changes in the topography caused by avalanches and rock falls, not only making advance route-planning more difficult, but even resulting in route changes over the same terrain from one day to the next. This kind of problem is evident in the Ice Fall section of the Khumbu Glacier on Mount Everest (Bonington, 1976).

Route judgment becomes a more serious activity when the walk or climb is in progress and when not only is detailed planning under investigation, but also the climber's ability to make difficult and often serious decisions as to the best line to take. A critical factor common to both walking and climbing is the need to relate the detail of the map to the terrain ahead (Cliff, 1978). This involves more than just visualising what the terrain will be like from reading the map contours; establishing a visual image. It also requires going a stage futher and recognising the surrounding terrain as visualised from the map. It is a two-stage process during which map detail is translated via the brain to detail on the ground. It is interesting to speculate where difficulties arise in this process because some individuals – especially novices – frequently have problems identifying features about them. It may be that their visual image of the features taken from the map is wrong and perhaps distorted in terms of distance estimation on gradient, or that they have difficulty in translating their image into objective features. One problem, of course, is that the image obtained from the map is based on a plan view, which does not correspond to the panoramic view obtained when situated in a valley or on a mountain top. The observer's task involves a visual prediction about where he estimates his position to be in relation to a much wider and more detailed world about him, known to be present but which is invisible. A technique sometimes used is to set the map by orientating it so that the map's features correspond in plan view to those of the terrain.

Assuming that a general line of travel has been chosen – perhaps the destination such as a mountain summit is visible – the walker is now faced with the ongoing task of making precise decisions about the route as he is walking. This involves always looking ahead, noting difficult, dangerous or time-wasting sections and planning how to effectively avoid them, for example by negotiating a succession of short crags by traversing along the dividing, grassy terraces, or avoiding a steep facing slope altogether by contouring to and ascending a side ridge. Decision-making involves a whole chain of actions where streams are crossed and re-crossed, gullies are climbed, crags are avoided and height is lost and gained repeatedly; all necessary in achieving a goal.

Central to making correct judgments such as these is the ability to *remember* the visual scene ahead and, in particular, the features which define the immediate route and are recognised as the route gradually unfolds. The reason for this lies in the fact that gross changes or *visual transformations* take place in the display as the walk continues. If the initial memory of the display is weak and the various transformations not accounted for, then the walker could very easily become disorientated, possibly lost. What may appear to be a two-dimensional picture from a distance, quickly changes into a dynamic, three-dimensional display where depth is exaggerated, colours become more distinct, steep slopes become shallower, crags take on huge proportions and other features may even disappear. The situation illustrates precisely the kinds of transformations which Gibson (1966) refers to in his theory of space perception, namely perspective transformations, kinetic occlusion and motion perspective. The problem is not so much being aware of these changes, but of taking account of them, and examples are shown in Figures 12.1 and 12.2.

A popular climb on the mountain (Figure 12.1) follows a minor ridge up the centre and has a distinctive curve throughout its length. The

Figure 12.1   View of Buachaille Etive Mor, Glencoe, Scotland from the roadside
(Broken line indicates the climb.)

Figure 12.2   View in the same direction as Figure 12.1, but taken from just below the
rock slab marked 'R'

walk from the road follows a well-worn path up to a large rock slab
inclined at about 45° and some 15 m wide, then proceeds to the right
below a steep buttress and finally up and across to the left to a triangular
snow patch at the foot of the climb. The entire approach route and the
climb itself, as well as the mountain summit, are clearly visible from the
road and to the uninitiated present no apparent difficulties. However,
having walked about 200 m from the road the picture begins to change.
Not only does the mountain dramatically appear much closer, but it
also begins to fall away and look less steep. By the time the rock slab is
approached both the summit and climb have disappeared and the
immediate view contains a threatening collection of major crags and
impenetrable gullies (Figure 12.2). For the climber who has not gauged
his distances accurately or remembered which buttress is which, the
route ahead presents an inordinate number of difficult, and possibly
serious, challenges. The problem is solved by accurately forecasting and
remembering the intended route and then *updating* this forecast by
taking note of changing shapes, relative distances and disappearing
features so that an accurate visual image of the route is always available.
   Similar problems also exist for the rock climber, although for him
distances are normally much shorter, but the consequences of taking a
bad line or wandering off route can be more serious. In the case of a

route being climbed for the first time anticipation is minimal and often the climber can only look to the immediate section above him to gauge whether 'it will go' or not. As already mentioned, some climbers are claimed to have a natural 'eye' for spotting a new route and certainly there are several well-known individuals who have put up many new routes, occasionally on crags and mountain buttresses previously thought to be exhausted. Such advances are doubtless due to new techniques and attitudes, but possibly also to the vision of certain personalities who can detect a line involving a sequence of cracks, slabs, chimneys or rock faces never previously noticed.

For those climbers who repeat the routes of others – the major pastime for most – the challenge of finding and staying on the route is reduced with the aid of guide-books, which not only give general details about a specific climbing area, but also detailed information about length of climb and individual pitches, where the difficulties lie and the standard of difficulty of the climb. Photographs or illustrations often accompany the route description, giving a visual guide to the line to be taken. The following is an example of a route on the mountain seen in Figure 12.1 (MacInnes, 1971):

Agag's Groove (350 feet, Grade IV)
Climb up corner of wall beside a rectangular block (just left of Grooved Arête). Up 90 ft to belay at start of groove. Short corner a little below block belay is crux. Follow groove 110 ft to belay. Follow groove to easy left traverse on open face beneath vertical nose. Up nose and left up to sloping top of block; 80 ft traverse left and 75 ft up face to ridge.

Once on the climb visual memory is recalled, together with the accompanying problem of interpreting the rock and its features which extend above and below the climber in relation to the internal visual image. As in walking, translation is made difficult by the absence of features obscured from view and changing perspectives as the climber moves. Distance judgment is a useful guide here, for if the climber knows that a particular pitch is, say, 80 ft and he can estimate this – by noting how much rope he has used, the time he has been climbing, or the approximate number of steps he has moved – then he has a concrete guide to use in locating himself from his visual memory of the route. Other details enhance the climber's knowledge of where he is; pitches angled in a particular way, cracks and chimneys clearly defined or difficult sections reported in the guide-book may be obvious when encountered. Detecting smooth and polished holds is also a useful clue, assuming that not too many routes intersect.

Navigation Skills

The most important technical aid in mountain navigation is the map
(Cliff, 1978) and, indeed, it is the only one required when the weather is
clear. If the map is used skilfully, then only in bad weather conditions is
there need to resort to other devices such as the compass, estimating
time, or pace judgment. Contrary to popular belief there is no need to
learn parrot-fashion all the conventional symbols shown in the legend.
It is sufficient to know something about the grid system and the difference between parish boundaries and footpaths, plus appreciation of the
scale of a map and methods for showing relief. Understanding a map's
scale does not present many difficulties and most people use a simple
rule of thumb such as $\frac{1}{4}$ in $= \frac{1}{4}$ mile or 1 mm $= 50$ m to estimate the
distance between two points from the map. This can be done 'by eye',
using a ruler, or by comparing the distance against the one kilometre
spaces between grid lines. The real difficulty lies in the confusion which
may arise when changing from one map to another with a different scale
and this is particularly so at present with three scales in common use,
the one inch to a mile and the two metric 1:50,000 and 1:25,000 scales.
An additional problem with metric scales is the presence of both First
and Second Series editions which have height represented in feet and
metres, respectively, but distance in metres for both.

Probably the most confusing aspect of larger scale maps is the extra
detail presented, not only in terms of number of features but also with
regard to contours and their precision. So much information can distort
an individual's perception of the terrain in such a way that distances
and features are exaggerated. The outcome is that time is overestimated
and route-finding takes on an unnecessarily cautious emphasis to avoid
apparent difficulties. However, both maps have their advantages and
limitations, for example the 1:50,000 scale allows the reader to visualise
the topography in a given area almost immediately; especially
important if time to consult the maps is limited and the walker is experi-
encing physical stress. The 1:25,000 map does not display the features
so quickly, but reveals them more accurately and in sharper contrast;
characteristics which the walker navigating in poor visibility would find
invaluable.

It has already been suggested that interpreting the map – that is,
constructing a visual image of the terrain from it – is a central skill in
navigation and gives the walker a *first approximation* of his position.
Not only are contours essential here, but also other signs such as crags
and their orientation, the manner in which streams flow into one
another, vegetation changes, the presence of scree, slopes and lakes,
footpaths and tracks and also place names for features such as mountain

summits, cols, glens and ridges. For the skilled navigator this is almost an immediate process where accurate judgments are made about the gradient of slopes, the difference between valleys and spurs and the distance between adjacent features. He might even have such a well-developed 'map memory' that from an initial survey of the map before the walk begins he can locate his position correctly without referring to the map again in any great detail.

For the less experienced navigator, or any walker wishing to confirm his location, the technique of 'setting' the map can be used. The map is rotated until its features correspond with those on the terrain. This can be achieved 'by eye' or by aligning grid lines with the compass needle. By taking an imaginary line from the present position through a specific feature on the map it is possible to continue one's gaze along this line and up to the skyline to note the actual feature. Such a procedure not only confirms or refutes present position, but is also an aid to identifying additional nearby features.

Perhaps the compass tests visual abilities more than anything. Para-doxically, despite the importance of its use, and especially in bad weather, it can be the cause of simple, yet quite serious, navigation errors when used incorrectly. The compass is invaluable when mist, cloud or heavy rain reduce visibility to such an extent that wayfinding by eye alone is impossible. In these situations the compass is used in conjunction with the map to estimate the bearing between two points, which can then be referred to the compass and used as a visual direction indicator when walking. The initial task of taking a bearing from the map simply involves aligning the side of the compass against the two points and rotating the compass housing until its grid lines are parallel with the map grid lines. Unless the map is dirty, or the grid lines feint, this is a straightforward comparison task, although height difference between the two sets of grid lines may cause parallax problems. The major problem arising is that the grid lines are aligned in opposite direc-tions and the walker finds himself travelling exactly 180° contrary to the intended direction. This kind of error can be avoided with care and by observing that grid lines are in correct alignment if North on the compass needle always points North on the map.

The second part of the task is to use the compass bearing as a guide for walking. This involves following an imaginary line extending from the compass centre through the direction-of-travel arrow and then on to the terrain into the mist or cloud ahead. It imposes a severe test of an individual's predictive skill, considering that he has to visually estimate the continuation of a line of up to, say 200–200 m from one only a few inches long on the compass. It is hardly surprising, therefore, that the task of following a bearing is affected by a variety of outside influences, all of which act to throw the walker off his intended direction of travel and force him to concentrate not only on the bearing to be followed, but also competing influences such as the wind, slope of the terrain, objects appearing through the mist and other walkers. A constant wind, for example, can displace the walker to one side of his bearing without him being aware of the change. An added complication is that if he is aware of the problem, overcompensation may occur; also applicable if the walker is 'contouring', where it is easy to lose or gain height. It is also easy to be drawn off the bearing if someone walking slightly ahead is off course, and a strong source of error may be a crag or boulder appearing through the cloud and acting as a source of attraction.

Walkers may unwittingly find themselves being 'dragged' toward objects when the terrain is otherwise featureless, almost as if they were seeking security from the only object within their vision. It would be interesting to determine whether those who are more prone to this kind of influence are the individuals that Witkin classifies as 'field-dependent' (see Peck & Whitlow, 1975). A comment by Boardman (1978) is also appropriate, because he emphasises the need in mountaineering, particularly when the situation becomes serious, to 'switch-off' from distracting stimuli and emotions and to concentrate fully on the problem and the techniques required in its solution:

> My strength was draining away, my arms felt like butter, my fingers were opening. Somehow I managed to tap last reserves of strength and heaved myself over, teetering dizzily, onto a tiny ledge . . . I was not going to die . . . But that was a rare moment of reflection. When you are going up a mountain, you cannot really have great thoughts. You have got to concentrate all the time on the job in hand. Until I reached the summit, I was involved only in surviving.

Returning to the task of walking on a bearing, one technique used to assist accuracy is to locate a near object on the imaginary line and use it as an objective reference point. Such a procedure works well if individual stages are kept short and suitable objects can be found, but it is limited when terrain undulates and selected objects keep disappearing or when 'white-out' conditions prevail. The latter occur when it is impossible to discriminate between snow and the cloud above; there is no skyline and all ground features are snow-covered. For some it is a disorientating and disturbing experience. With no visual reference the walker's sense of direction is tested to its limit and if it is known that there are steep crags in the vicinity then strict safety precautions need to be enforced, roping together or tossing snowballs in front to see whether or not they land in snow. A useful technique is to appoint someone to walk on the prescribed bearing while a second person remains stationary and observes whether or not the walker remains true. Through verbal communication the second man directs the walker and just before the latter disappears, informs him to stop then catches him up. While such 'leap-frogging' techniques provide an objective visual reference point and increase navigation accuracy, they are time-consuming and involve the additional problem of finding a volunteer to walk into the unknown.

The compass can also give a second, and more precise, approximation through a reversing of the procedure required when taking a bearing from the map. The observer is required to imagine a line between himself and a known feature and then to align the compass so that its side is parallel with the line. The procedure is repeated and the two bearings are transferred to the maps, providing intersection lines to indicate the walker's position.

Climbing Skills

The detection and recognition of important cues is a central feature of all 'open' skills, and even if mountaineering is not considered 'open' in the strict sense that it would be applied to fast ball games (Whiting, 1975), it is quite obvious that safe and enjoyable movement in a mountain environment demands precise and unequivocal judgments about the terrain and its ever-changing features. Accurate judgments involve a precise understanding of the medium one is working with and being able to make fine discriminations about the weather, rock and snow forms. Chouinard (1978) made the following point in relation to winter climbing:

> One of the joys of climbing comes from a growing intimacy with the medium. Learning rock climbing has been described as a process of becoming increasingly sensitive to the forms of the rock. Technique follows awareness, and climbing on snow and ice takes more awareness because it is so much more complex and variable than rock.

Success in rock climbing is achieved through understanding the nature of the rock, the accompanying types of climb and hand- and foot-holds to be expected. Granite, because of its round and weathered texture, tends not to offer small holds and hence climbing demands effort involving friction, pressure and jamming methods. Schist on the other hand, because of its rippled and crystalline structure, offers plenty of scope for pinch grips and incut holds which result in more balanced climbing. Given that the climber is aware of this he can visually – and also kinaesthetically, because he may not be in a position to see all likely holds – *anticipate* the nature and possible locations of holds.

A difficulty frequently encountered is a detection problem caused by the sun shining on rock. A section can look blank and featureless, especially if the sun is shining on it directly. Late in the day, however, when the sun is at a low angle, textures in the rock become differentiated and shadows reveal a variety of ledges, cracks, holes and irregularities useful as holds. Looking at a section from a different viewpoint can also be revealing in this respect and a good example occurs when a climber looks down and notices the holds and 'jughandles' (a good hold around which the entire hand can grip) that would have made his movements so much easier and more efficient had he noticed them. Sometimes the climber can benefit by elevating himself to look around for possible holds before stepping down again. The novice often has difficulty appreciating this fundamental technique of spending time looking for holds and mentally rehearsing moves before they are executed. Blackshaw (1968) referred to ". . . planning ahead, so that you can anticipate the difficulties and work out the best way of solving them", and "when you reach each resting place calculate exactly how to do the next bit". Kemp (1975) succinctly expressed a similar point in the instruction, "you climb the rock first with eye and brain, then with muscle and movement".

Similar considerations apply when searching for suitable locations for running belays (metal safety devices jammed in cracks and through which a rope is threaded as the climber ascends). It is important that the climber should gauge whether the placement of a 'runner' will cause undue friction on the rope as it is pulled through, or will allow it to run freely in a more or less direct line. He needs to anticipate how the rope will lie with a particular sequence of runners so that drag is reduced to a minimum. Furthermore, he needs to anticipate whether or not runners will pull free if he falls and the rope comes under tension. Accordingly, the placing of running belays demands a precise visual analysis to account for strength, rope-drag and stability under tension.

Safe climbing in winter also involves finely tuned anticipation of the possibility of avalanches or cornice breakage and, as Chouinard (1968) pointed out, a knowledge of ice and snow types and textures. Snow is infinite in its variety and the Canadian Eskimos have up to a dozen words that describe newly fallen snow according to how it affects the running of their sleds. While the climber does not need to be so discriminating, he needs to have a respect for snow, especially in relation to avalanche formation. The best clues in avalanche prediction come from the snow's history, type of terrain and time of day, but also from a close visual inspection. By digging a snow pit, successive layers can be properly analysed and even a magnifying glass used to detect whether ice crystals are locked or frozen together. Finger pressure will help to determine whether adjacent layers differ in their resistance and recognising layers of 'graupel' (hail) are sure signs of instability in the snow pack.

The analysis of snow and ice by firmness and colour, respectively, is also important in ascertaining correct belay methods. Ice must be the correct hardness and colour before an ice screw becomes a good anchor point. Similarly, 'deadmen' (aluminium plates) placed in the snow will only hold if the snow is firm enough. The angle of insertion for both items of equipment is also critical (March, 1973), demanding accurate angular judgment in relation to the ice or snow surface. It is tentatively suggested that the field-dependent person may be prone to making errors, as his perception could be distorted by inaccuracies in judgment of spatial dimensions in both horizontal and vertical orientations.

Observation Skills

Informed and accurate observation is important in a variety of moun-taineering situations, not the least of which is weather prediction. Although general weather forecasts are highly reliable (Scott, 1979), in mountainous terrain local topography can create unpredictable weather patterns thereby creating difficulties for the unprepared climber or walker. Watching for changes in wind direction, for example, is important in detecting the advance of fronts, and recog-nising specific changes in cloud formation is essential in predicting the timing of depressions which bring heavy rain and poor visibility. Most experienced walkers do this automatically, but the novice has difficulty in making absolute judgments about changes in wind speed, cloud formation and altitude. Through comparing his observations with the weather forecast, and in particular the associated synoptic chart, he learns to recognise weather patterns which help to develop a 'set' for possible problems.

Learning to recognise the weather is only one of the novice's problems. The would-be climber has to learn rope-handling skills, demanding keen visual awareness of different knots and how they look, together with an understanding of the methods used for tying oneself to the rope, rock and of belaying. The climber constantly uses his eyes and while much of his rope handling utilises kinaesthetic information –

where touch and feel are important – he is always sensitive to simple errors which could prove fatal.

Finally, it is important to emphasise the relevance of observation in assessing the wellbeing of fellow walkers, particularly from the point of view of being party leader. As well as being technically articulate the leader must be sensitive to how people feel and how they are coping with the elements. It is important, for example, that the leader is able to perceive danger signs of exposure and be able to differentiate between those acts of behaviour from a party member which are normal and those more subtle responses which indicate that exposure is taking over. Observation of first aid is important in assessing the nature and severity of some injuries. Perhaps the most fundamental skill is the power to see situations through the eyes of others in the party so as to appreciate their difficulties and feelings. Yet for all those skills discussed in this chapter, visual information alone is insufficient for accurate decision-making in mountaineering. Correct judgment is based upon a combination of sights, sounds, feelings, technical knowledge and, above all, experience.

References

Blackshaw, A. (1968) *Mountaineering*, London: Kaye & Ward.

Boardman, P. (1978) "A westerner's luxury", *The Listener*, March, 266–7.

Bonington, C. (1976) *Everest the Hard Way*, London: Hodder & Stoughton.

Chouinard, Y. (1978) *Climbing Ice*, London: Hodder & Stoughton.

Cliff, P. (1978) *Mountain Navigation*, Edinburgh: Cliff.

Gibson, J. J. (1966) *The Senses Considered as Perceptual Systems*, Boston: Houghton Mifflin.

Gillette, N. (1979) "A trek around Mount McKinlay", *National Geographic Magazine*, 156: 66–79.

Kemp, D. (1975) *Rock Climbing*, Wakefield: Educational Productions.

MacInnes, H. (1971) *Scottish Climbs:* Vol 1, London: Constable.

March, B. (1973) *Modern Snow and Ice Techniques*, Manchester: Cicerone Press.

Peck, D. & Whitlow, D. (1975) *Approaches to Personality Theory*, London: Methuen.

Scott, J. (1979) BBC TV weather forecast, August.

Whiting, H. T. A. (1975) *Concepts in Skill Learning*, London: Lepus.

13

Providing the Visual – Motor Match for Young Players

G. S. Don Morris

Within the sporting world one is constantly required to rely upon visual cues in order to perform particular movement skills successfully. It goes without saying, perhaps, that performance is significantly affected by the ability to process visual information. If a batsman can't *see* the object approaching then the likelihood of striking it successfully is drastically reduced. Objects must be clearly *visible* to performers and it is important for coaches and teachers to understand the relationship that exists between a player's ability to process visual information and the resulting action. This relationship is greatly enhanced if the coach or teacher can design instructional movement tasks that *match* each player's developmental visual processing status. This chapter will introduce the notion that movement tasks can be matched according to each player's ability to process visual information. Procedures that enable coaches and teachers to accommodate individual differences during instructional time, that is practice sessions, will also be discussed.

Seeing – What Is It?

Recognising that other authors in this book have already addressed themselves to this question, it is stated briefly here that in the present context seeing is attaching meaning to visual stimuli, thereby affording

the ability to 'act upon' those stimuli. Implicit within this definition is
the suggestion that seeing is *learned*.

One well-known procedure used to describe the visual process is to
identify it via an information-processing model. Marteniuk's (1976)
model (Figure 13.1) clearly establishes the relationship that exists
between visual stimuli and resultant motor response.

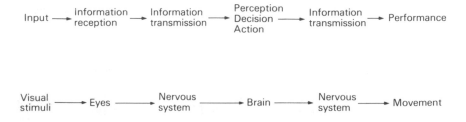

Fig. 13.1*   Visual Information Processing Paradigm
*Adaptation of Human Performance Model from R. G. Marteniuk, *Information Processing in
Motor Skills,* New York: Holt, Rinehart & Winston, 1976

The model suggests that a player must (a) receive information from
the external environment then (b) process and act upon the information
before (c) movement occurs. This model, however, only suggests how a
performer might process visual information and by no means represents
a complete picture of human performance.

It becomes apparent that 'acting upon' visual information involves
the efficient use and co-ordination of the eyes as well as effectively
processing visual stimuli in the brain, followed by appropriate decisions
effecting the activation of correct muscle groups. The result of this
entire process is movement and the present chapter focuses upon the
effects that external visual stimuli (input) have upon the visual
perceptual process and, thus, its effect upon a player's movement.

Accordingly, it is a necessary prerequisite to understand the operational schemata upon which the remainder of this chapter is
predicated. Attending primarily to the effects that external visual stimuli
have upon movement performance should help coaches develop tasks for
use with players during practice, and should facilitate performance and
learning by adjusting visual stimuli to specific movement skills.

The Effect of External Stimuli
upon Motor Performance

Focusing attention upon those factors that influence the reception of input data makes it possible to identify several environmental factors that can influence the visibility of objects travelling within a player's visual space field. For example, the colour of a ball may be considered an environmental factor that can make the ball more or less visible to performers (see Chapter 14).

Also, by focusing attention only upon the visual environmental factors that coaches can control, several operational procedures may be demonstrated that improve the visibility of three-dimensional objects. It is recognised that other external factors exist which also influence object perception, but only those that have been researched and/or properly field tested will be reported. The following items represent some of the issues to be discussed: object colour, background colour, speed of object movement, object trajectory angle, object size and object directionality relative to the performer.

By manipulating these variables a coach can vary the quantity and/or quality of the visual stimuli presented to a player, thereby influencing performance. For example, in Morris's (1976) study the manipulation of ball and background colour affected the catching performance of children aged 8, 10 and 12 years. They were able to catch blue and yellow balls significantly better than they caught white balls. Moran (1976) investigated the effects ball and background colour had upon striking skills of children 8 to 12 years of age and found similar results. Children could strike blue and yellow balls more successfully than white balls. There was further evidence to indicate that background colour and its interaction with ball colour reveals a trend in catching and striking results, but that using a solid colour background produces the best catching and striking scores. If a high colour contrast between ball and background is used, catching and striking improves and by avoiding complex visual backgrounds a coach can assist novice players with the acquisition of such skills.

It is important to understand also that both type and amount of illumination affects a player's colour perception as well as affecting the general visibility of a ball. As dusk approaches the amount of light available greatly diminishes, thus affecting the visibility of a ball, although it is interesting to note that many youth programmes seem to hold practices that coincide with this period. Table 13.1 identifies other factors that may influence the input data a player receives from the external environment and represents research conducted on the effect of input data upon the information-processing system and the resulting performance of players. While many of the findings are common sense, an interesting point is that it is possible for a coach to manipulate each factor with the outcome of making movement tasks more or less difficult. The research may assist the coach by enabling him to help a

Table 13.1   Some Factors Affecting Ball-Skill Performance

Factor	Effect	Reference
1 Object Size	Up to the point of diminishing returns the larger the ball the better the catching, kicking and striking scores	Ridenour (1974)
2 Object Trajectory Angle	Children up to age 6 can only visually track a horizontally moving ball effectively. From age 6 to 8 they can track a vertically moving object, by age 8 they can track a ball moving in an arc, and by age 9½ to 10 they can move to a point of interception and catch a ball moving in an arc	Williams (1968)
3 Direction of Object Flight	Young players can most easily catch a ball thrown directly toward the body's midline, followed next by catching a ball thrown to the preferred hand	Williams (1968)
4 Object Speed	A broad generalisation would be that slower moving objects are easier to track and manage perceptually than faster moving objects	Ridenour (1974)

youngster improve a particular skill, by increasing task difficulty, for example, or by providing practice tasks that match the player's level of development.

Task Complexity Spectrum

Based upon the information about external stimuli (input data), it is easy to demonstrate how a teacher or coach might sequence a series of movement tasks rendering them more or less difficult. To do this one simply establishes a task complexity spectrum (TCS) for a movement. For example, a TCS for catching might appear as in Table 13.2.

Table 13.2   Task Complexity Spectrum for Catching (i)

Degree of Difficulty	Visuo-spatial factors		
	Ball size	Ball colour	Angle of trajectory
Simple (easy)	Large	Blue	Horizontal
Moderate	Medium	Yellow	Vertical
Complex (difficult)	Small	White	Arc

This spectrum indicates that it is easiest to catch a large blue ball thrown on a horizontal trajectory. At the complex end of the spectrum it is most difficult to catch a small white ball thrown through an arc.

The concept of developing a task complexity spectrum represents a procedure that enables teachers and coaches to design properly sequenced movement tasks for their players. It may now be possible to design movement tasks utilising information from the TCS. Coaches could present tasks to accommodate each player's current movement status by taking him only as far along a continuum as his skill level permits, while at the same time stimulating each player to try the next more difficult task on the continuum. Accordingly, practice sessions can be structured to profit every player.

The following stages need to be followed to adopt the TCS procedure:

1. identify the movement task for analysis, for example catching, striking, kicking;
2. identify the environmental factors that affect the performance of the movement task;
3. establish a task complexity spectrum for each factor;
4. develop a series of tasks for each identified factor that can be presented to players during practice;
5. present the tasks during practice.

The following spectra (Tables 13.3 and 13.4) are presented to assist teachers and coaches with the task compexity procedure and with additions made to each spectrum as new research findings become available.

Table 13.3   Task Complexity Spectrum for Catching (ii)

Degree of difficulty	Visuo-spatial factors				
	Ball colour	Background colour	Ball speed	Ball size	Angle of trajectory
Simple (easy)	Blue	Dark	Slow	Large	Horizontal
	Yellow	Light	Medium	Medium	Vertical
Complex (difficult)	Red, White	Multi-coloured	Fast	Small	Arc

Table 13.4   Task Complexity Spectrum for Striking

Degree difficulty	Factors			
	Ball colour	Background colour	Ball speed	Ball size
Simple	Yellow	Dark	Stationary Slow	Large
	Blue	Light	Medium	Medium
Complex	White	Multi-coloured	Fast	Small

Example A: Sequenced Catching Tasks

Factor 1 used for task design: Ball Colour

Tasks

Simple (i) Throw a blue ball to a player ten times; expect him to catch it on eight out of ten attempts.

(ii) Throw a yellow ball to a player ten times; expect him to catch it on eight out of ten attempts.

Complex (iii) Throw a white ball to a player ten times; expect him to catch it on eight out of ten attempts.

Factor 2 used for task design: Ball Size

Tasks

Simple (i) Throw a softball (large) to a player ten times; expect the player to catch it on eight out of ten attempts.

(ii) Throw a baseball (medium) to a player ten times; expect the player to catch it on eight out of ten attempts.

Complex (iii) Throw a tennis ball (small) to a player ten times; expect the player to catch it on eight out of ten attempts.

It is, of course, possible that a coach will combine two or more factors in order to develop a movement task appropriate to a player's skill.

Example B: Sequenced Catching Tasks

Factors used for task design: Ball Speed, Ball Size, Angle of Trajectory.

Tasks

Simple (i) Throw a large ball slowly on a horizontal trajectory; expect a player to catch it eight out of ten attempts.

       (ii) Throw a large ball vertically at medium speed; expect a player to catch it eight out of ten attempts.

May require (iii) Throw a large ball in an arc at a fast speed; expect a
intermediate   player to catch it eight out of ten attempts.
stage

       (iv) Throw a medium size ball vertically at medium speed; expect a player to catch it eight out of ten attempts.

       (v) Throw a medium size ball in an arc at a fast speed; expect a player to catch it eight out of ten attempts.

       (vi) Throw a small ball in an arc at medium speed; expect a player to catch it eight out of ten attempts.

These activities are representative of catching tasks that might accommodate most eight- to nine-year-old children. By no means do they account for every individual difference that exists among young players. Rather, a system of task design has been proposed and it is up to coaches to fit the system to their own players' needs. A coach may be required to design intermediate tasks in order to allow a player to move to the next, more difficult, level.

Visual – Motor Match

If a coach wants his players to improve it is imperative that he matches the task to a player's skilfulness in processing certain external visual stimuli. How does a coach recognise each player's skill level? There are basically two ways of determining this. First, a coach can read the available literature that will suggest performance expectancy levels young players might demonstrate when processing certain visual stimuli. For example, children aged six can visually track a horizontally moving ball; between six and eight they can also track a vertically moving ball; between eight and nine years they can track a ball moving in an arc (Morris, 1980a). Second, and perhaps more appropriate, a coach can assess the player's developmental status. The procedure to accomplish this is reasonably simple and is in two parts. Initially the factors that seem to be influencing or limiting the motor performance most are identified (Morris, 1980b) and a series of tasks using the preceding information is then developed. Assuming the coach has determined that the limiting factors affecting a player's striking performance are ball speed and ball size, the series of tasks might appear as follows:

1. Strike a large ball that is stationary.
2. Strike a large ball that is moving slowly.
3. Strike a large ball that is moving at medium speed.
4. Strike a medium size ball that is stationary.
5. Strike a medium size ball that is moving slowly.
6. Strike a medium size ball that is moving at medium speed.
7. Strike a small ball that is stationary.

By asking a player to perform several of these tasks a coach discovers his pupil's developmental status when the latter is unable to successfully perform two consecutive tasks. For example, a player performs 1–4 successfully but not 5 or 6; thus task 4 represents his performance level. Once a coach has established the players status he can develop intermediate tasks to enable the player to move to the next, more difficult, level. Thus, the visual–motor match has been made.

This precedure may appear difficult and time consuming, but need not be either. Once a coach understands the principles behind the development of task complexity spectra and possesses developmental data, it becomes relatively simple to design appropriate visual–motor matches. Effective coaches already design intermediate tasks that assist their players in moving to the next level of performance. A player need not formalise this procedure by attempting to use all the information presented here. However, during initial learning it is strongly recommended that a coach formalises his procedures in order to structure his thinking and the operations he intends to adopt.

Practical Applications

An examination of baseball practices will demonstrate how it is possible to effect performance change in children using the methods already described.

Baseball

Utilising skills learned in this chapter a coach may have found that a child of eight years of age has difficulty catching a fly ball while moving in any direction. The coach may have also discovered that the child has difficulty tracking a ball moving in an arc towards him. The coach moves the child to second base where he develops into an adequate infielder. By the end of the child's ninth or tenth year he may be ready to return to the outfield. A simple change in position may have ensured the child's continued participation in the game. All too often youngsters become discouraged with a movement activity before they are developmentally prepared for the tasks.

By examining the performance of the eight-year-old in the light of developmental data the coach might be able to match the child's skill level with a fielding position that requires him to process a ball that will normally travel on a horizontal flight path. The match is appropriate for the player; the child will experience success and will probably be willing to attempt more difficult tasks at some other time.

An important feature of coaching is repeating successes and eliminating failures. In order that young players can improve, practice time in any sport needs to be well organised and it must focus attention upon learning additional movement skills. To that end, the notion of *training centres* is put forward for consideration. The centres need not be used during the entire practice, but rather during the time that is usually devoted to individual skill development when a group of players may be evenly divided among the number of available training centres. Assume that a coach has 24 players and decides upon six centres. By having four players working at each station all players will have a greater amount of on-task practice time. Using a rotation system that enables each group to visit four or more stations in a 30-minute period, players will have valuable opportunities for individual learning. The design of the movement tasks at a centre is of paramount importance and a schema for each centre is presented in Table 13.5.

Table 13.5   Training Centres to Develop Ball Catching

1 Catching balls thrown horizontally to players	2 Catching balls thrown vertically	3 Catching balls moving in an arc
4 Catching balls thrown slowly and in an arc	5 Catching balls moving across a multi-coloured background	6 Catching balls moving across a visually 'noisy' background, and in an arc that necessitates a player moving to intercept

The six centres represent use of the TCS for developing catching and the intent is to foster improvement of this particular skill by focusing much of the practice upon catching performances. A coach might establish specific performance criteria for measuring success and before the player moves to the next centre he must master this criteria. For example, the player might be required to 'catch five balls thrown horizontally. It is the coaches' job to determine when a player moves to the next centre. Thus, once a procedure has been established more than four players at one time may be operating at any location. An alternative is to allow each group to move from one centre to another after a suitable period of time. It should also be stated that a coach might want to work on more than one skill, say both catching and hitting, during the individual practice time. This is not only permitted, but strongly recommended. Accordingly, three centres might consider the skill of catching, while the remainder could be involved with striking skills.

Important to the success of this training concept is to design tasks that accommodate a range of skill levels. By using the task complexity spectrum practice time will become more effective. Without spending a great deal of time indicating management steps for the operation of such a system, one piece of advice might be helpful. For each centre place the desired movement task descriptions on large poster board, making sure the tasks are properly sequenced, and teach players to perform the tasks according to the instructions. The coach can move from one group to another offering assistance as appropriate. This concept may be applied to any other movement task that requires a visual-motor match. A further use of the visual-motor match and the visual task complexity spectrum is to permit coaches to gradually increase the degree of difficulty for movement skills performed during practice. By formalising this process, players will demonstrate rapid skill development due to the programmed change.

Recognising that a multitude of factors influence a player's ability to accurately perceive three-dimensional objects travelling in his visual field can enable coaches to manage particular components of a practice more effectively. The time of day a practice should be held, particularly for players between the ages of six and twelve, should coincide with daylight hours. To hold practices in late afternoons or early evening, when the ambient light proves difficult for young players to track a ball, makes little sense. Furthermore, always provide a high colour contrast between the object and the background against which it is viewed. This means that grass-stained or brown-coloured baseballs should not be used with young children. The players who *should* get the 'better' equipment are the youngsters, but they invariably receive hand-me-downs from older players.

If a coach is attempting to teach a young novice to catch or strike a ball but is having limited success, he might consider the background against which the ball is moving. Perhaps positioning himself with his back to a solid background, for example a school-building wall, before delivering the ball to the player may facilitate the acquisition of ball skills. To ask inexperienced players to track a ball against the foliage of a tree or other complex background is, for example, counterproductive to the development of catching.

Finally, it is useful to reflect upon the design of sporting activities and to speculate about possible developments. Based upon information presented in this and other chapters of *Vision and Sport,* it may be possible to promote continued sport participation by altering some aspects of game design (Morris, 1980b). Hockey and soccer netting could be coloured blue, yellow or orange and with the supports painted in a contrasting colour. Volleyball nets and stands could also be colour contrasted. Balls used for a variety of sports might be produced in colours that various age groups perceive more easily, while basketball rims, nets and backboards could be similarly painted.

Trajectory angles for sports such as baseball can be controlled; at least for the batters. This is easily accomplished by placing the ball on a batting tee or swinging a ball from a pendulum stand. Players might also be afforded opportunities to determine how a ball is to be delivered to them. Although not all these ideas would be acceptable to all age groups, it is possible that they might help to generate greater interest in, and enthusiasm for, sport participation among young players.

References

Marteniuk, R. G. (1976) *Information Processing in Motor Skills,* New York: Rinehart & Winston.

Moran, G. T. (1976) The effect of ball colour and background colour on pursuit tracking and motion prediction as demonstrated by movement interdiction. Unpublished Doctoral Thesis, University of Oregon.

Morris, G. S. Don (1976) "Effects ball and background colour have upon the catching performance of elementary school children", *Research Quarterly,* 47: 409–16.

Morris, G. S. Don (1980a) *Elementary Physical Education Toward Inclusion,* Salt Lake City: Brighton Publishing.

Morris, G. S. Don (1980b) *How to Change the Games Children Play* (2nd edn.), Minneapolis: Burgess Publishing.

Ridenour, M. V. (1974) "The influence of object size, speed and direction on perception of moving objects", *Research Quarterly,* 45: 293–301.

Williams, H. G. (1968) The effects of systematic variation of speed and direction of object flight and of skill and age upon visuo-perceptual judgments of moving objects in three-dimensional space. Unpublished Doctoral Thesis, University of Wisconsin, Madison.

14

Colour Perception and Sports Performance

Ian M. Cockerill and William W. MacGillivary

The Determinants of Colour Vision

Human beings live within the context of complex and incompletely understood states and physical processes. Any relationship with the surrounding environment demands an accurate system for processing afferent information and subsequent decision-making about the energy sources that continually impinge upon our bodies. Gavrisky (1969) pointed out that approximately 85 per cent of sensation is obtained through the visual system. This fact is clearly acknowledged by motor skills researchers by virtue of their interest in vision and its function within the context of learning and performing perceptual-motor tasks. Yet it is perhaps remarkable that while references are continually made to such problems as movement speed, occlusion, attention, acuity and the perception of proximal space in vision studies, little interest has been shown in colour perception and its consequent influence upon psychomotor behaviour. Knapp (1963), Whiting (1969), Robb (1972), Singer (1973), Schmidt (1975) and Marteniuk (1976), for example, are among the more noted authors who have failed to recognise the possible relationship between colour and skilful performance.

Colour is a property of light conveyed through the eyes and different colours are produced by variation in sensation due to light of different wavelengths and frequencies. Electromagnetic energy, the stimulus for seeing, is propagated in the form of waves of energy. The two conventions used to describe the periodicity of electromagnetic radiation are *wavelength* and the *frequency* at which energy waves are propagated; red light, for example, has a frequency of approximately 10^{14} cycles per second. Colour is perceived in the brain when an object reflects light of a specific wavelength and some of the earliest experiments with colour were conducted and recorded by Newton (1704). He allowed a beam of sunlight to shine through a hole about a third of an inch in diameter made in a window shutter. A triangular prism was held against the hole, the resultant beam was projected on to white paper and the seven spectral colours were identified.

Colour perception is part of normal vision and although deficient colour vision is not uncommon among males – about 8–10 per cent – its incidence is relatively rare in the female population; probably less than one per cent. The term 'colour blind' is a misnomer, for there are few sighted individuals who are totally unable to experience colour sensation. There is generally only a partial deficiency, usually in distinguishing red and green, and particularly the more subtle tones of both.

Theories of colour tend to vary according to whether the argument is for three or four basic colours. Taylor (1962) appears to have resolved the difficulty by explaining:

. . . two apparently conflicting methods are fundamentally the same principle that red, green and blue are the basic constituents of colour, and that yellow becomes a primary chemical colour because, as its purity can not be obtained by chemical mixture of red and green pigments, it must be made separately as are red and blue, which are also basic chemical colours.

It can be said, then, that light has *three* constituents, red, green and blue, but as Bloomer (1976) indicated, this major postulation, the Young–Helmholtz theory, does not easily explain why people tend to perceive *four* fundamental colours, namely, red, yellow, blue and green. The addition of yellow, a pigment or chemical colour, to the other three helps one to recognise that perhaps a four-colour theory provides an acceptable compromise, if not an altogether perfect solution. Certainly in sport, four colours plus black and white are most frequently used for team identification purposes, while the Olympic flag incorporates interlocking rings in red, yellow, blue, green and black on a white background to represent all nations of the five continents within the Olympic movement. Moreover, in those British schools operating a house system, each of the four "houses" adopts not only a different name, but also a colour; usually red, yellow, blue and green.

The colour wheel (Figure 14.1) is an interesting device used to illustrate relationships between colours and is a common artifact of colour technology. It can be seen that the three primary pigments are equidistant, with the secondary colours placed between those from which they originate. Finally, tertiary colours are mixed from adjacent primary and secondary colours.

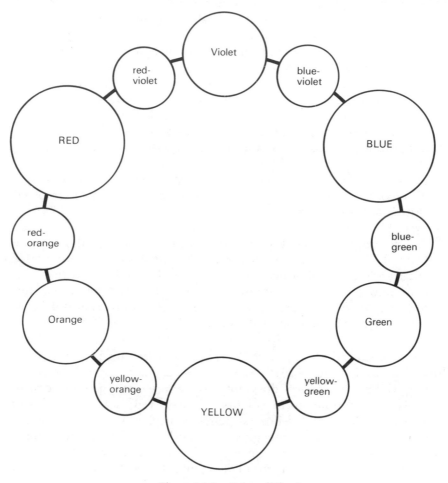

Figure 14.1   Colour Wheel

One further major aspect of colour to be considered before referring to research data in this field is to determine the most appropriate means of identifying a specific colour. Discriminating between geometric shapes, lengths of objects or the areas of two-dimensional forms is relatively straightforward in comparison with colour discrimination. It is undeniable that a three-sided figure is a triangle and that a figure with four sides of equal length is a square, but for one person to say that the plumage of a bird is blue may elicit the response from another that it is green; particularly if the bird is flying, or the background varies as the judgment is made.

Of the several available systems, perhaps that devised by the artist Albert Munsell has proved the most reliable. It is assumed (Evans, 1974) that three perceptual variables are necessary and sufficient to describe all possible colours. The three Munsell variables are Hue, or what is usually understood as *colour*, Value, which indicates *brightness* and Chroma, referring to the degree of *richness* of a particular hue. Fisher (1968) has provided succinct examples of possible variations in explaining that the hue of a tomato is usually referred to as red and the sea as blue. The value of a tomato can be bright red and the sea a dull blue. Finally, an unripe tomato might be described as pale red, while the Mediterranean is vivid blue. A form of notation is used to identify any colour precisely, with 5BG/4/9 specifying a blue-green of medium value and fairly high chroma and 5R/3/12 describing a medium red of low value and high chroma. Confusion in nomenclature can sometimes arise, however, particularly with value and chroma. The former may be termed luminosity in other systems, denoting the amount of light a particular colour appears to emit or reflect. Chroma may be directly referred to as saturation, extending from full saturation to reduced, or dilute, saturation.

Unlike variations in handedness and intelligence within a normal population, and where environmental and cultural influences are considered to be influential, deficiency in colour vision is believed not to be affected in this way. That is, the major defects in this facet of vision are inherited. As pointed out earlier, as many as 10 per cent of males may reveal a colour vision defect, whereas females remain relatively unaffected. The main defect appears to lie within the red–green zone, two complementary colours, and there are several tests available purporting to identify abnormalities. Probably the best known procedure is to use pseudo-isochromatic plates as in the Ishihara (1977) test. This test has been widely adopted and claims a quick and accurate assessment of congenital colour deficiency. However, while proving satisfactory for the diagnosis of general colour deficiencies in a given population, it may be inadequate as a more specialised research tool, being somewhat insensitive to both kind and degree of defect that an individual might possess.

In suggesting that a more reliable test can be constructed by limiting the number of embedded figure-type plates used in a set, Pickford & Lakowski (1961) have proposed that the Pickford–Nicholson anomaloscope is a more reliable and valid means of diagnosing colour defects. This particular instrument is portable and operates in daylight conditions. It is able to identify a variety of important features within the red–green, blue–green and yellow–blue colour zones, thereby accounting for almost any eventuality. Even using the embedded figure form of display the present authors were able to identify three out of 21 male members of a national squad of team game players who revealed defects in the red–green colour zone. Only one of the players was aware of the presence of any abnormality in his colour vision.

Those individuals who experience difficulties in colour identification and discrimination in their lives should clearly not choose occupations where their defect could prove hazardous. In considering the data obtained from the games players, above, it may be argued that even within a fast ball game played at international level, being unaware of the colour of team uniforms and background will not necessarily prove a handicap, and that identification is more readily made on the basis of stimulus pattern and contrast than upon colour. At the present time this is, of course, speculation and provides an interesting area for future research, although there have already been a limited number of investigations already carried out and these will be referred to later in the chapter.

Interesting data were obtained by Connors & Kelsey (1961) concerning the red–green colour zone which, it has been mentioned, produces the greatest defects. Particularly in team games, it may be important to determine the range over which red and green may be readily identified. It is necessary to be able to ascertain whether a player to the left or right is 'friend' or 'foe' and being able to quickly make an accurate judgment may be a contributing factor influencing individual team game skill. Logically, it might appear that because competing teams are both searching for a player to pass to as well as avoiding opponents, the effect of one colour being more easily recognisable than another will be cancelled out. Connors & Kelsey (1961) demonstrated that the colour zone for green is narrow compared with that for red, whose colour zone extends in a reliable, yet irregular, manner into the far periphery. Sensitivity to both colours was shown to have a sharp cut-off, while for others it diminished gradually as in the case of blue and yellow. This research is mentioned in order to illustrate that basic work already carried out on colour could have implications for sport. It is clear that colour perception varies for both the colours themselves and in respect of differences among subjects who have taken part in experiments.

Processing Colour Information

Human information-processing models have become a popular basis for research into psychomotor behaviour, with arguments having been developed from the standpoint that skilful performance is largely dependent upon efficient perception. Students of physical education and sport are repeatedly reminded that a learner must be directed to attend to appropriate information (see Chapter 5).

Laboratory research frequently employs psychophysical procedures to study the limitations of a person's perceptual processing capacity. A subject is usually required to compare a variable stimulus with a standard for similarity or difference, with stimuli varying according to the sense modality under consideration. In sports research it is usual for vision, proprioception and, to a limited extent, audition to be investigated. Psychophysical studies of vision almost always involve linear dimensions and, therefore, experimentation with colour has been limited. Furthermore, with one or two exceptions, the possible relevance of colour space in sport has not previously been considered.

It is early to make positive statements about the precise relevance to sport of research in colour perception already published, but there is some work that should be reported. Miller (1956) produced evidence to support the notion that humans are only able to classify information into about seven different categories. However, it was noted that absolute judgments of colours were more accurate than judgments about the brightness of light, size of visual stimuli or sound intensity. The implications are that colour may prove a superior method of coding information than, say, size or shape. In practical terms it may be better strategy to direct children to a 'red line' or a 'blue line' than to a 'dotted line' or a 'double line' on a running track if colour is processed most efficiently. The maze of lines superimposed upon a sports hall floor rarely confuse when each playing area is identified by a different coloured line. When all lines are white the problem of disembedding can be a difficult one for the field-dependent person.

Notwithstanding Miller's (1956) claims that human channel capacity is strictly limited, a study by Chapanis & Overbey (1971) indicated that it is possible to identify individual colours with remarkable accuracy. Using 36 randomly selected Munsell colour chips, both male and female adult subjects were able to correctly identify each of the stimuli by the twelfth and eighth completed trials respectively. It was concluded that channel capacity for processing information is less restricted than is generally supposed. Using colour in a visual display makes for more accurate information processing and it is likely that learners will maintain interest over a relatively lengthy period. Even following several hours of testing, Chapanis & Overbey (1971) had to exclude only one subject through disinterest in the experiment.

Although span of absolute judgment and immediate memory impose severe limitations upon the amount of information that humans are able to receive, process, remember and act upon, there is little doubt that this is largely overcome by *coding* information. That is to say, information is organised along several dimensions or into various categories. Green & Anderson (1956), for example, reported search times for two-digit numbers coloured either red or green and superimposed upon a black background. When subjects knew the colour of the target, search time was proportional to the number of symbols bearing the known colour. However, when target colour was not known, search time was dependent upon the total number of items in the display. Implications are that in common with perception generally, a colour 'set' operates. Irrelevant colour information can be easily discarded, although it is probable that multi-coloured displays will reflect longer search times. Anecdotal evidence in support of a colour 'set' relates to a recent occasion when an English first division football team wore unfamiliar blue and black stripes for a home game instead of its usual red shirts. Spectators were heard to remark that although they could easily identify the team as a whole, difficulty was experienced in recognising individual players within it.

Most sporting competitions are usually organised in a formal way, and the game is played according to a well-defined code of rules. In team competition there are only two groups on the playing area at one time and, despite the possibility of being unable to discriminate quickly between individuals, there is little likelihood of confusing either team. However, a television sports commentator's main observation about a football match played between England and Argentina in 1980 was that the predominantly white shirts and dark blue shorts of the former were easily confused with the light-blue and white striped shirts and black shorts of their opponents. Problems tend to occur when trying to identify one individual from among a group of competitors wearing a variety of coloured uniforms. Middle- and long-distance track and road races, and particularly horse racing, probably provide the greatest source of confusion and potential error. Although a perceptual 'set' operates when seeking to identify, say, one's club or national colours, it is difficult to select one from among a group of unfamiliar, coloured uniforms.

Smith & Thomas (1964) have stated that "colour coding is a powerful means of discriminating among classes of items presented in unstructured visual displays". They tested the claim in a comparative study of colour and shape for a counting task. Five each of military symbols, aircraft shapes and geometric shapes were coloured red, blue, green, yellow and white. It was demonstrated that counting was faster and more accurate when based upon the five colour categories than upon any of the three shape codes. Moreover, colour counting was unaffected by the particular shape code upon which colours were superimposed, and when red, yellow or white was incorporated, counting was faster than for either blue or green. Finally, for geometric shapes stars were counted fastest, followed by circles, semi-circles, diamonds and triangles. The latter finding is surprising in the light of studies by Fisher & Foster (1967) and Cockerill (1969) who showed that a two-dimensional triangle is perceived to be greater than a circle, which in turn was judged to be greater than a square when all three were of equal area.

Thus, if an object tends to be recognised more quickly than another because of colour differences, and if some shapes are perceived as greater than others and thereby facilitate recognition when each is of similar size, then it is useful to combine colour with other forms of information as an aid to processing. Rather than attempting to answer the quesiton "do we use colour or something else for ease of recognition?", possibilities should be exploited for combining colour with another variable to obtain the best answer. The facility with which stimuli can be recognised in sport tends to be synonymous with speed of movement. It is increasingly apparent, therefore, that the part played by colour in motor performance extends beyond that of simple discrimination between two teams of players.

Which Colour Do You Prefer?

Colour preference and its commercial importance was recognised following the statement by Henry Ford that those who bought his cars could have any colour they wished so long as it was black! If it is possible to determine with reasonable accuracy which are the more 'popular' hues, and particularly with regard to their value and chroma, then the psychological effect of colour upon motor skill acquisition and performance is worthy of consideration.

It has been suggested by Bjersted (1960) that there is no general support for the view that colour preference relates to an individual's personality. He tested the hypothesis that those who generally prefer 'warm' colours have a different personality from those whose preference is for 'cool' colours. With regard to work behaviour, are the former more easily activated and do they respond relatively quickly to a stimulus? Do they perceive situations easily and accurately, with a predisposition for enjoying life? Bjersted (1960) showed that those who preferred 'warm' colours had faster response times and tapping task scores than 'cool' colour preferent subjects, but were also more subject to environmental distractions.

An interesting report by Guilford & Smith (1959) proposed a system of colour preferences based upon reliable longitudinal data that claimed a high degree of predictability of colour preference. They used a large number of Munsell samples and required subjects to judge the pleasantness – affective value – of each sample on an eleven-point scale from zero to ten. Their main findings indicated that bright colours are preferred and that achromatic colours are rated as being relatively unpleasant; perhaps surprisingly, black was rated as being pleasanter than white. The most preferred colour was shown to be in the blue–green zone and greenish-yellow was the least popular. As a general principle, colours tended to be most preferred when both value and chroma were high.

It is often useful to be able to predict colour preference; for example, when purchasing small apparatus for motor skills teaching with young children. For this purpose isohedonic charts, first proposed by Guilford (1939), facilitate plotting preference for value against saturation for a given hue. The main value of isohedonic charts is claimed to lie in their use as norms for predicting the effective values of colours for both sexes. Bearing in mind that Guilford & Smith's (1959) studies were laboratory based, extrapolating results to practical situations should be considered with caution. There are, however, good reasons for extending research of this nature into the area of motor learning. Implications are likely to exist for the design of sports equipment and clothing with the aim of facilitating and increasing the rate of skill acquisition. As both authors pointed out, the area of effective reaction to colour combination is virtually untapped and here lie opportunities for sports psychology research.

Finally, attention is drawn to work on colour preference by Granger (1955). He also used Munsell-based stimuli in attempting to identify a general order of colour preference and his study is particularly relevant in that it provides a comprehensive review of much of the work on colour preference up to that time. Hue, value and chroma were considered both separately and in combination. Hue preference confirmed that there is a general liking for blue through green, red and orange to yellow. Secondly, for value, background was shown to be an important factor in preference. When stimulus brightness was more or less equal to its background, irrespective of hue, it was preferred less than when there was contrast. The background against which an object is superimposed has particular relevance in sport, especially in dynamic ball-game situations, and related issues will be discussed in the final section. Granger (1955) demonstrated that chroma preference increased to eight on a ten-point scale. The two upper levels of saturation were afforded low preference because they were seen to be 'too vivid'.

Thus, not only is it probable that a general order of colour preference does not exist, but the order of preference for one attribute, say chroma, remains invariant despite changes in the level of the other two. No marked sex differences in colour preference are usually identifiable, but it is possible that scores on any reliable test of colour preference have a predictive use. Finally, it is worth noting that many years ago Eysenck (1947) pointed out that the predisposition of an individual for preferring one colour over another tends to be biologically determined and that cultural factors play little part.

If colour preference is a more or less stable parameter, whether biologically or otherwise determined, it would be prudent for studies in psychomotor behaviour to take account of this factor in appropriate instances. Multiple-choice displays in response time studies, for example, usually incorporate lights that may vary along the three Munsell dimensions. Developmental studies, in particular, frequently refer to the need to use equipment of a particular colour to facilitate skill learning (see Chapter 13). Acknowledging that colour may contribute in various ways to motor behaviour it is insufficient to suggest that 'a blue ball is easiest to catch' or 'a yellow target is easiest to hit'. Not only hue, but also the value and chroma of the display, may require equal consideration when deciding upon the best programme of activities to develop skill in both beginners and experienced players.

Age and Sex Differences in Colour Responding

It is a fact of life that with increasing age, beliefs, interests and preferences also change. Likewise, both biologically and culturally determined sex differences are noticed in general psychological behaviour. It would not be surprising to learn, therefore, that male and female response to colour also differs and that the ways in which colour is used varies for both according to age.

In attempting to identify the more important cues associated with concept formation in young children, Suchman & Trabasso (1966) showed that at three years of age children were likely to be either colour-preferent or form-preferent when required to choose within these two dimensions. Furthermore, up to the age of four years colour was preferred to form, with a reversal beyond this age. Despite the widely held belief in colourful toys for young children, it was demonstrated that colour-preferent children have an increased choice of form over size with age, while form-preferent children did not reveal a later preference for colour over size.

On the basis of these findings it would be interesting to discover whether preference for colour over other dimensions varies with older children and whether sex differences are also apparent. An investigation by Corah (1964) confirmed that younger children prefer matching by colour rather than form, but he was not able to identify sex differences in colour matching. It was argued that the results may have reflected the inability of five-year-olds to consider equally all the features in a display and to make a decision based upon the most *relevant* feature, rather than that which *perceptually dominates*. Although this argument is reasonable, it conflicts with ideas about selective attention (see Chapter 5), wherein motor performance improves if an individual chooses the relevant response cues and ignores those that are unimportant.

Research that has attempted to identify and isolate differences in colour perception according to age has, in the main, been equivocal, if not unrewarding. A study by Child, Hansen & Hornbeck (1968), for example, produced few conclusive results and generally confirmed what was already known. The paper is an important reference, however, inasmuch as the authors draw attention to the problems that arise when stimuli varying in hue, value and chroma are randomly presented without maintaining two variables constant while modifying the other. The findings support the view that there is a tendency for preference to favour cooler hues with increasing age, although sex differences in this respect are unreliable. Brighter colours were shown to be preferred by both sexes, and particularly by girls, with a reduction in high value preference at adolescence. Up to about the age of nine years more highly saturated colours were selected, but once again this effect reduced with increasing age. The main outcome of this study by Child and his colleagues was to identify the importance of the relative influence of hue over value and chroma among younger children, but with no apparent preferred difference between sexes.

While marked performance differences according to sex tend to occur for physiological measures, it is unlikely that vision research in the area of colour perception has so far yielded much that is directly useful to maturing athletes or their coaches. That is not to say that future investigations, designed with the raising of skill levels in mind, will not prove helpful. It is only unfortunate that the majority of studies relating to colour perception and age have failed to consider subjects beyond the age of about ten to twelve. Kagan & Lemkin (1961), for example, investigated children's relative preference for colour over shape and size. They showed that the pre-school child classifies according to shape and with size chosen less often than colour. The oldest children in the research were, not atypically, nine years of age and boys of nine were found to use colour for object classification more often than girls. There is no reason, however, why apparatus used in motor-skills teaching should be made less colourful for girls than boys, or why there should be relatively less variety in the size and shape of apparatus used to teach motor skills to boys. Research tends to confirm that the universal practice of teaching physical education to both sexes in the same class is, with regard to equipment design, a sound procedure.

Contrary to popular belief, the perceptual mechanism of a young child does not necessarily function in an inferior way to that of an adult. Cockerill (1969), for example, showed that several features of so-called 'immature' space perception are not distorted to a greater degree than those of adults. Conventional accounts of space perception and its development (Gibson, 1950; Piaget & Inhelder, 1956) suggest that distortion of perceptual judgment in childhood is gradually overcome as the result of actively manipulating the spatial environment rather than from any 'reading-off' of the situation by the perceptual apparatus. In other words, all human beings come to perceive objects accurately through actions built up and organised with experience. Yet a curious feature of these theoretical formulations has been an apparent refusal to recognise that when evidence for a systematic distortion of visual space exists among adults, it must be reconcilable with the claims referred to above as to how perception develops and yields an accurate account of reality. Regrettably, Piaget and his colleagues placed little emphasis upon the role of colour in perceptual development and it has been left to those adopting a non-Piagetian approach (Cuisenaire & Cattegno, 1955) to explore the possibilities of using colour in work with children.

A comprehensive study by Gaines (1972) supported the view that the 'immature' colour perception of children with a mean age of less than six years is equally reliable as that of adults. She expressed the opinion that studies in colour perception should incorporate balanced colour stimuli within each of the three dimensions. Furthermore, attention was drawn to her young subjects' skilfulness in being able to "distinguish between extremely small variations in value and chroma". It was emphasised that:

It is possible that colour discrimination is not a function of age. Instead, colour discrimination could appear to improve with age because of an increasing ability to match the cognitive aspects of a task rather than because of an increasing perceptual ability.

Here an argument is presented in accordance with the probable rationale behind much of the experimental work of Piaget, namely the investigation of the ways in which children *represent*, rather than actually *perceive*, space. Thus, his research is essentially concerned more with cognitive development than the function of the perceptual mechanism; thereby querying the difference, if any, between perception and cognition.

A perennial, but nevertheless important, issue has been raised by Gramza (1969) with reference to laboratory studies of colour preference. While a laboratory setting may not be the best predictor of the way in which humans manipulate colour in real life, attempts have been made to overcome the laboratory-field problem. It is worthwhile referring to some of these before the final section identifies research on colour perception in a sports context.

The effect of ball colour and target colour in aiming and catching tasks has proved to be an interesting, although not entirely fruitful, area of investigation. Morris (1976) showed that while ball and background colour influenced catching among young children, with few exceptions performance was best when *contrast* between ball and background was great irrespective of colour; not an unexpected outcome. Davis's (1978) work with five baseball players and fifteen non-players found no significant differences between groups on a perceptual task or on a hitting task for the baseball players when orange, yellow and white balls were used. Apart from the inclusion of 'cool' colours throughout, the low number of trials and few subjects probably precluded the likelihood of anything of real interest being revealed. Eason & Smith (1979) found that practice improved the performance of two groups of subjects who aimed at either a chromatic or an achromatic target. The main finding was a significant performance *decrement* when changing from chromatic to achromatic target and vice versa.

Morris (1976) was possibly the innovator of studies in the area under consideration, but there are certain features of his work which are overlooked in discussion. First, high catching scores with a blue ball were consistent with blue being the most preferred colour for the majority of individuals. Second, high scores with a yellow baseball may have been attributed to the use of a novel colour in preference to the traditional white. As in all psychological experiments the selection of particular independent variables, and also instructions to subjects, can markedly affect results. This was recently demonstrated by Bartells, Beck & Clayson (1979) who showed that indicating to subjects that red stimuli give a faster response time than blue, blue faster than red or that there is no difference, produced results coincident with variations in the instructions given.

It might reasonably be concluded that while research investigating the parameters associated with colour perception and human performance has been unspectacular, there may be cause for optimism in the future. The studies conducted so far have perhaps paid insufficient attention to detail in the careful selection of stimuli. Furthermore, it is for those interested to seek out for themselves the avenues that may prove fruitful in demonstrating that colour has an important role in our sporting lives. Possibly the relationship between personality and colour perception may yet prove a rewarding area for investigation. Much of the work in the field has related to clinical aspects, but research using normal subjects is increasing. Studies by Krishna & Ahmad (1971), Birren (1973), Gotz & Gotz (1975) and Robinson (1975) are among those published in recent years, while Schick (1977) is probably alone in attempting to compare colour, personality and motor performance within a single experiment.

Practical Applications

The modern sports arena is replete with a spectrum of colour that includes not only the uniforms of athletes, but also the contrasting and often contradictory colour schemes of playing surfaces, seating areas and advertising displays. It is interesting to speculate on the effects of such a montage of colour upon the performance of athletes in this environment.

It is well known that demands placed upon the visual system during sports performance are somewhat different from those encountered in the normal daily routine, particularly inasmuch as the margin for error during decision-making in sport is usually reduced considerably. Accordingly, there may be a case for placing greater emphasis upon the role that colour perception can play in the learning and performance of sports skills. Neglecting this aspect of vision, particularly as it relates to the immediate environment and equipment, might produce unnecessary delays in skill acquisition. A disregard for the impact of colour in a gymnasium may induce fatigue with its associated effects on performance, while there is a need to choose carefully the combinations of colours that are used. One would gain little from using white balls, white uniforms and a light coloured surround in a ball-type activity; although this sometimes occurs.

There is a dearth of published research on the effects of colour on

Cockerill, I. M. (1969) The development of perceptual and sensori-motor skills. Unpublished Master's Thesis, University of Newcastle upon Tyne.

Connors, M. M. & Kelsey, P. A. (1961) "Shape of the red and green color zone gradients", *Journal of the Optical Society of America*, 51: 874–7.

Corah, N. (1964) "Colour and form in children's perceptual behaviour", *Perceptual and Motor Skills*, 18: 313–16

Cuisenaire, G. & Cattegno, C. (1955) *Numbers in Colour: A New Method of Teaching the Processess of Arithmetic to all Levels of the Primary School* (2nd edn.), London: Heinemann.

Davis, D. R. (1978) The effects of yellow, orange and white baseballs upon the visual perception and hitting effectiveness of college baseball players. Unpublished Master's Thesis, Middle Tennessee State University.

Eason, B. L. & Smith, T. C. (1979) "Effects of chromatic targets on a throwing task on subjects referred for learning disability", *Perceptual and Motor Skills*, 48: 229–30.

Evans, R. M. (1974) *The Perception of Colour*, London: John Wiley & Sons.

Eysenck, H. J. (1947) *Dimensions of Personality*, London: Routledge & Kegan Paul.

Fisher, G. H. & Foster, J. J. (1967) "Apparent sizes of different shapes and the facility with which they can be identified", *Nature*, 219: 653–4.

Gaines, R. (1972) "Variables in colour perception of young children", *Journal of Experimental Child Psychology*, 14: 196–218.

Gavrisky, V. S. (1969) "The colours and colour vision in sport", *Journal of Sports Medicine and Physical Fitness*, 9: 43–53.

Gavrisky, V. S. (1970) "Vision and sporting results", *Journal of Sports Medicine and Physical Fitness*, 10: 260–4.

Gibson, J. J. (1950) *The Perception of the Visual World*, Boston: Houghton Mifflin.

Gotz, K. O. & Gotz, K. (1975) "Color preferences, extraversion and neuroticism of art students", *Perceptual and Motor Skills*, 41: 919–30.

Gramza, A. (1969) "Choice of coloured blocks in the play of pre-school children", *Perceptual and Motor Skills*, 29: 783–7.

Granger, G. W. (1955) "An experimental study of color preferences", *Journal of General Psychology*, 52: 3–20.

Green, B. F. & Anderson, L. K. (1956) "Colour coding in a visual search task", *Journal of Experimental Psychology*, 51: 19–24.

Guilford, J. P. (1939) "A study of psychodynamics", *Psychometrica*, 4: 1023.

Guilford, J. P. & Smith, P. C. (1959) "A system of color-preferences", *American Journal of Psychology*, 72: 487–502.

Ishihara, S. (1977) *Tests for Colour-blindness*, Tokyo: Kanehara Shuppan Company.

Kagan, J. & Lemkin, J. (1961) "Form, color and size in children's conceptual behavior", *Child Development*, 39: 237–47.

Knapp, B. N. (1963) *Skill in Sport*, London: Routledge & Kegan Paul.

Krishna, K. P. & Ahmad, I. (1971) "Personality adjustment and colour preferences", *Behaviorometric*, 1: 99–102.

Marteniuk, R. G. (1976) *Information Processing in Motor Skills*, New York: Holt, Rinehart & Winston.

Miller, G. A. (1956) "The magical number seven plus or minus two: some limits on our capacity for processing information", *Psychological Review*, 63: 81–97.

Morris, G. S. D. (1976) "Effects ball and background color have upon the catching performance of elementary schoolchildren", *Research Quarterly*, 47: 409–16.

Munsell, A. H. (1979) *A Color Notation* (13th edn.), Baltimore: Munsell Color Co.

Newton, I. (1704) *Opticks*, in D. L. MacAdam (Ed.) (1970) *Sources of Color Science*, Cambridge, Mass: MIT Press, pp. 16–39.

Piaget, J. & Inhelder, B. (1956) *The Child's Conception of Space*, London: Routledge & Kegan Paul.

Pickford, R. W. & Lakowski, R. (1961) "The Pickford–Nicholson anomaloscope for testing and measuring colour sensitivity and colour blindness and other tests and experiments", *British Journal of Physiological Optics*, 17: 131–50.

Robb, M. D. (1972) *The Dynamics of Motor Skill Acquisition*, Englewood Cliffs, N.J.: Prentice Hall.

Robinson, C. (1975) "Colour preference as a function of introversion and extraversion", *Perceptual and Motor Skills*, 40: 702.

Schick, J. (1977) "Relationship between personality and color in the performance of a gross motor skill", *Journal of the Association for the Study of Perception*, 12: 19–22.

Schmidt, R. A. (1975) *Motor Skills*, New York: Harper & Row.

Singer, R. N. (1973) *Motor Learning and Human Performance* (2nd edn.), New York: Macmillan.

Smith, S. L. & Thomas, D. W. (1964) "Color versus shape coding in information displays", *Journal of Applied Psychology*, 48: 137–46.

Suchman, R. & Trabasso, T. (1966) "Colour and form preference in young children", *Journal of Experimental Child Psychology*, 3: 177–87.

Tayor, F. A. (1962) *Colour Technology*, London: Oxford University Press.

Whiting, H. T. A. (1960) *Acquiring Ball Skill: A Psychological Interpretation*. London: Bell.

15

The Use of Demonstrations and Videotape Recorders in Sport and Physical Education

Leslie Burwitz

A majority of sports coaches and physical education teachers believe that demonstrations and videotape recordings benefit the acquisition and performance of physical skills. One need only consider how often "watch me", "watch this film" or "watch this videotape recording of yourself" is pronounced to verify this belief. Intuition tells that it is possible to improve someone's performance much more effectively when demonstrations and videotape recordings are used. In short, there appears to be no doubt that such techniques are useful to the performer who wishes to attain higher levels of skill.

The final chapter seeks to investigate the effectiveness of demonstrations and videotape recordings in sports-related situations. An attempt is made to be objective, to avoid personal bias and to consider evidence available from relevant research. Such evidence is not always supportive of intuitively based opinions, and as a consequence a theoretical model is outlined to allow one to speculate about how the effectiveness of demonstrations and videotape recordings might be improved.

The Function of Demonstrations and Videotape Recordings

Both provide visual information feedback to the instructor, coach and performer. This information is analysed by the brain (decision-making mechanism) before a particular response is made (output). Figure 15.1 illustrates the relationship and also presents a clear visual image of the varied and differing functions offered by this form of feedback. Demonstrations are a means of providing what is referred to in the diagram as input information. That is, demonstrations are potentially valuable *prior to* the performance of a particular skill or task. Videotape recorders, on the other hand, provide information via the feedback loop. That is, some attempt must be made to perform a skill before relevant information can be recorded and played back, either immediately or after some period of delay.

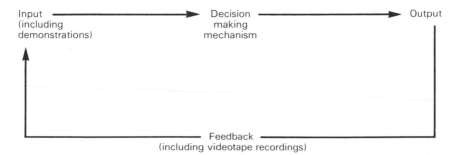

Figure 15.1   The Human Performance Model

Demonstration Research

Demonstrations are usually provided by a live model or film of an 'expert'. They may be performed at normal speed, or in slow motion for further clarification; they may be presented prior to a performer's first attempt at a skill, or at any stage thereafter; they may be accompanied by verbal cues or presented without verbal feedback; they may show the entire skill, or break it down into it's constituent components.

If asked to describe the most effective form of demonstration the reply might be that demonstrations, such as films of an 'expert', are essential. This form of demonstration should include the 'expert' performing the entire skill in slow motion, or a real-life expert performing the skill at a normal pace. Teachers are forced to develop such answers as they are faced with situations which have an applied connotation. They must believe that their answers are absolutely correct or else they could not be considered appropriate.

If the reported research is analysed with respect to the topic of demonstration, it might be found that there are no easy answers such as the one noted earlier. Few of the issues raised in the previous paragraph have ever been investigated and the available evidence is equivocal. For example, those studies which have reported that demonstrations are beneficial to motor performance (Lockhart, 1944; Gray & Brumbach, 1967; Landers & Landers, 1973; Burwitz, 1975) are countered by those that have found an opposite trend, or no difference, in final level of proficiency between two groups trained with or without the use of demonstrations (Brown & Messersmith, 1948; Nelson, 1958; Burwitz, 1975; Martens, Burwitz & Zuckerman, 1976).

In trying to analyse why such a conflict occurs, experimental procedures must initially be considered. Early research attempted to observe skilled performance in the field and the effect of demonstrations was tested using classes of beginning bowlers (Lockhart, 1944), tumblers (Brown & Messersmith, 1948), golfers (Nelson, 1958) and badminton players (Gray & Brumbach, 1967). There are obvious advantages to be gained from this approach, but there are also problems such as the use of inadequate randomisation procedures, the lack of appropriate control conditions, particularly in situations where individuals can observe each other, and the effect of previous experience, or practice, between experimental sessions which take place over a prescribed period.

The more recent demonstration research has, for the most part, been conducted in a laboratory environment. As a consequence many of the problems mentioned above have been eliminated or, at worst, reduced. There are other problems, however, which have yet to be overcome, such as the appropriate application of the research findings to real-life sports situations. The research reported by Burwitz (1975) is particularly relevant in that he found demonstrations to be beneficial in certain situations and detrimental in others. Thirty-six university students were tested on their ability to climb as many consecutive Bachman ladder steps as possible in eight, 30-second trials (Figure 15.2). Live demonstrations were given to one half of the group before the first and fifth trials and results indicated that the demonstrations were beneficial to performance.

Figure 15.2   The Bachman Ladder Apparatus

In a second experiment, thirty-two university students were given eight, 20-second trials on a rotary pursuit task (Figure 15.3). Live demonstrations were again provided and half the group benefited on the first and fifth trials as before. There was no positive effect on this task as there had been with the Bachman ladder task. Those who received the live demonstration in the rotary pursuit task were inferior to their peers, who only received instructions about the task demands.

In an attempt to explain the conflicting and confusing evidence Burwitz (1975) referred to the information obtained during a post-experimental interview. Apparently the students who received the Bachman ladder demonstration were able to observe clearly the strategy that governs the successful execution of the task. That is, they were able

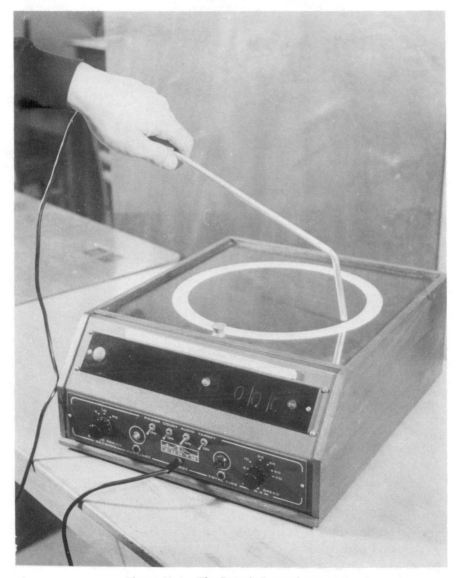

Figure 15.3   The Pursuit-Rotor Apparatus

to see that climbing high produced disequilibrium and low scores due to overbalancing, thus causing time losses; whereas climbing the lower three rungs repeatedly enabled good balance to be maintained and higher scores achieved. With respect to the rotary pursuit task, students reported that they were unable to observe the technique that was required to maintain the stylus on the rotating beam of light while watching the demonstration. Burwitz (1975) concluded that the strategy, or technique, governing successful performance must be visible to the performer who is observing the task if such demonstration is to benefit future performance.

In a follow-up experiment Burwitz (1975) found that viewing the correct strategy was not the only prerequisite for the group of subjects who utilised a demonstration successfully. He tested 48 university students on sixty trials of the shoot-the-moon task (Figure 15.4). The object of this commercially available game is to roll a ball uphill between two inclined rods, and at its farthest point drop the ball into one of seven holes located in the base of the apparatus. High scores can only be achieved by using a particular strategy and this was clearly visible to those students who observed a film of seven successful trials prior to their first attempt, and also after every ten attempts. Results revealed that the demonstrations were of no real benefit to task performance. Those who watched the demonstrations had the lowest average score at the conclusion of the experiment. This finding was explained with reference to the nature of the task. It was argued that being able to imitate the necessary action was limited by the inherent task difficulty, claiming that good shoot-the-moon performance relies heavily upon certain kinaesthetic cues or 'touch' that can only be developed with lengthy practice.

Finally, Burwitz (1975) compared the effect of a film of seven perfect trials on the shoot-the-moon task with live demonstrations. The live demonstrations attempted to display the correct strategy, but generally resulted in less than perfect scores. Results revealed that there were no differences between the two approaches. Apparently demonstrations did not need to be performed by 'experts' provided that those who were demonstrating could convey relevant information to the observer about the strategy needed for success.

In extrapolating from the four experiments Burwitz (1975) stated that there are at least two prerequisite conditions for the successful utilisation of demonstrations in motor skill learning, namely:

1. the strategy or technique which governs successful performance must be visible to the performer;
2. the observer must have an innate, or acquired, ability to imitate the demonstrated action.

Figure 15.4   The Shoot-the-Moon Apparatus

Both factors will be discussed later in the context of a theoretical model, offering a parsimonious explanation for the conflict between the demonstration literature and that which exists in the area that is considered next.

Videotape Recorder Research

Fitts & Posner (1967) have claimed that videotape recording is one of the most promising techniques for use in skill training as it enables performers to see themselves immediately after attempting to execute a particular action. Thus, they suggest that it has a feedback function. Feedback may be defined as an all-inclusive term referring to the information that performers receive about their own previous actions. It is generally believed to be one of the strongest and most important variables controlling performance. Consequently, the videotape recorder has intuitive appeal. This fact, together with equipment developments which have reduced purchase costs, has encouraged coaches and physical educators to use videotape recorders widely; especially for such activities as tennis, swimming, golf and gymnastics.

If existent videotape recorder research is critically evaluated, a similar situation is found to that reported for demonstrations. That is, the experimental evidence on videotape recorders is not completely supportive of their use and value. There is, once again, a good deal of conflict in the completed research. Del Rey (1973) reported results which support the contention that the videotape recorder benefits motor performance, but the majority of published research (Caine, 1966; Gasson, 1969 and Penman, 1969) indicates that viewing one's own performance will produce no greater improvement than is possible without the videotape recorder.

The quality of most of the published research is also questionable. Each study, with the exception of Del Rey's (1973) work, is a field experiment and so there are unavoidable errors resulting from the use of established groups, the loss of physical practice time for the students to watch the videotape recordings and the difficulty in accurately assessing the performance of tumbling, trampolining, bowling and badminton skills in a normal teaching environment. Del Rey (1973) revealed none of these problems as the study was well conceived and rigorously controlled. The results may be accepted with more confidence than those of the field experiments and the investigation merits a detailed examination.

The study was designed to consider the effect of the videotape recorder on the acquisition of a modified fencing lunge. Forty-eight right-hand preferent female university students were randomly assigned to one of two groups.* Both groups performed 18 lunges on each of three consecutive days and form, accuracy and latency were measured prior to, midway through and at the end of the experiment. Following

*The actual design was more complex than this, but it has been simplified in order that the relevant videotape results may be interpreted more easily.

the sixth and twelfth lunge on each day, half the students read cue
cards directing the attention to the key points of form, while the other
half also read these and then analysed a videotape recording of their
previous six attempts, with instructions to note discrepancies between
their form and that of the required standard. Form was assessed by
three trained judges who used a rating scale. Accuracy was determined
by discrete scoring involving a 3–2–1 system based upon three
concentric circles and latency was measured by a millisecond timer
which quantified the interval between target illumination and foil-
target contact.

The data revealed that the videotape recorder improved both lunge
form and lunge latency. It helped students to reduce the deviation
between the imposed standard form and their own style, and this in turn
appeared to increase the speed of lunge action. One other notable
finding was the lack of any relationship between form and accuracy
scores. Del Rey (1973) originally hypothesised that accuracy would
improve as form matched the externally imposed standard more closely.
This was not the case, since form improvement was followed by
deterioration in accuracy. Such an observation is particularly relevant
to the concept of goal confusion as outlined by Gentile (1972). She
suggested that coaches and physical education teachers often confuse
the goal of a task that is established for beginners. The object of a unit
may be to score a basket, but it is often minimised by over-emphasising
such features as 'good style'. Presumably this is done because it is felt
that better form produces better results, that is, more accuracy. Clearly
this was not the case in Del Rey's (1973) study because it was apparent
that accurate lunges could be achieved without depending upon a
'textbook' style.

An attempt to explain the discrepancies within videotape recorder
research results has been made recently by Burwitz (1980). His
arguments are based on Bandura's (1969) contiguity-mediational
theory of imitation and, as is shown in the next section of this chapter,
they apply equally well to demonstrations. In addition to reducing some
of the confusion in two important areas of study the Bandura model also
encourages speculation about how the effectiveness of demonstrations
and videotape recorders might be increased. The latter point is of
critical importance to the coach and physical education teacher, but
before outlining some practical applications it might be worthwhile to
consider the Bandura theory in greater detail.

Bandura's (1969) contiguity-mediational theory was designed to
explain imitation, or the tendency to reproduce the actions exhibited by
a real-life or symbolised model. He believed that a model's actions are
coded into images or words for storage in the memory and that these will

later serve as mediators for the retrieval of appropriate responses. He argued that the amount of imitation will depend upon four specific components. The first two are believed to influence the actual acquisition of a response, while the remainder are thought to affect the performance of a learned type of response. The four components are:

1. attention processes;
2. retention processes;
3. motor reproduction processes;
4. incentive conditions.

With respect to the attention processes, Bandura (1969) claimed that an observer must attend to modelled responses if they are to be properly imitated at another time. In generalising from this hypothesis to motor performance it might be assumed that demonstrations and videotape recordings are beneficial, but only if the performer attends to the visually presented information.

Attention requires not only that the eyes are focused upon a particular visual display, but also that relevant information is extracted from it. It may be relatively easy to ensure that the student observes either a demonstration or a videotape recording of himself, but the extent to which relevant information is extracted appears more problematic. As discussed earlier, Burwitz (1975) found that university students could not always attend to the relevant cues contained in a demonstration. Accordingly, there is no reason to suspect that students who watch videotape recordings of themselves are any better at detecting and attending to those aspects of their performance that require modification than those who do not watch such recordings.

It may be that the confusing evidence in the demonstration and videotape recording literature is a function of differential attention aspects. That is, those studies which report that the aids are beneficial may have directed attention to the important aspects of the display, while those that report contradictory results have not. This explanation is plausible, but can not be accepted without reservation, because in the majority of the research reports there is insufficient information about the quantity and quality of verbal directing cues to make a judgment. It is interesting to note, however, that Lockhart (1944), Gray & Brumbach (1966) and Del Rey (1973) used some of the attention directing cues and their findings support the use of demonstrations and videotape recorders.

Information which is extracted from a demonstration or videotape recording must, if it is to be of value, be retained until additional physical practice can be undertaken. In ideal situations this time period is less than two minutes, but short-term memory research indicates that substantial forgetting can occur over such a period. Whether short-term forgetting influenced the demonstration and videotape recording research findings is impossible to detect. It seems reasonable to suppose that visual information has a more forceful impact in those situations where care is taken to ensure that as much information as possible is retained over short periods of time.

Bandura (1969) believed that the role of motor performance reproduction processes in imitation is crucial. He argued that a modelled response which has been attended to and retained in representational form in memory may not be reproduced because of physical limitations. Generalising from this concept, beginners may extract the relevant information from demonstrations or videotape recordings and they may be able to retain it until the next opportunity for practice, but unless they have the physical capability to reproduce the desired action there will be no improvement in performance.

Burwitz (1975) suggested that the conflicting demonstration research results may be partially explained by referring to the motor reproduction process. It was claimed that innate or acquired ability to imitate a desired action is a necessary condition for the effective utilisation of demonstrations. Burwitz (1980) has extended this argument to videotape recorder research using 'videotape recorder' and control groups who were tested at college level and where no differences were reported; this being contrary to those studies which reported demonstrations and videotape recordings to be effective. In the earlier investigations beginners were used in contrast with the latter which involved subjects who found the skills relatively easy to perform. Additional research is obviously required to confirm or refute the assertion that conflict in the demonstration and videotape recording literature is a function of motor reproduction processes. It may be reasonable to suggest, however, that demonstrations and videotape recordings can benefit the performance of those who do not possess the capacity to move in the desired fashion.

The final factor in Bandura's contiguity-mediational theory is incentive. He claims that attention, retention and ability do not guarantee imitation. Generalising from this statement, students may be able to visualise what to do after having watched a demonstration or videotape recording and they may have the capacity to perform the required skill, but lack the motivation required to produce the appropriate action. Incentives can influence both the acquisition of new skills and the performance of previously learned movements. They may be applied directly to a subject watching a demonstration or a videotape recording, or vicariously to the person who is performing the demonstration. In both cases it might be assumed that incentives would be beneficial although, once again, further research is required in order to substantiate or reject such an assertion.

Practical Applications

Sports coaches and physical education teachers believe intuitively that demonstration and videotape recordings benefit those who perform motor skills. The research evidence does not totally support such an assumption, since in both areas there is conflict between those studies which report beneficial effects and those that do not. Explanations for the conflicting evidence can be based upon Bandura's (1969) contiguity–mediational theory of imitation, although they remain to be confirmed.

Bandura's (1969) theory has one other important function. It provides a framework for considering how the effectiveness of demonstrations and videotape recordings can be increased. This is a practical problem and although the statements that follow could be criticised as being too speculative, they are included here in an attempt to stimulate both the practitioner and the research worker to assess their validity in appropriate situations. Thus, the understanding of how to best use demonstrations and videotape recordings to maximum advantage may be facilitated.

In conclusion, demonstrations and videotape recordings appear to be most effective when:

1. the strategy governing successful performance is visible to the observer and attention is directed by verbal cues to the most important aspects of the visual display;
2. relevant visual information is retained over both short and long periods of time;
3. students have the necessary innate or acquired ability to reproduce the desired skill;
4. the incentive to perform the required skill is above a specified minimum threshold level.

Provided that the above conditions are met there seems little, if any, advantage to be gained from slow motion versus normal speed demonstrations and videotape recordings, or from the use of 'experts', either 'live' or on film, versus 'non-experts' in live demonstrations.

References

Bandura, A. (1969) *Principles of Behavior Modification*, New York: Holt, Rinehart & Winston.

Brown, H. S. & Messersmith, L. (1948) "An experiment in teaching tumbling with and without motion pictures", *Research Quarterly*, 19: 304–7.

Burwitz, L. (1975) "Observational learning and motor performance", *FEPSAC Conference Proceedings*, Edinburgh.

Burwitz, L. (1980) "A critical review of videotape recorder research", *Physical Education Review* (submitted).

Caine, J. (1966) Effects of instant analysis and reinforcement of motor performance through the use of cinematography techniques related to television. Unpublished Doctoral Thesis, Colorado State University. Cited by P. Del Rey, 1973.

Del Rey, P. (1973) The effects of videotape feedback and environmental certainty on form, accuracy and latency during skill acquisition. Unpublished Doctoral Thesis, Columbia University, Eugene, Oregon: Microform Publications, 1973, No. BF295.

Fitts, P. M. & Posner, M. I. (1967) *Human Performance*, Belmont, Calif.: Brooks/Cole.

Gasson, I. (1969) "Relative effectiveness of teaching badminton with and without an instant replay videotape recorder", *Perceptual and Motor Skills*, 29: 499–502.

Gentile, A. M. (1972) "A working model of skill acquisition with application to teaching", *Quest*, 17: 3–23.

Gray, C. A. & Brumbach, W. B. (1967) "Effect of daylight projection of film loops on learning badminton", *Research Quarterly*, 38: 562–9.

Landers, D. M. & Landers, D. M. (1973) "Teacher versus peer models: effects of model's presence and performance level on motor behavior", *Journal of Motor Behavior*, 5: 129–39.

Lockhart, A. (1944) "The value of the motion picture as an instructional device in learning a motor skill", *Research Quarterly*, 15: 181–7.

Martens, R., Burwitz, L. & Zuckerman, J. (1976) "Modelling effects on motor performance", *Research Quarterly*, 47: 277–92.

Nelson, D. O. (1958) "Effect of slow-motion loopfilms on the learning of golf", *Research Quarterly*, 29: 37–45.

Penman, K. (1969) "Relative effectiveness of teaching beginning tumbling with and without an instant replay videotape recorder", *Perceptual and Motor Skills*, 29: 45–6.

AUTHOR INDEX

SUBJECT INDEX